THANK YOU, MR. DEBARTOLO

By Thomas Rossetti

ACKNOWLEDGEMENTS

This book is dedicated to the late Edward J. DeBartolo, Sr., whose council and confidence in me allowed me to experience the heights and achievements mentioned in this book, as evidenced by the title. The title also applies to Edward J. DeBartolo, Jr. for his role in helping in my development and success over the years. Thanks also to Marie Denise DeBartolo York for her friendship and support during my tenure in Youngstown and well beyond.

I also want to thank all the members of my staff who worked with me for so many of those years. There's too many to mention here, but you all know who you are, and I'll never forget you.

Finally, I'd like to acknowledge my family: wife Chris and sons Mike, Chip and Tommy, who took most of this trip with me and experienced many of the highlights and good times mentioned herein. Special thanks to Mike, who guided me through the complex process of getting this six-year project written, proofread and published. I could not have made it through without all of you.

Cover photo of Edward J. DeBartolo, Jr. by Bill Serne

ISBN: 978-0-692-16850-9

Thank You, Mr. DeBartolo

PROLOGUE

September 13, 1973 was the day that changed my life. To begin with, it was my first child's first birthday – a momentous occasion for any parent. We celebrated his birthday on a Thursday with family in our two-bedroom duplex apartment in Garfield, New Jersey. It was a proud and happy day for a 25-year-old father and his 23-year-old wife.

However, there was also some anxiety that evening. Over the previous few weeks, I was looking for a new job out of town. I interviewed with Westinghouse in Baltimore for their nuclear defense plant and was offered a position there.

I also interviewed with the Edward J. DeBartolo Corporation in Youngstown, Ohio and gave them a deadline of nine o'clock that night to make me an offer. As we put our son to bed and the deadline passed, I accepted the fact I would be calling Westinghouse on Monday morning and we would be Baltimore-bound.

I wasn't really surprised I might not be offered the Youngstown job because the Controller at DeBartolo, Bob Munro, told me he felt I was too young for the job. But, he left open the possibility he might reconsider.

We were a bit disappointed not to get a call. The Baltimore job required extensive travel – as much as 80 percent, while the Youngstown job required only minimal travel. Plus, Youngstown was only an hour from my wife's Pittsburgh hometown and she relished the idea of being closer to her family.

We talked awhile and then decided to call it a night. No sooner had we turned off the lights, when the phone rang. It was 10:15 and

Bob Munro was on the line. He was traveling, and his plane was delayed in the air in Chicago. He offered me the job. I told him I would consider the offer and call him Monday. Three days later we hammered out some minor issues and I accepted the job.

Thus began the phenomenal journey working for Edward J. DeBartolo, a mysterious, powerful and often misunderstood man. Along the way I experienced incredible highs and depressing lows, and over time worked closely with this man and his family. I had insights as part of his "inner circle" and grew to love him as a father figure, as well as a boss. I experienced his kindness and generosity, as well as sometimes ruthless demands and cutthroat business decisions made in his pursuit of perfection and success. Along the way, I also grew to love and respect his two children, Edward J. DeBartolo, Jr. and Marie Denise DeBartolo York, who worked with me and supported me in my climb to heights in the corporation I never would have guessed possible.

The stories you will read throughout this book are all true and factual. In a few instances, I have chosen to change the names of certain individuals. You will note an asterisk (*) exists in those rare occurrences.

CHAPTER 1

THE ESTABLISHMENT OF PRINCIPLES

I was born April 10, 1948 in Brooklyn, NY, the second of six children. My parents were Julius Rossetti, the only son of two Italian immigrants, and Cecelia Anita Rossetti, one of many children born to parents of Swedish and French ancestry. My dad was born and raised in Brooklyn and graduated from Fordham University, while my mother grew up in the Upper Peninsula of Michigan. They met in Washington, D.C., where my mother went to work for an ordnance company during World War II. My dad was there on business.

My paternal grandmother died the year before I was born, but my paternal grandfather was alive throughout my entire childhood. Since neither I, nor any of my siblings knew my grandmother, our Gramps (Curiazio Rossetti) was our link to my father's side of the family. He owned a butcher shop and was a gifted weaver of tales that could keep his grandchildren entertained for hours, particularly when he told us about growing up in Italy. He was also a gifted musician, proficient in guitar, banjo and the accordion.

My maternal grandparents weren't as well known to my siblings and me. To begin with, they still lived in the "U.P." and rarely traveled. My mother's father was a carpenter by trade who died in 1955. Since we only saw him a few times on summer vacations to the U.P., his influence in our lives was minimal.

I do, however, remember him carving toy guns for us to play with while we visited. My grandmother, of French descent, was a standoffish farm woman who rarely showed emotion. She wasn't the "soft and cuddly" type of grandma, but we loved her just the same. She was a hard-working woman who chopped the wood to fuel the kitchen stove and the house furnace and tended to her garden that supplied the wide array of fruits and vegetables that always showed up on the dinner table.

My older brother Mark, my newborn sister, Pam and I, along with my parents, shared an apartment with my grandfather in Brooklyn until 1950 when my parents bought a house in East Paterson, N.J., and the five of us moved out of the city and into the suburbs. Gramps stayed in Brooklyn to work in his shop and drove out on weekends to visit.

East Paterson was across the river and not part of Paterson, the "silk city" known for its silk factories. Many years later, East Paterson changed its name to Elmwood Park to distance itself from its crime-ridden neighbor on the other side of the Passaic River.

My other three siblings, brothers Charles, John and Bill were all born in New Jersey. We had a normal childhood, with a lot of laughing and bickering that comes with being part of a large family. We all loved sports, including Pam, who with five brothers was doomed to become the tomboy she was during childhood.

My parents were practicing Catholics. My dad was an usher at St. Anne's Church in neighboring Fair Lawn, but my mother was much more devout than dad. She was a stay-at-home mom while dad commuted back and forth to New York for work. My mom instilled many of the values my siblings and I share, while dad was the disciplinarian. It was a role which suited him. He had a trigger temper and we felt the sting of his strap often when we stepped out of line.

We all went to St. Anne's Catholic grammar school, The fear of God instilled in us by our teachers - the Sisters of St. Joseph. There was more corporal punishment there when we got into trouble, which in my case was all too frequent. However, the combination of my parent's up-bringing and the nuns' supporting roles instilled honesty and integrity in us, a trait I have carried with me all my life.

My parents also had a strong work ethic. Being a mother of six young kids kept my mother busy all day, and my father worked hard to keep us fed, educated and clothed. I picked up their work ethic early and worked hard, helping my father with chores around the house and doing odd jobs for the neighbors, mowing lawns and shoveling snow, often utilizing Pam and Chas.

As soon as I was old enough, perhaps 10 or so, my parents allowed me to get a paper route delivering the Bergen Evening Record six days a week from Monday to Saturday. To add to my income, I delivered the Newark Star Ledger on Sundays when the Bergen Evening Record wasn't published. Both routes were developed from scratch and provided me with a nice income. The Record cost $.33 per week then, $.03 of which I got to keep, but the bulk of my income came from tips.

Rain, snow or freezing cold didn't matter. If the papers got to me, I delivered them. I remember a blizzard in December 1960 that dumped more than 2 feet of snow on our part of the state. The Record papers were dropped off at a spot a half mile from my house because most roads were impassable. I trudged through unplowed streets to get the papers and then delivered them to my customers.

Non-customers saw me that day and offered me money to give them a paper. I apologized and told them I only had enough for my customers. That week I got nearly a dozen new customers from the competing Paterson Evening News because the neighbors were impressed with my delivery effort.

My parents taught me savings at an early age and I listened. Most of the money I made delivering papers went into a savings account. I could take money out to buy birthday and Christmas gifts, but the bulk of the funds were earmarked for college.

After graduating from St. Anne's grammar school in 1962, I was accepted to and entered Bergen Catholic High School in Oradell, New Jersey. The bus commute, together with extra-curricular activities (sports and clubs) didn't allow me the time to deliver papers, so I turned the route over to my younger brother, Chas.

Bergen Catholic was and still is, run by the Irish Christian Brothers. The school is, to this day, one of the top prep schools in the Northeast, with a history of great sports teams since opening in the late 1950s. The Brothers were also known as rigid disciplinarians, and again honesty, integrity and ethics were emphasized. Transgressions from these core values were often dealt with quickly and harshly.

I was a good athlete in pre-high school days particularly in Little League and Babe Ruth Baseball. I dabbled in football at Bergen Catholic, but the school could recruit the best athletes throughout the county and I just wasn't good enough. I had a bit more success at baseball, and I played on the school's freshman team. Unfortunately, I had trouble hitting curve balls and when word got out, my baseball career was over.

My first involvement in any form of sports management started my freshman year. The high school baseball season was over and the academic year was ending. One evening, I received a call from a man named Mr. Hauseman, who ran a baseball league for St. Anne's School. St. Anne's parish was so big it had its own league filled with students of the school and other public school Catholic children. I had played in that league as well as the local public Little League. Mr. Hauseman was the manager of the team I played on as an 8th grader.

When he called, he told me he had a problem. It was mid-season and he needed a coach for one of his teams. The former coach quit abruptly because the players on the team wouldn't listen to him. The team was 0 and 7, none of the parents wanted to take over, and Hauseman was desperate. He felt that I, at the age of 15, was mature enough to manage the boys. I told him I wasn't even old enough to drive and my Dad didn't get home before six p.m., about the time when the games would start. I wanted to do it, but I didn't think it possible.

He then asked to speak with my parents. They conferred and Hauseman asked to speak with me again. He told my parents he would pick me up and bring me home if it was okay with them, and they agreed. My mother also offered to take me if she was available on a day. Hauseman gave me the field for the weekend so I could meet and work with the boys. I spoke with them that first session, told them the past was over, and they should consider the next game as the start of a new season.

I immediately realized the former coach hadn't given these kids any real instruction. Some were talented and some not so much. The talented ones were my base and I concentrated on working on the basics with the other boys. I encouraged them to work hard and tried to instill in them the confidence they could succeed. Some responded immediately and some didn't, but I wouldn't give up. I wanted to help them.

The league required all boys play in each game and must bat at least once per game. After the weekend of practice, Hauseman picked me up for the first game and introduced me to the umpires and opposing coach. We won that game, the team's first of the season. We won again three nights later, and the boys' confidence soared. I encouraged them to enjoy it and work hard. Over the next three weeks, we won all six of our games, moving to 8 and 7 for the season, and the boys were flying high.

One by one, the less talented boys began to have varying amounts of success except for one – a boy by the name of Albert Jacobs. Albert was facially scarred on his face from what appeared to be burn marks. As a result, he was extremely self-conscious, shy and introverted. I continued to work with him and encourage him, but his talent level was almost non-existent. As the games went on and other players experienced some success, Jacob's teammates joined me in encouraging him. Even though they shunned him in the beginning, probably because they were afraid of his disfigurement, one by one they accepted him as a teammate and rooted him on.

In the fifth inning of our 15th game and my eighth as his coach, Albert came up to bat. I had worked with him for 5 weeks, but his swing was still timid and weak. He just wasn't a ballplayer. He never moved his bat as the pitcher's first offering was called a strike and then watched another strike go by to fall behind 0 and 2.

I called timeout and went over to speak with him. I told him "the next pitch that's near the plate I want you to swing. I don't care if you miss it as long as you try. YOU CAN DO THIS!"

He nodded and stepped back to the plate and then the miracle happened. He swung at the next pitch and grounded a clean single over second base and into center field. Every player on the bench and every fan in the stands erupted in a cheer that sounded like he hit a grand slam to win the World Series. Albert raced to first base and stood on the bag with the biggest smile I've ever seen on a kid's face – except for maybe my own. I looked at his parents. His dad was clapping wildly, and his mother was smiling and crying. At that moment, I knew the season was a smashing success.

Compared to my freshman year, the final 3 years of my high school tenure were anti-climactic. I went out for baseball in the spring of my sophomore year, but the "curve ball issue" came up again and I eventually withdrew. My grades were only average, and it was time to start thinking about studying more and getting into a good college.

I studied harder the last two years and made honor roll the second half of my junior year and all my senior year, even being exempted from having to take a few of my senior final exams. My SAT and ACT scores were better than average and I was accepted into the three colleges to which I applied.

Colleges paid close attention to extra-curricular activities then, as they do now. I had spent a few years on Bergen Catholic's bowling team, belonged to some clubs, worked on the class newspaper and worked a part time job during the summers and school breaks. One summer I worked three jobs – full time at a paper mill, part time as a Little League umpire and delivering chicken for a Chicken Delight franchise. Most of the money went into my savings account for college.

The paper mill job is an interesting story. My father was a waste paper broker. He bought train car loads of old newspaper, books and cardboard and sold them to mills that essentially ground them up like oatmeal in big vats and mixed them with various chemicals, which produced another form of paper or cardboard. So, my father had connections with the mills including one in Paterson, called Morris Paper Board.

The General Manager at Morris was a man named Jerry Rose. He was a big, gruff guy who dealt with a very rough element of laborers who worked there. The mill was a union shop. Rose hired me for the summer of my junior year as an assistant to the electrician in the maintenance department.

Essentially, I followed the electrician around, carried and handed him tools, ran errands and did anything else he asked me to. The mill was a hot place, but the work wasn't too hard, and I was paid minimum wage. When I first started, the union shop boss wanted me to join and pay dues. Rose refused, and they threatened to strike. The union officials came in and they went into Rose's office. There was a lot of shouting and then the meeting ended. Rose came out and told me I was now a "Management apprentice," and thus was exempt from joining the union. He reassigned me to work for the electrician.

The paper mill was a big, foul-smelling place. It was hot and dirty with roaches nearly the size of baseballs. I worked there for several summers and part of some or all my breaks from school. Most of the men who worked there were crude people. Pornography, something I had never been exposed to, was rampant and a lot of the men drank on the job.

After the first summer, I asked Rose if I could work on some of the higher paying jobs. I finally did join the union and started to get union scale. I worked some of the hottest, dirtiest jobs imaginable. One job I did regularly was clean out the basement. The excess "oatmeal," which was like mush in the vats, would be drained into the basement where it sat like an ocean of thick glue.

One or more times a day, I donned hip boots and waded into the sea of goo. Using high pressure hoses, I and another "apprentice" would push the sludge into drains. I'd like to think it was recycled again but I'm pretty sure it ended up in the Passaic River. To break the monotony of this two- to three-hour job, we'd take turns trying to knock the enormous roaches off the wall with the high-pressure hose's spray.

I did a lot of other mindless, menial jobs in the many weeks I worked at Morris over the years, but it was a good experience. I'm pretty sure my Dad got me that job as an incentive to stay in school and get a good education, and it worked. I knew I wouldn't want to do that for the rest of my life. The money was good, though.

I also learned something else about myself over that time. I learned no matter what I did, whether it was delivering papers or chicken, umpiring baseball games or spraying goo, I wanted to be the best at it. I never slacked off, took a nap or hid to get out of work. I gave an honest day's work for the wage and never cheated my bosses or stole from them. Clearly, the lessons from my parents and teachers had taken hold.

Having documented my educational and work habits through high school, I'd like to tell you a bit about my leisure activities growing up – sports. From my earliest memories, baseball was my love. It seems I spent most of my spare time on baseball – playing or watching. My dad was a die-hard Brooklyn Dodgers fan and so, I too, became a Dodgers fan. In 1957, he took me to Ebbets Field in Brooklyn, where I saw Pee Wee Reese, my first idol, Duke Snider, Gil Hodges, Roy Campanella and the rest of that great Dodger team of the 1950s. I met Pee Wee and Campy that day and my rooting interest was solidified. Unfortunately, the team left Brooklyn after that season and moved to Los Angeles. My dad lost interest, but I loved the Dodgers and after Pee Wee retired, Don Drysdale replaced him as my favorite player.

Around that same time, I remember one Sunday watching an NFL football game on TV. It turned out to be the NFL Championship Game of 1958, often referred to as the "Greatest Game of All Time". Watching that game, I fell in love with Johnny Unitas and the Baltimore Colts. They beat the local New York Football Giants, but I didn't care. I had no rooting interest in the Giants. The Colts became my favorite football team.

In the 1960's I became an avid New York Knicks fan. My brothers and I went to numerous Knicks games in the old Madison Square Garden. The Knicks were bad in those days, but they were "our Knicks" and we loved them. For several years they won every game we attended, and we thought we were "good luck charms".

So, my love for sports was cemented at an early age, and even though I knew I would never play professionally, I could still hope that maybe I could be involved in some other manner.

My college selection process was simple. I knew I wanted to follow my dad into business management, so we visited only a few schools. Dad graduated from Fordham University and took all his boys to the annual Father and Son days. We walked the campus, shot rifles, swam in the indoor pool (a special treat since it was winter) and went to a Fordham basketball game in the field house. So, Fordham went on the list.

The next school of interest was Manhattan College, also in New York. I picked that school after a brief visit with the dean of their business school. This was an alternate in the event I didn't get accepted to Fordham.

The third and last school I applied to was Saint Francis College in Loretto, Pennsylvania. During my junior year of high school, Joe Gilson, a business associate of my father, told my dad and Ralph Gaccione, another of my dad's business associates, about his alma mater. Ralph's son, Joe, who I knew from bowling and playing baseball, was a year ahead of me and trying to get into a college. Unfortunately, Joe's grades weren't great, but he was hoping perhaps St. Francis might accept him. We scheduled a weekend visit, and Ralph, Joe, my dad and I made the six-hour drive to Loretto, which sits on top of one of the Allegheny Mountains between Altoona and Johnstown.

What a difference from the New York City schools, to which I'd also applied. It was in the middle of nowhere, but it was beautiful. We met with the president of the school, and after looking at our grades he told Joe his academic record was not strong enough for him to be accepted. He then looked at me and said, "if you keep your grades up, we would be interested in you." The school was known for its Business and Accounting departments, and my dad was impressed with Mr. Gilson, so St. Francis went on the list.

As it turned out, I got accepted to all three, so Manhattan was immediately eliminated. My decision was between Fordham and St. Francis, and to my dad's credit, he didn't try to influence me one way or another. Both schools were good ones, and dad told me he could afford to send me to either one, so it was my decision to make. I was 18 years old and ready to leave the nest. I went to Loretto.

My four years of college were great. Of course, I was lonely at first and had to learn some discipline that comes with being away from parental supervision. We weren't allowed to go home until after Parents Weekend, which wasn't for six weeks, so all the new freshmen were in the same boat. About half of the incoming freshmen were from the east coast, so I had a lot of common acquaintances from the New York area.

My incoming advisor recommended I major in Accounting because of my interest in being in business. His logic was that a successful business manager must have a good understanding of financials and economics of the business, and an emphasis on accounting with legal, insurance and management courses was mapped out. It made sense to me.

Part of the adjustment going from high school to college is to learn HOW to study. For most people, and I was one of them, the study habits that got us through high school don't work in college. Throw in some partying and nobody nagging me to study, and I got off on the wrong foot. I struggled from the outset.

My parents came up for Parents Weekend and I was never so happy to see them. We went out to dinner, went to a movie and just enjoyed each other's company. I knew I'd see them again in a month for Thanksgiving, so when they left on Sunday I was in a much better frame of mind. I went back to my studies and improved some, but it wasn't good enough for Dr. Albert Zanzuccki, the head of the Accounting Department. During my mid-semester review he suggested that perhaps I should rethink my major, and he didn't think I was the "proper material" for the business world. Well, not only was I crushed, but I was also furious at Dr. Zan for giving up on me so easily. I decided I would prove him wrong and eventually I did. It wasn't until a few years later I learned Dr. Zan used the same speech and tactic on nearly every one of his students.

All my business professors at St. Francis taught me well, but most of the good instructors stressed ethics and honesty in business.

They emphasized any smart person can be good in business but at the end of the day, if you can't look at yourself in the mirror and be proud of what you see, then you can never really be successful. I had no idea my future would see me being tested early on those values.

I loved my four years in college. I learned how to think, how to take care of myself, how to party within reason, and I joined the Tau Kappa Epsilon fraternity and graduated with good grades.

But, college is more than that. It's also about memories and lasting relationships and I have a great deal of those. But one relationship stands out among all the rest. St. Francis is where I met the love of my life, and the now 50-year relationship has resulted in 46 years of marriage, three great sons of whom I couldn't be prouder, four granddaughters who light up my life in my senior years, three beautiful daughters-in-law, who keep my boys in line, and a whole host of extended family members and friends who make getting older much more manageable.

I met Chris Weber in October of 1967. She was dating a fraternity brother of mine at the time, a relationship that would soon end. I asked her to go out with me and she agreed. The rest is history.

We dated throughout college. I was a year ahead of her. We married after she graduated in 1971, and through the years she has been instrumental in balancing my life between work and home. While I was out getting recognition, success and sometimes glory, she was raising the family and keeping my head from getting too big.

We had our ups and downs along the way and, thank God, there were many more ups than downs. She was the rudder that kept the ship on course. She shared many of the good times mentioned in this book and suffered or agonized through some of the leaner times. I could not have accomplished what I have without her at my side.

In the spring of 1970 as my college career was coming to an end, I began to think about the kind of job I would like to get. St. Francis' reputation for accounting was well known in the business community. All the "Big Eight" CPA firms came on campus to recruit. I interviewed with many of them and, with graduation looming I had nine job offers, seven of them in New York City, one in Baltimore, and one in Pittsburgh. I visited each of their offices and selected one of the New York firms – Ernst & Ernst, one of the Big Eight. I was ready to apply my skills in the business world and the next step of my future was about to begin. Unfortunately, it wouldn't be long before the ethics issue would raise its head.

CHAPTER 2

MY EARLY PROFESSIONAL YEARS

I started with Ernst & Ernst on June 1, 1970. The job was unusual from the start. The firm had hired several dozen recruits, all of whom started in the summer after graduation. Summer was also a slower time for CPA firms, so there wouldn't be enough work to keep that many inexperienced rookies busy.

The first couple of days we all filled out paperwork, learned the layout of the office, met key personnel and generally just received a good introduction to the firm and its policies. We spent most of our time in the staff room, an enormous room with 60-80 desks. The rookies held introductions and got to know each other. A few guys got assigned to jobs right away but the rest of us had nothing to do. On Wednesday of our first week, Dan O'Mara, the human resources person in charge of the staff accountants came in and told us we could go home for the rest of the week and return Monday morning.

The following Monday we returned, at which time a couple of staff accountants were assigned to jobs, while the rest were sent home for the week. A few of us went to the shore. It felt strange to be paid to go to the beach.

This continued throughout the summer. Eventually we all got some minor assignments, and that gave us a chance to show what we could do and got exposure to the regular staff of managers and supervisors. As we made these connections, we got work and became part of their teams. By mid-fall, I was working regularly.

Over the next several months, I worked on audits of some of the country's largest firms. The first significant one was for Goodbody & Co.,

Wall Street's fifth-largest brokerage firm. Goodbody was founded in the 1880's and flourished with offices all around the country. The corporate office was headquartered in New York City. Ernst & Ernst was to audit the firm's financial records.

The late 1960's was a tumultuous time in the securities industry. Trading volume on the New York Stock Exchange surged, taking many Wall Street firms by surprise. This was before computers became commonplace and many firms still handled trades manually, issuing paper documents only. Goodbody & Co. had begun the process of converting their accounting records to a computerized system.

My assignment was to verify the company's cash section of the balance sheet. There were many dozen bank accounts with balances on the books. My job was to reconcile those accounts. It sounds easier than it was, however, because many of those accounts didn't exist. When the conversion of the accounting from manual to computer was taking place, errors were made. Some accounts were set-up in duplicate, and when Goodbody personnel went to correct the duplicates, they sometimes did it backwards, creating still more accounts. It also didn't help that these accounts were located all over the country, so most of our verification was done by mail. We were, however, able to sift through and many accounts were deleted.

But Goodbody's problems didn't end there. The surge in trading volume caused the company to fall far behind in keeping up with the avalanche of stock certificates and orders to process. Many were lost, and the company was going to go under. The conventional thought was if Goodbody collapsed, the New York Stock Exchange would have a serious panic. Desperate, the NYSE turned to Merrill Lynch, the only firm capable of handling such a large acquisition. Merrill, which already had a solid technological foundation, came to the rescue and absorbed Goodbody. Very quietly Wall Street avoided a possible disaster.

Ernst & Ernst required evaluations of its associates after every job. I scored outstandingly across the board, which led to more varied assignments over the next several months. Each evaluation I received was excellent and I got great experience in all facets of auditing. I settled into a pattern of working on a couple teams on a regular basis, and my billing hours began to skyrocket. The days of getting paid to go to the beach were over.

On July 1, 1971, I was promoted to the next level at Ernst & Ernst. I received a healthy raise, my new title of In-Charge Accountant gave me a little more responsibility, and I would have the opportunity to supervise some of that year's recruits.

E&E also involved me during the recruiting and interview process. I took recruits from other Catholic universities out to lunch and then accompanied them back to the office. It was the earliest form of profiling. After handing them off to the next interviewer, I had to fill out evaluation forms and rate the candidate. This part of the job was not optional. Whenever I was in the metropolitan area I was required to drop whatever I was doing and return to the office for "lunch duty." It affected my billable hours and I was forced to make up the time, usually on a weekend.

On July 3, 1971 Chris and I were married in Pittsburgh. We immediately left for our honeymoon in Tidewater, Virginia. A week later we moved into an apartment in Garfield, N.J. She got a job teaching third grade at a Catholic school in West New York, N.J., across the Hudson River from New York City.

My daily commute from Garfield started at seven each morning. I walked a short distance to catch an Erie Lackawanna train to Hoboken. From there I took a Port Authority train under the river, which dropped me off at the still-under-construction World Trade Center. Next, I either walked to my office at 140 Broadway or to a client's office, if located in the Wall Street area. If I was assigned to a mid-town client, it was another subway ride to the north. If all went well, and that meant no transit strikes or slowdowns or other delays, I would get to my destination in two hours. It was reversed at night.

Two days after the wedding, my grandfather took ill and was hospitalized in Brooklyn. The diagnosis turned out to be cancer. The doctors attempted surgery and determined the cancer was too far spread to do anything. Gramps had complications during the surgery and was kept in the hospital. I was very close to my grandfather my entire childhood. Since my dad and I both worked in the city, it was easier for us to visit him after work and then commute back to New Jersey, usually arriving home at nine p.m. or later. This meant that Chris and I didn't see much of each other during the week, not an ideal situation for newlyweds.

To make matters worse, my supervisors advised me to come to work on Saturdays. Even when I told them I had nothing to do on Saturdays, they told me I should still come in "for show." Being seen in the office on the weekends would enhance my standing with the firm.

My grandfather passed away on September 1, and it was a sad time for all of us. Gramps was our link to our Italian ancestry, and his passing was a blow to the family. Ultimately, I believe it may have contributed to the breakup of my parent's marriage. The only good thing that came out of it was I would get home a few hours earlier on work days.

Since I lived in New Jersey, I applied to work on jobs at E&E's clients on the New Jersey side of the river. That would eliminate some of the commute and perhaps get me home a bit earlier. Finally, in the fall of 1971, I got an assignment working in the Newark area. It would also put me with a new team, enhancing my visibility in the firm. The client was a large container shipping company. My assignment was to evaluate certain current assets that could be easily converted to cash. This would include assets such as deposits made to utilities and insurance companies, advances to employees and executives, and similar assets.

Most of the subject assets were cut and dry. I looked at contracts and agreements and verified the amounts, but there was one asset that stood out – a $400,000 Workers Compensation deposit. This took some time to evaluate. I verified the amount and interviewed the company's risk manager, spoke to representatives of the various workers compensation carriers, and researched laws of the various states where the company did business.

The conclusion was clear to me – the $400,000 could not be easily converted to cash. In fact, the risk manager told me it would be on the books for "several years." The company had a lot of truck drivers and longshoremen who did a lot of lifting, and back injuries were common. Many back injuries surfaced much later due to cumulative "wear and tear." There was no way ,the carriers were going to refund those deposits anytime soon.

I documented all my research in the audit work papers and proposed an adjustment to reclassify the $400,000 to a section of the balance sheet designated for long-term assets. My work was reviewed, approved and signed off on by all my superiors – a senior accountant, a supervisor and the manager on the job. I finished that job, received an outstanding review and moved onto my next assignment. A few weeks later, the senior accountant on the Newark job called me into his office.

He explained the partner on the audit, Mr. Goldfarb,* met with the client's financial management to review the audited financial statements before their release. Some of the E&E adjustments proposed in the audit, including the $400,000 adjustment I authored, would put the client in violation of its working capital requirement with a major lender. Goldfarb* instructed the senior to have me delete my proposed adjustment and all supporting records and memos relating to the adjustment. I asked him if my work was in error, and he assured me everything I did was correct, but I still needed to remove all vestiges of the work.

This presented the first ethical dilemma of my professional career. If I removed something that was correct and assisted in the issuance of incorrect and misleading financial statements being disseminated to the public, I would be as guilty as anyone else involved. I refused to remove my work.

Individually over the next couple of days, the supervisor and manager met with me and asked me to remove the work. I refused and explained it was ethically wrong in my opinion. Finally, I was summoned to Mr. Goldfarb's* office. He wasn't interested in my reasoning. He just ordered me to remove every paper relating to my work on the $400,000. I refused, and he ordered me out of his office.

I learned a few days later the entry was deleted and all evidence of my work was removed from the files. The audited financial statements were issued with the worker's compensation deposit reflected as a current asset. I figured that would spell the end of my career at Ernst & Ernst, but, initially nothing happened. I was assigned to my next job and nothing further was said to me about the previous job.

It was now the first quarter of 1972, and I picked up several assignments working as support for corporate tax returns, which had a filing deadline of March 15th. Each tax assignment was relatively short compared to the audit assignments, and my reviews after each one were all good.

In mid-January, Chris had a doctor's appointment and we learned we were going to become parents. It was a wonderful revelation and we immediately started planning. We signed a lease for a new apartment and began working on turning the extra bedroom into a nursery. We painted and/or wallpapered all the rooms and laid carpet over some of the linoleum floors. Chris was due in September, and she was going to finish the current school year. I was working a heavy schedule during tax season.

On March 17, 1972, I was fired by Ernst & Ernst. I was told I was being laid-off because I didn't figure into the firm's plans. I anticipated there might be some backlash from the container company matter, but as the months went by with nothing happening, I forgot about it. Clearly, now the other shoe had dropped. Goldfarb* had exacted his revenge.

There was a lot of confusion over my being let go. Many of the managers, supervisors and seniors I had worked for, and who had given me very high grades in my reviews, were shocked when they saw my name on the list of the subordinates being let go. CPA firms commonly hired dozens of college graduates each year and then would quickly weed out the ones they felt would never be "partner material." So, it wasn't unusual for that type of list to be published, but seeing my name on that list was somewhat surprising to them, since I was highly regarded in all my reviews.

Only one manager stood up for me, however. A manager is one step away from being a partner and having an ownership interest in the firm. The manager's name was Ted Pincus, and I had worked for Ted on several assignments. He always requested me on his jobs. The day the list came out and I was told I was out of a job, Ted called me to his office.

"I'm sure it's a mistake," Ted told me. "I reviewed your file and there are only outstanding reviews in there. I'll get to the bottom of this. Come and see me in the morning."

In those days, there was more paperwork to fill out when an employee was terminated, and E&E told me I could use the office in my search for another job. So, it wasn't unusual for ex-employees to be in the office.

The next morning, I reported to Ted's office. The first thing he said to me was, "You butted heads with Goldfarb.*"

I gave him my version of the story. After listening to what I said he told me he heard pretty much the same story but, unfortunately, because a partner insisted I be let go, there was nothing he could do. He offered to get me a job with one of his clients in the city and I told him I would let him know, but I was really interested in getting a job in New Jersey so I didn't have such a long commute. We shook hands, and I left 140 Broadway and never returned.

I had experienced the politics of working in a big CPA firm in the big city. I was taught in school CPA firms had the highest ethical responsibility but learned the real world presented a different reality. I didn't blame Ted Pincus or any of the other professionals I worked with on the various assignments I received at Ernst & Ernst, other than Goldfarb*.

At the end of the day everyone involved in that political environment had to look out for their own futures. I only hoped what I experienced on the Newark job was an anomaly. Ernst & Ernst was the only company I ever worked for that fired me. But, when I looked in the mirror that night I wasn't ashamed of what I saw.

It didn't take me long to find a job in New Jersey. After slightly more than two months I hooked on with a company in Passaic, only a few miles from where I lived. Popular Services, Inc. was a privately held conglomerate, predominately in retail. The company's main business was mail-order out of a catalog.

What set it apart from other mail-order companies was the Popular Club Plan, which allowed customers who didn't have the money, to buy products on a monthly payment plan. The company sold everything from socks to furniture, all available on monthly payment plans. It was buy-to-own before there was rent-to-own, and the interest was calculated in the payment.

In addition to three mail-order divisions, the company also had four retail chain store divisions; a banking division; a data processing, sales and system division; and a commercial credit division. The corporate offices were in a campus featuring very old red brick buildings in an industrial area. I came on board as an internal auditor.

I started on May 25, 1972, and didn't care for the job from day one. However, we spent two months living on my wife's $4,500 per year salary and some unemployment, so I needed to bring in some money since the birth of our first child was less than four months away.

I just didn't like the retail environment. When you sell at retail, it is important to make sure controls are in place and strictly adhered to. The nickels and dimes add up, and the owners of the company wanted to count every one of them.

It wasn't the people. I worked for, and with, some wonderful people including the man who hired me, Ray Bacek. When Ray hired me, he knew I wouldn't stay long but he really needed help. I pledged to him I would give him 100 percent effort until the day I left. He promoted me within six months and treated me fairly, but he knew it was a matter of time. I was already looking for the next "right" opportunity.

Michael Thomas Rossetti was born into the world on September 13, 1972, and Chris' and my lives changed forever. He was the joy of our lives and I was grateful I could share in his earliest years, but I was traveling quite a bit all over the East Coast and Midwest. The three of us and a dog lived on the second floor of a duplex in Garfield, and Chris and I dreamed of owning a house for little Mike to grow up in.

I was making decent money – about $14,000 per year but had little savings and with the cost of housing in the New York metropolitan area, the likelihood of being able to buy something decent was remote. We decided to consider moving away from the New York area to a smaller, more affordable area. I employed the Robert Half search firm to look for positions in cities such as Baltimore, Pittsburgh, Kansas City, St. Louis and other areas where housing in the suburbs would be more affordable.

The first job offer I received in the new search came from a tool company in Syracuse. The Crouse-Hinds company flew Chris and I out to see the area, but in the end the prospect of severe winters combined with the state taxes in New York caused us to rethink it, and I turned down the offer.

The next interview was in the Baltimore/Washington area. Westinghouse was looking for an internal auditor based out of their plant between the two cities. The company's reputation was impeccable, and it was obviously stable financially. But there was a drawback – the job was going to require me to travel 80-90 percent of the time, not the best for a family man. We gave serious consideration for Chris and Mike to move in with her parents in Pittsburgh, and I would fly into and out of that airport. On the few nights that I'd be in the Maryland area, I'd get an inexpensive room in a boarding house. The money we'd save over a year or two would be used to buy a house. Westinghouse offered me a job pending an investigative background check on me, which would take a week to ten days.

At the same time as the Westinghouse interview, I interviewed in Youngstown, Ohio, with the Edward J. DeBartolo Corporation, a shopping center developer. We parlayed both interviews with a visit to my in-laws, driving from New Jersey to Baltimore for a Friday interview with Westinghouse, then to Pittsburgh for the family visit. The DeBartolo interview was the following Monday.

When I arrived at the DeBartolo office I was ushered into Bob Munro's office, the Controller for the company. Munro was looking for a Manager of Special Projects. Munro told me about his own background.

Prior to joining DeBartolo, he worked at Crown Construction of Johnstown, Pennsylvania, about 20 miles from St. Francis College, where I got my degree. The owner of Crown was a man named Frank Pasquerilla who was very involved with St. Francis. Pasquerilla had been on the St. Francis Board of Trustees and donated thousands of dollars to the college. Munro told me he wanted to see what a graduate of St. Francis would be like, so he interviewed me. Munro was also born in New York.

We chatted for quite a while. He told me what he was looking for, and I fit every requirement. When the interview neared its end, I told him I enjoyed the discussion, and asked "do I have the job?" He smiled and told me he was impressed, but he was looking for someone older – around 30. I was 25. I asked him to reconsider and he said he would think about it. He would call me after he finished interviewing and made his decision. I told him I was very interested. We shook hands and I left.

The DeBartolo position moved to the forefront. I was intrigued by Munro's enthusiasm for the company and the job sounded interesting. There was minimal travel involved, and the money was comparable to the Westinghouse offer. It was now up to Munro to get over the age issue.

A week later, the Westinghouse people called. My background check was clean and they would send me a letter formalizing their offer. I received it early the next week and I called Munro. I told him I was considering another offer and I needed to hear from him by Thursday. Late Thursday night, Munro made the offer. The following Monday I accepted and the next step of my life was about to begin.

The final caveat to this part of my life arose from a phone call several months later from a former colleague, who was still employed by Ernst & Ernst. E&E had been sued for malpractice on the container company audit. Apparently, the client had defaulted on its loan and the lender sued E&E. It was settled for several million and Goldfarb* quietly retired.

CHAPTER 3

1973-1974 - THE EARLY DEBARTOLO YEARS

During the same time I was in my job search, so too was my father. My dad got his job first – a partnership interest in a waste paper brokerage company in Chicago. He was over 50 and this was his first chance at some big money. In early 1973, he, my mother and my two youngest brothers moved to Northbrook, Illinois.

As a partner in his new firm, he signed a partnership agreement that had a successor clause in it. Upon his retirement, if he had a family member to succeed him he would reap better benefits than he would without a successor. Since I was his first son with a college degree, I was a natural candidate and, since he knew I was looking, he called and offered me a job. This was right about the time the Westinghouse and DeBartolo job offers were imminent.

My dad called and we discussed the possibility of my working for his company. He told me it would be necessary to learn the business first by running a paper mill in Green Bay, Wisconsin. After two years, I would join his firm in Chicago. I was considering it, but the prospect of two winters in Green Bay was not particularly appealing. When the DeBartolo offer came in I politely told my dad I wasn't interested in Green Bay, and I'd be moving to Youngstown.

Chris and I began winding up our affairs in New Jersey preparatory to the move to Ohio. In the meantime, my dad was checking out the DeBartolo Corporation with his contacts in New York. My father had some connections through his union involvements on the East Coast with certain elements in organized crime. A few days later he advised me he checked out DeBartolo and was told he wasn't involved in organized crime. That hadn't really crossed my mind at that point, but it was nice to know.

One funny aside relating to that point: just prior to leaving for Youngstown, Chris and I were watching an episode of the original "Hawaii 5-0," and Jack Lord apprehended a Mafia member from the mainland. The criminal was wanted for murdering a man in Youngstown, Ohio, in a car bombing. The victim's name was Rossetti. We looked at each other and started laughing, but we hoped that wasn't going to be an omen.

I arrived in Youngstown on Saturday, October 13, 1973, and started work the following Monday. Chris and I made an offer on a home in Austintown, a suburb of Youngstown. We needed to apply for a mortgage, and Bob Munro hooked us up with the bank the corporation used. That bank was the Dollar Savings and Trust Company, and the loan officer we met with was Bill Jayne. His office was in the Southern Park Mall across the street from DeBartolo's office. The mall was a DeBartolo property.

We introduced ourselves to Mr. Jayne, and the first thing he said to me was, "So, you're the newest hot shot from New York?" His choice of words surprised us a bit, but I acknowledged I was from New York. Then he said, "Let me tell you something, son. You are going to learn more in one year working for that man across the street that you'd learn in 10 years working in New York."

I was pretty cocky in those days, but I kept my opinion to myself. Little did I know how prophetic Mr. Jayne's words would turn out.

The DeBartolo Corporation was started in 1948 when Edward J. DeBartolo left his father's business and struck out on his own to build shopping plazas in the suburbs. DeBartolo, a Notre Dame graduate, was a World War II veteran who was born and grew up in an Italian neighborhood on the south side of Youngstown.

He recognized the post -war exodus from the cities into the surrounding areas and began building homes in those areas for the returning soldiers and their families. He also recognized the need for stores and services for those families, so he built the area's first outdoor shopping center in Boardman Township in 1951. The center's success spawned dozens of similar projects throughout the Midwest over the next decade.

Those shopping plazas built in the 1950's led to the next step in retail - the enclosed shopping mall. DeBartolo pioneered that concept as well. When I joined the corporation in the fall of 1973, Mr. DeBartolo's company was widely considered to be the largest shopping center developer in the world. He also branched out into horse racing with Thistledown Racetrack in Cleveland and, about the time of my arrival, he purchased Balmoral Park Racetrack, south of Chicago in the town of Crete, Illinois. A third racetrack, Louisiana Downs was under construction, soon to open in Shreveport. The company also had two new Holiday Inns in the Cleveland suburbs and managed a foreign trade zone operation in Toledo, Ohio.

My first position was Manager of Special Projects, and my initial project was to research and implement a document storage system. The company had millions of paper documents in filing cabinets in-house and in storage, and they were out of room. I would spend several weeks evaluating the newest document storage systems and visiting companies that already made the conversion. I finally settled on a micro-fiche system, which we implemented.

In November, the company expanded the Toledo operation, from initially managing the Foreign Trade Zone, to include the stevedoring operation – the loading and unloading of Great Lakes freighters. Munro and I drove to Toledo and I met Walter T. Zeplien, a fascinating man who managed our Foreign Trade Zone operation and who would also oversee the stevedoring operation.

Zeplien was a German-born U.S. citizen and a former U-boat captain for Germany in World War II. He immigrated to the U.S. after the war and met Mr. DeBartolo in the 50's. The men developed a friendship and in 1960, Captain Zeplien (as he was known to his staff) began working for Mr. D. Both men had a deep respect for each other and Zeplien broached the prospect of taking over the stevedoring operation to Mr. D., who gave his approval.

We set up the entity and controls for Toledo Overseas Terminal, Inc., the newly-formed stevedoring company. Over the next several years, I made many additional trips to Toledo and worked closely with Captain Zeplien and his people. The captain was always good for interesting stories and I always enjoyed the trips.

At the time, I was considered lower middle management on a level with other department heads who reported to the Controller. Two associates on a similar level became my first friends in Youngstown -- Dave Gehrich who was the Director of Taxation for the company and Dick Korby*, who oversaw the accounting for Thistledown and the two new racetracks.

I first met Marie Denise DeBartolo shortly after I joined the company. MDD (many of us in the company used initials for the family members and other executives) was the Vice-President of Personnel. Marie Denise was friendly and was very good at what she did. However, she had a habit of engaging you with her eyes, and over the years I often felt like I had to look away to avoid a staring contest. She was very pleasant, however, and became a strong ally and friend in the years to come.

I met Edward J. DeBartolo, Jr. (EJD, Jr.) at the company Christmas party the week before Christmas. He seemed friendly but was surrounded by friends, and we didn't really have any kind of discussion. That would come a bit later in our relationship.

I encountered Mr. DeBartolo Sr. (EJD) a few weeks prior under a comical and somewhat unnerving experience. I had occasionally seen him around the office but never had the opportunity to introduce myself. Mr. D. was usually hurrying somewhere or walking with someone else in conversation. Bill Pfaus, who was the company's Chief Financial Officer and Bob Munro's boss, had promised to introduce me to Mr. D. when the opportunity arose. Pfaus' office was adjacent to Mr. DeBartolo's.

One day in early December I was summoned to Pfaus' office while he was meeting with Munro. I answered a couple of questions for them and then was dismissed. As I walked out the door, Pfaus called out to me. I turned around and he asked me another question. I answered, he thanked me, and I was free to go.

I turned quickly and walked right into a small gentleman standing behind me. I outweighed him by a good 50 pounds, and he lost his balance and stumbled back against the wall. I quickly apologized and introduced myself. From behind me, Pfaus offered "Oh Tom, meet Mr. DeBartolo. Fortunately for you he likes aggressive people!" Blushing I headed down the hall toward my desk. The sound of laughter followed me from Pfaus' office.

In late January 1974, Munro determined there was enough work to warrant setting up a new accounting department for the company's non-shopping center operations. On January 31, 1974, I was promoted to Manager of Diversified Operations Accounting to initially oversee the Toledo Operations, Thistledown Racetrack and two Cleveland Holiday Inns. I would also have some limited involvement with a new venture; Fun -N- Games Associates, a partnership involving EJD, Jr, MDD and another executive of the company, William Moses. Fun-N-Games had a family amusement center (we used to call them pinball parlors) in Boardman Plaza, and the company planned to build a string of them, primarily in DeBartolo malls across the country.

Shortly after my promotion I encountered another new challenge. The manager of the development and mall management accounting department left, and Munro asked me to take over on an interim basis. The corporation had five or six degreed accountants who did the accounting for the DeBartolo Corporation's 100 or so business entities. The year-end accounting work was very labor- intensive, getting all those entities completed for the tax returns and the corporation's consolidated financial statements.

The entire procedure had dragged into October for the previous year, and a repeat was unacceptable to management. I decided to split the workload up among the five or six accountants and put them on a schedule to each have two or three entities done on a weekly basis, the target being to have all the year-end accounting done by the end of March. Due to the complexity of some of the entities the consensus was it wasn't possible. I stuck to the deadline and told them they had no choice. I would review their completed work and monitor each of the associate's progress.

When one of the accountants would fall behind, I'd review his status and reassign some work to another accountant who was ahead of schedule. If none of them was ahead of schedule, I'd jump in and do some or all the work myself. After some initial grumbling, the guys began to see progress and the enthusiasm caught on. We all worked as a team and the preliminary work got completed on time.

The review logjam then hit Bob Munro and me, but we worked through it, and before April was over, we'd given DeBartolo's CPA firm 90 percent of what they needed to do the certified financial statements. The other 10 percent required input and decisions from top management, which was out of my hands. I commended the staff for their efforts and hard work and turned the department over to the recently hired new manager. Munro rewarded me with a 10 percent pay increase.

While all of that was going on, Louisiana Downs opened down in Shreveport, Louisiana, and it was a disaster. The clubhouse wasn't finished before opening day and the track started bleeding money. Mr. DeBartolo had partnered with two other wealthy men – Kemmons Wilson, the founder of the Holiday Inn chain, and John Wolcott, a Texas oilman.

Wolcott was running the track, and he was in over his head. There were frantic calls from Wolcott for capital to cover the operating expenses, and the unpaid construction bills were piling up. Munro dispatched Dick Korby* to monitor the finances and report back on the financial operations. Munro instructed me to take over Korby's* responsibility for Thistledown Racetrack in North Randall, Ohio, a suburb of Cleveland.

I began making the 75-minute drive to the track where I worked with Keith Simon, the track's new Controller. This was the initial racing experience for both Keith and I, so we were learning together. We learned from each other's strengths – Keith worked the operations side with the track's department heads while I worked the financial side, teaching him the controls and financial tools he needed to do his job for Munro. Keith, in turn, taught me the operational side of the racing business, which served me greatly in the years that followed. We made a good team, not only at Thistledown, but throughout many future projects in the years to come.

With me making several trips to Cleveland each month, Munro felt that it was also time for me to get involved in the company's Hotel Division in Cleveland. As I mentioned earlier, the company had two Holiday Inns in the area – a 280-room, 10-story property across from Thistledown, and a 150-room motel about 10 miles up the road in Beachwood.

A third property with 120 rooms was under construction in Mayfield Heights, a few miles north of Beachwood. The two existing hotels, as well as Thistledown, were all losing money.

The country was in a recession in 1974 and, as a developer, the DeBartolo Corporation was understandably hard-hit. Money became very tight and Mr. DeBartolo called for cost cutting. This procedure became commonplace during my tenure at DeBartolo, but this time was the first for me. It required a full understanding of all the operations, so my learning curve was short. Mr. D wanted operations "lean and mean", which was a statement I would hear many times over the years.

That spring, I also experienced a personal crisis that solidified for the first time my loyalty to the DeBartolo family. In April, my mother called from Chicago, and she was very upset. My father had left her and moved out after more than 25 years of marriage and six children. She was alone with my two youngest brothers and was devastated.

I went to Munro and told him I had to get to Chicago and help my mother through this crisis. I offered to take an unpaid leave of absence since I had been with the company for less than seven months. Munro went to Marie Denise DeBartolo and explained my predicament.

Marie Denise went to Mr. DeBartolo and then told me he approved my leave of absence, except I would continue to be paid for the time I was gone. About an hour later, Munro called me at home while I was packing. Apparently, Mr. D had second thoughts about my trip.

He suggested to Munro that I visit the newly-acquired Balmoral Park racetrack, "if I had the time," and the company would pick up my expenses for the trip to Chicago. Mr. DeBartolo also told Munro to tell me that "family is the top priority in this company" and I had to do whatever was necessary to resolve my (and my mother's) problems. I was blown away by Mr. D's compassion. But that was only the beginning of what I experienced with the family. The bonds of loyalty were tightening.

I couldn't resolve the issues between my parents and they eventually divorced, although my mother fought the divorce to the bitter end. But, I could help her and my brothers cope, as best as they were able. My mother never remarried and, to the best of my knowledge, she never dated after that.

I did make a couple of visits to Balmoral that week, and now I was actively involved in the management of both Thistledown and Balmoral, the Cleveland Hotel Division, and the two Toledo operations, as well as my duties in the home office. Bill Jayne's prognostication during our mortgage process was quickly becoming a reality.

Next up would be Louisiana Downs. The track completed the racing schedule for the year and it had been disastrous. The racing meet resulted in a several million-dollar loss, the clubhouse construction was still incomplete, and the racing surface -- the track itself -- was sub-standard and considered unsafe for the horses and jockeys . The horse-men notified management they wouldn't run their horses there unless it was replaced. Management was incompetent and in over their heads, and there were rumors of corruption and mismanagement of money. Compounding matters, many of the original construction bills still hadn't been paid, and the workers and contractors had pulled off the job.

The three partners met to discuss their options. They agreed only a large influx of cash could begin solving the problems. And then, Mr. DeBartolo received a few nasty surprises.

First, the Texas oilman, John Wolcott, who was also the track's General Manager, revealed he was broke and reportedly had less than $20,000 in assets to his name. Then, Kemmons Wilson, the Holiday Inn founder, revealed all his net worth was tied-up in Holiday Inn stock, which was severely depressed in value due to the recession. He had no additional funds available to contribute to the joint venture. If the track was going to survive, it would do so on Mr. DeBartolo's slender shoulders.

Mr. DeBartolo was a risk taker, but this would be the biggest gamble of his life, so far. He decided to go "all in." He would cover the existing debts and attempt to turn the track around, a severe gamble given that the company was in a cash bind of its own. He fired Walcott and took assignment of both Walcott's and Wilson's stock.

DeBartolo began a search for a new General Manager to manage the debt-ridden track, but it was a hard sell. The track had a bad reputation within the racing community. The racing industry had watched everything unfold and few, if any, expected the track to survive. Most viable candidates weren't interested in the job.

DeBartolo's search eventually took him to Vincent J. Bartimo, a former journalist from New England, with experience running Green Mountain Racetrack in Southern Vermont. It would be Bartimo's job to find and install a management team, sort through the cascade of bills and get them paid, get the racing surface rebuilt to safe standards, complete the clubhouse construction, repair the reputation of the track, and staff the operation to get it profitable – all during a recession!

What Bartimo quickly learned was the situation he inherited was even worse than previously thought. The corruption and graft he found involved many of the department heads, and he had to fire some of the management people he had planned to keep, including Dick Korby*, the DeBartolo watchdog Munro had sent down. He also discovered some of DeBartolo's construction people had dropped the ball and were responsible for many of the construction flaws. Bartimo advised Mr. D. he would have no further use for Youngstown personnel.

Bartimo set to work and began to build his own staff. To the extent he could get funds from the home office, he was able to start making payments to the contractors and get them back on the job. Slowly, the clubhouse was completed. Likewise, he got a racing track expert from Texas to come to Louisiana Downs, and Tex Tankersly engineered and supervised the reconstruction of the racing surface. It would still be several months, however, before all the old construction bills were paid off.

Bartimo had the expertise and powers of persuasion to build the staff he needed and, after firing Korby, he felt his two bookkeepers could handle the financial matters for him. The women, though hard workers, simply didn't have the expertise to devise and prepare the sophisticated reports Mr. DeBartolo demanded. Bob Munro and Bartimo would argue over what was needed, and Munro let DeBartolo know Bartimo was in over his head on the financial side.

DeBartolo, caught between Bartimo's distain for Youngstown involvement and Munro's insistence that the company needed to get somebody down there to straighten out the finances, reluctantly agreed to allow Youngstown involvement, but on a very short lease. Bartimo would still have final say on everything.

DeBartolo, mindful of the history of bungled Youngstown involvement, warned Munro that whomever he sent to Shreveport "better not screw it up!" Munro delegated me to take the trip. On a hunch, I requested that the Thistledown Controller, Keith Simon, accompany me, and Munro and DeBartolo agreed. It would be good to have Keith's operational expertise to help guide me. We left for Shreveport on a Sunday, rented a car and headed to the Hilton, which was convenient to the track. When we walked into the lobby, I was surprised to see Korby* waiting for us. Obviously, someone from the track had tipped him off that we were coming down. From there, he probably used his connections to find out where we were staying.

After checking-in, we reluctantly agreed to have a drink with Dick. There was no subterfuge here. Korby* wanted me to get his Louisiana Downs job back, or at least get back into his former job in the corporation. I listened to his story and told him I had to do some research and hear the other side of the story. He made it clear Bartimo was ruining the track's chance to succeed with his "heavy handed ways." At this point, I hadn't even spoken with Bartimo, so I put Korby* off. I agreed to call him after I met with Bartimo.

The following morning, Keith and I got to the track and we were escorted to Bartimo's office by security guards. Given Bartimo's experience with Youngstown personnel, we did not expect a warm welcome, and we certainly didn't get one. Bartimo railed about the incompetence of the DeBartolo representatives he had dealt with, and he made it clear we were there only "as a favor to Mr. DeBartolo."

We told him what we planned to do, and he ordered us not to change anything without his express approval. He reiterated his two bookkeepers were adequate for what he needed and instructed I meet with him twice each day, once at mid-day and again at the end of the day. If I failed to follow his instructions, Keith and I would be escorted off the property.

Bartimo then dismissed us and Keith and I split up. I went to meet with the financial people and Keith went to meet with the various department heads to evaluate the control aspects of their departments. I felt we had to come up with something significant quickly to blunt or soften Bartimo's hostility and, hopefully, gain his support. We got it quickly in a big way.

With the track in so much debt, Bartimo would meet with one of the bookkeepers each morning to review the outstanding bills and determine who would get paid that day. That was his primary view of what his financial people should do. After that morning's meeting between Bartimo and the bookkeeper, I asked the bookkeeper if I could see the unpaid bills file she just reviewed with Bartimo. The file included not only operating expenses, but also many of the unpaid construction bills, as well.

I decided to trace a few of the bills back to the original and/or revised contracts. I immediately found a couple of huge discrepancies. Some change orders to the contracts were not included in the bills Bartimo was reviewing. In nearly all the cases, the change orders had reduced the amount of the contract and the amount due. The bills Bartimo was looking at were overstated – by well over a million dollars, just in these cases. When I met with Bartimo a few hours later, in my first mid-day meeting, he was shocked at what I had found. He gratefully advised me to continue.

We made more inroads the rest of the day and week. We built up a good rapport with the department heads, thanks to Keith's "folksy" way and our recommendations to help track management run more efficiently. As we neared the end of the week and were due to return up north, Bartimo asked if we could stay. I was unable to stay but I promised Vince (as he instructed us to call him now) I would return in a week or two. Keith could and agreed to stay until I returned. By the time I returned a week later, Keith had made great progress in implementing controls and reports. Vince was duly impressed, and he asked if one of us would stay on permanently.

Neither Keith nor I was interested in moving to Louisiana. Both of us had only recently moved to Ohio and Keith's wife had grown up and had family in Cleveland. I offered to find a suitable professional for Louisiana Downs, subject to Vince's approval. Bartimo took me up on the offer. Korby* would not be considered.

I contacted my representative at Robert Half and he started lining up interviews. There were not many locals in the area that were interested in the racing business (Shreveport was in the heart of the so-called "Bible Belt"), so we had to expand our search area. With the Shreveport/Bossier City communities in that strict religious area, many of the residents hadn't wanted the track there to begin with.

Also, given the bad blood the track's first year had created with local contractors not being paid, people being laid-off and fired, and all the negative publicity the first season created, most likely kept many of the qualified candidates on the sidelines. The few locals that responded didn't have the personality or experience, and I knew Bartimo would need to be comfortable with his Controller as a person and professional. The solution would come from out of state. I flew home for the week-end.

The Robert Half representative we used was the same one who placed me with DeBartolo. He called while I was in Shreveport the next week and told me he found a young man in Memphis who had all the credentials I required. He wasn't afraid of the racing business and would relocate. I changed my homebound flight to arrange a stopover in Memphis to interview Thomas B. Donahue.

We met at a hotel near the airport, hit it off immediately, agreed upon a salary, and I arranged for him to meet Vince Bartimo in Shreveport. Bartimo liked Donahue, as well, and we finally had a Controller at Louisiana Downs. The track was still bleeding money, but big changes were in the works.

CHAPTER FOUR

1975-76 - CHANGE TAKES PLACE

With Louisiana Downs stabilized, at least from a management position, I fell into a routine that didn't require as much travel. Bob Munro asked me to devote more time on our Cleveland operations – Thistledown Racetrack and the Holiday Inns. As each day went by, my responsibilities were evolving away from purely financial and more into management.

Thistledown was an old track located in North Randall, a Cleveland suburb south of the city. In the 50's and 60's, DeBartolo purchased four racetracks in the Cleveland-Akron area – Summit Park, Thistledown, Randall Park and Cranwood Park. All four tracks ran thoroughbreds and were old and worn, and eventually, Mr. D closed three of the tracks and consolidated the racing licenses to Thistledown, the lone survivor. DeBartolo wanted the land occupied by the tracks for future mall sites and the enormous acreage racetracks required was perfect. By consolidating the four tracks to one, this freed up the other land for development and allowed DeBartolo to run four separate racing meets at Thistledown, comprising more than 200 racing dates per year.

Mr. DeBartolo loved thoroughbred racing. Aside from his work, it was his only activity that might be called a hobby. In the years to come, I would learn how true that statement was, but for the time being all I knew was Thistledown was dear to him. The track was across the street from the former Randall Park Racetrack.

DeBartolo had razed the old track years before and, now the company was in the process of constructing the country's largest shopping center – the Randall Park Mall on that site. Also on that site was the first of DeBartolo's hotels – the Randall Park Holiday Inn, the 10-story hotel . It had 250 rooms, a full-service restaurant and bar, large meeting rooms and a car rental company among its amenities. Right outside the door was the massive construction site that would eventually be the mall. Thistledown was across the street from the hotel and the mall.

There was always a method to Mr. DeBartolo's manner and this area was no different. The track served as a place where he could fly into and have lunch and wager on the horses at the same time. He had a private suite at the hotel where he could rest and freshen up, and the car rental agency would supply him with a vehicle he could use to roam around the area, conducting meetings and overseeing the several construction projects he had going on in the Cleveland area.

When weather conditions were acceptable, Mr. DeBartolo would fly to the Thistledown track. The company owned a small one-engine airplane known as a STOL (Short Take-Off & Landing), sometimes called a helio plane, that could get airborne in a few hundred feet. EJD Corp. had a small grass runway adjacent to the office, and the Thistledown infield was perfect for landing and take-off, as well. DeBartolo always had at least three pilots on the payroll to fly the STOL and the corporate Lear Jet housed at the Youngstown Airport. When EJD flew to Cleveland, the rental company at the Holiday Inn would shuttle a car to the track for his use.

One typical hot summer day in 1975, EJD flew to Cleveland, landed at the track, jumped into the rental car and drove out of the track parking lot toward the mall construction site to review the progress. Mr. D went perhaps a quarter of a mile when the rental car stalled – it was out of gas. Mr. DeBartolo got out of the car and walked toward the Holiday Inn, a few hundred yards away.

It was a hot windy summer afternoon, and Mr. D was wearing his typical dark suit –either black or charcoal grey. Unfortunately, the earth movers on the mall site were working on the parking lot and the dust was blowing right toward the street where Mr. D was walking. By the time he got to the hotel, the sweaty man was covered with so much dust it appeared his suit was white. I heard from the hotel management his confrontation with the owner of the rental car agency was not very pleasant, to say the least.

The next day I was called into Bob Munro's office. He told me what happened to Mr. D, handed me a copy of the lease, and instructed me to audit the car rental company and get enough information to terminate the lease with cause. I called the rental agency owner and scheduled the audit.

A few days later, I drove up to the hotel and went over the agency's books. His hand-written ledger and numbers exactly matched the reports that he had provided the hotel and on which his rent was paid. However, I had also checked EJD Corporation's records to see what the company paid that agency for Mr. DeBartolo's car usage. Those numbers also exactly matched, meaning the owner had only reported transactions initiated by our company.

Now, I also knew for a fact Thistledown occasionally rented vehicles from that agency, as well, so I confronted the owner with that fact and asked for the correct set of ledgers. The embarrassed owner reluctantly opened a desk drawer and produced a second ledger that had different numbers for his five or six car rental fleet. Those numbers showed the track's usage, but no cash or credit card sales. I mentioned that to him and casually added that the IRS and State of Ohio might be interested in the results of my audit. Even I was surprised when the man then produced a third set of records that "included all of my revenue!" My question as to why he had three sets of records produced no answer.

By now, the owner realized he was in trouble, and he offered me cash if I wouldn't report him to anyone. I declined his offer and went on calculating what back rent he would owe. He then offered his daughter, an attractive woman who worked for him, for "a date." Again, I politely refused and told him the best thing he could do would be to pay the back rent and perhaps the company would not terminate his lease. He owed us seven or eight thousand dollars, and he immediately wrote a check for the rent. I gave the check to the hotel controller for deposit and drove back to Youngstown to write my report. The following week, his lease was terminated.

It was now late summer, and my next surprise was an unpleasant one. Bob Munro resigned as Controller of the Edward J. DeBartolo Corporation. Before the news was released, Munro called me into his office and confided that his successor would be Peter S. Frank, the gentleman recently hired to head up the Mall and Development Accounting Department.

Munro told me he seriously considered me for the Controller position, but he felt I was "too young for the responsibility." He explained I earned consideration through my performance, but he felt my age was too much of a deterrent. Pete Frank was 10 years my senior and had been with the company less than a year. My only consolation was that I was promoted to Assistant Controller, a new position, and given a 24 percent raise.

Over the next couple weeks before Munro left, he asked me several times to "stick around awhile" and help Pete make the transition. I don't remember exactly how I felt at the time, but I told Munro I would help Pete, but the message to me was clear – my future with the company wasn't as solid as I thought, and future promotions would probably be limited. Ironically, the age issue that made my initial hiring questionable was still on somebody's mind. I wondered if it was just Munro or somebody higher up the ladder.

I had no clear-cut feelings about my future, so I decided to wait and see how the new relationship with Pete would work out. Pete was a low-key guy I had gotten along with to date, including the time he spent with Hill, Barth and King, the CPA firm that audited the company's books. Pete had good credentials as an accountant, but his management talents were an unknown at this point. He pretty much left me alone while he adjusted to his new position.

The highlight of 1976 was the Grand Opening of Randall Park Mall, "the world's largest and most beautiful shopping complex", according to a quote from Cleveland Magazine. Chris and I were invited to the grand opening, and we both felt the more than two million square-foot mall was impressive not only in its size, but its grandeur as well. I was proud to be a part of the company that built the magnificent edifice and I was happy for the DeBartolo family for the achievement.

1976 was also noteworthy for us due to the birth of my second son, Chip, born on April 7th. I was in a meeting in the conference room with the DeBartolos and others when Mr. D's secretary, Edy, interrupted us to tell me Chris was going into labor. Mr. D immediately told me to "get my ass going" to join her.

Professionally, 1976 had been an interesting year, but nothing special. I had gotten more involved with Balmoral and Thistledown Racetracks and the Cleveland hotel operation, which added a third Holiday Inn in Mayfield Heights. I also made occasional trips to Shreveport and Toledo, but there were no real crises in any of the Diversified Operations, and progress was being made across the board. It may have been a little boring, but at least I had more family time as the travel demands were less. But, as quiet as 1976 may have been, 1977 would prove to be anything but.

CHAPTER 5

1977 – MY FUTURE BECOMES CLEARER (MAYBE)

1977 started off quiet enough, but it wasn't going to last. Since my primary responsibilities were financial related to the Diversified Operations, the year-end accounting for the entities I was responsible took center stage. Since 1974, I built a department of a handful of good accountants and clerks to handle the day-to-day accounting. My manager was a young man named Marty Hamer, a quiet, loyal and competent family man, who was also going to night school at Youngstown State University for his accounting degree.

He also had a family with children, and where he found the time to do his job, go to school at night and raise a family baffled me. But it never became an issue with his work, so I was fine with him. Marty did much of the accounting for two of the tracks (Thistledown & Balmoral) and the Toledo operations. He previously worked at the company as Manager of Accounts Receivable and jumped at the opportunity to join my staff in 1974. When I left some 15 years after we started together, he was still there.

Christine Bilski was a degreed accountant we hired a year or two later. Chris was ambitious and reliable and quickly took over the accounting for the hotels and Fun-N-Games Associates, the family-owned amusement centers that were rapidly multiplying. When I left EJD Corporation years later, there were 84 game rooms to go with a handful of hotels and a few other odds and ends. Chris was also still there when I left, handling that part of the Diversified Operations.

I also had a few clerical people who assisted all of us where needed. My secretary at the time (I went through several over the years) was Debbie Loupe, and she was one of my best secretaries. This secretary position was one of the toughest in the company due to the sheer volume of work that crossed her desk with the telephone ringing constantly.

The DeBartolo Corporation kept all accounting in Youngstown at that time, except for Louisiana Downs, which, at the start, was a public company. Later, the sports teams would have their accounting kept on-site with heavy visitation from the home office. This was before the days of desktop computers, and DeBartolo's computer was a massive compilation of equipment that took up a large part of the second floor at 7620 Market Street. All the mall accounting was also done in-house, and there were more than a dozen degreed accountants on staff always.

Mr. DeBartolo firmly believed in "hands-on" management, and this included the accounting departments. Absolutely no major decisions were made without his input and approval, and when he wanted answers, he wanted them immediately. Having people in-house with the answers, required each one of us had direct lines to our responsible operations always. I had a Controller in Cleveland for the Hotel operations, another at Thistledown for the track, a third in Toledo for those operations, a fourth at Balmoral for that racetrack, and a fifth at Louisiana Downs. Later, our sports teams would be added.

Each of those controllers had direct responsibility to me and dotted line responsibility to their respective General Managers. The General Managers, in most cases, all had direct line responsibility to Mr. DeBartolo and dotted line responsibility to me on anything that might affect the bottom line. My Youngstown staff handled most of the run of the mill day-to-day accounting matters and reported to me on those matters.

Further compounding matters was when construction was needed at any of the entities. Then, our construction department got involved, and they would report to Mr. DeBartolo independently. It sounds cumbersome and it was, but it really worked out most of the time. With so many of the Diversified Operations GM's reporting to Mr. DeBartolo daily, I had to make sure to stay in touch with them and the controllers at the properties on a constant basis to make sure I was up to speed on what was going on currently.

As I indicated, it worked out most of the time, but there were more than a few times when Mr. D sent me a memo asking why he had to hear of a matter from someone other than me. In time, however, the GM's and I all got on the same page and copied each other on memos relating to the types of situations that would prevent confrontations with Mr. D.

Obviously, with this type of organization, it was imperative I spend considerable telephone time with the GM's and Controllers. When in the office, I averaged six to seven hours per day on the phone. I found the best "quiet time" was from seven to eight a.m. and from five to six p.m. (at least until the 49ers came on board), when the office was closed.

That was before the days of cell phones, but when I was travel-ling, or out of the office for any reason, I knew there would be a price to pay when I returned. I did have a recording device on my phone and many times had my secretary transcribe certain phone calls to keep track of some of the decisions made.

I also had good people in the field – Keith Simon at Thistledown, Tom Donahue at Louisiana Downs, Steve Williams at Balmoral, George Wenzlick in Toledo, and Diane Bernard handling the hotels. My rapport with the GM's was good, and between all of those, with constant input from Marty and Chris Bilski, we had it buttoned down.

That was why I was surprised when, in March of 1977, the Corporation announced to the world the family had bought a 90 percent interest in the San Francisco 49ers NFL football team. It was the best kept secret in the office, and later the company revealed Mr. DeBartolo bought a one third interest in the Pittsburgh Penguins of the National Hockey League over the past few months.

The company had entered big time sports. Reportedly, watching the 49ers press conference, Mr. DeBartolo commented "I build $100 million malls all over the country and nobody knows my name. Then, we buy a $14 million football team and suddenly everyone knows who I am."

The 49er announcement had a direct impact on me. Eddie, Jr. drafted Steve Williams in Chicago as his Controller and Business Manager in San Francisco.. He had met with Eddie, Jr. and soon was on his way to the West Coast.

So, I began a search for a new Controller at Balmoral. Out west there was some turbulence in San Francisco right off the bat when Eddie announced he was replacing the current 49er head coach, Monte Clark. Clark was very popular in San Francisco and served not only as coach but was also responsible for player development. When Eddie installed Joe Thomas as his General Manager, Thomas and Clark clashed over the player development duties. Eddie wanted to keep Clark, but Clark refused to stay if he had to cede control over the players. Clark left, and the DeBartolo era began. As excited as I was for the family, I was disappointed that Joe Thomas was named GM.

Joe Thomas was most famous for trading away Johnny Unitas from the Baltimore Colts. Joe had a reputation for being a cutthroat football man who believed in trading star players one year before their skills declined due to age. It may have been sound business, but it was very unpopular with the fans.

Eddie sent me to San Francisco that spring to work with Steve Williams in setting up the controls and communications with the home office. The team was owned by Eddie and he chose to bypass the usual reporting policies back to the corporate office. I would be responsible to report to Eddie for the financial operations of the 49ers, and I would be the go-between for financial reports to be sent to Eddie in Youngstown.

Aside from that, it was business as usual for me, and there wasn't anything particularly interesting going on. With summer approaching, Chris and I planned a camping trip to the Colorado Rockies. We bought a pop-up camper a few years earlier and would take weekend trips locally and longer trips to South Carolina to visit the ocean. This would be the longest yet and we planned to take a full two weeks.

Now, Mr. DeBartolo had a thing about vacations. He didn't take them and he didn't like them. He couldn't stand to be away from the office. There was a story in the office about when Eddie, Jr. and Denise were young, Mrs. DeBartolo convinced her husband to take the family to Italy on vacation. As the story goes, as soon as they landed in Italy, Mr. D called the office to check-in and continued to call almost hourly. This continued for a day or so and reportedly, Mr. DeBartolo returned to Youngstown because he felt he needed to be in the office. The rest of the family stayed on in Italy.

In fact, an article in Cleveland Magazine, which interviewed Mr. DeBartolo prior to the Grand Opening of Randall Park Mall, stated "DeBartolo boasts, in fact, of having never taken a vacation in his life. The very concept of vacation is alien to him, and he merely tolerates such desires by his employees."

Given that scenario, in my early years, Bob Munro would approve my vacation requests and apparently, I wasn't high enough on the radar screen to be noticed. But now, as Assistant Controller, I needed EJD's approval to go. Pete Frank approved my request, but EJD responded to my request with "You should schedule requests for vacation during the slow time of year or not at all!" I had no idea what that really meant since we never had a "slow time", but Pete told me that it was approved, so we went.

It was common when I was away from the office on business or pleasure that I would check back with the home office often, especially if I wasn't at a place where I could be contacted immediately. This was a policy that my wife objected to strenuously, while on vacation, as that was considered "family time." She was right, of course, but she didn't have to deal with Edward J. DeBartolo.

Nevertheless, I've always been an early riser and I would get up before the family and call the office before they woke up. The routine was pretty much the same each time I called. My secretary, Debbie at the time, would prioritize my calls and give me a list of calls I needed to return, read me memos I had received since my last call, and whatever other issues needed my input. Some I would delegate and some I would have to deal with.

One morning, we were camping in Durango, Colorado and I got up at six a.m. and walked to the camp store, where there was a pay phone. I got my list of calls, returned some and delegated a few others for Marty to handle. When we got to the memos, Debbie read one that really bothered me. That one came from EJD and announced that Tom Sweeney, the GM at Thistledown, was transferring to Balmoral in Chicago. This was somewhat expected since Sweeney and I had discussed it prior to my trip.

It was the next part of the announcement that bothered me – Keith Simon was promoted to General Manager of Thistledown. No input from me and no warning. Apparently, Sweeney made the recommendation and EJD approved it, most likely with Pete Frank's acquiescence. Pete hadn't even given me a heads-up.

I dictated a memo to EJD, Pete and Sweeney expressing my reservations with the Simon promotion. Keith was only a few years older than me and had no experience dealing with the powerful unions that controlled all the non-management jobs at the track. Management and the unions clashed numerous times over the years. I liked Keith a lot and had a great deal of respect for his talents, but I didn't think he would be ready to deal with the unions. I also indicated I felt I should have been consulted prior to the decision and announcement. Only Pete Frank responded.

The following Monday, I was in Pete's office and gave him my reasoning. Pete had no comment other than the decision was made. He didn't apologize for not consulting me when Keith's name came up. Later that week, I visited Keith at Thistledown. He was excited in his new role, and I pledged I would help him any way I could. That was in the late summer. Unfortunately, Keith would be gone by the end of the year. I filled his Controller position in-house, through the Internal Audit Department. I also called my contact at Robert Half and had him put out feelers for a new job for me.

September came, and the new DeBartolo-owned 49ers first regular season game was on the road against the powerhouse Pittsburgh Steelers, just 60 miles from the Youngstown office. The DeBartolo family purchased many tickets and every employee could bring a guest to the game. The company leased a fleet of buses, and a significant Youngstown contingent was on hand to view Eddie DeBartolo's newest asset. But, the Steelers spoiled the party, pounding us 27-0 and holding the 49er offense to 8 first downs and only 101 yards gained. The team then lost its next 4 games, starting 0-5. Three of the games were settled by seven points or less, but the DeBartolo/Joe Thomas era wasn't starting well.

While this occurred, the Randall Park Holiday Inn underwent some roof repair work. The Director for the Cleveland hotel group, Jack Black*, was new, having been hired a year or two before this. Another of DeBartolo's Youngstown Vice-Presidents, R. Lynn Squire, hired Black*. Squire assumed operational responsibility for the hotels before my arrival, and I would copy him on various reports and memos relating to the hotels. I was acquainted with Lynn only on a peripheral basis. The bulk of his responsibilities related to the department stores, but Lynn was currently responsible for the hotel operations, at least on a titular basis.

Very early one September morning, I was in the office and received a call from an individual, who refused to give his name. The caller said Jack Black* was having roof work on his house in the Cleveland suburbs that was being billed to the hotel under the roofing contract.

The caller then hung up. I had a habit of being in the office an hour early and the call came in on my private direct line.

Only a few people had that number and only a select few knew I arrived in the office that early. The anonymous caller must have gotten my number from one of those few. Later that morning, I walked over to Lynn Squire's office and told him about the call. He asked me if I had reason to believe the caller and I told him I did not. He told me to disregard the call. Apparently, it was not unusual for anonymous callers to call the company, and they were almost always crank calls. I went back to my office, but I couldn't get the call out of my mind.

I was in a bit of a quandary. I had to work with Black* on a day-to-day basis and I was concerned about discussing the call with him. If he was innocent, he might resent me for not trusting him, and our relationship could be strained or even ruined. I didn't need him to like me, but I did need him to work with me and, currently in my DeBartolo career, my confidence in my future with the company wasn't very high.

I decided to go to my supervisor, Pete Frank, with an idea. Several months before, the corporation added an Internal Audit Department under control of Pete and his supervisor, Vice-President of Finance William D. Pfaus. I had minimal contact with Pfaus through the years, primarily in meetings that included other department heads. Our relationship was cordial.

In my meeting with Pete, I told him about the anonymous call, my discussion with Lynn Squire and my concerns about destroying my relationship with Black* in the event the call was a hoax. I suggested this would be a perfect situation to involve Internal Audit, sending them in under the guise of something else. Pete said he would take up the matter with Pfaus and let me know. I felt confident they would go along with the recommendation.

Ever since Bob Munro's departure in late 1975, Pete and I had a cordial professional working relationship. But, the two of us were very different - Pete was the classic accountant, while I was more interested in the management aspects of the business. Pete was non-confrontational, and I was much more blunt and emotional in my beliefs. Our two styles occasionally clashed. Pete wasn't too happy with my outspoken manner and, given the recent situation with the Keith Simon promotion, I had lost some respect for Pete; not as an accountant, but as a manager. Plus, I was quietly looking for another job. This was a classic situation for me to look the other way and let the issue drop.

But, that wasn't necessary. Bill Pfaus did it for me. He turned down my request for Internal Audit involvement and had Pete relay to me that it was my problem. If I felt there was an issue with Jack Black*, I was on my own to handle it. I argued with Pete and asked to speak with Pfaus, but Pete just said, "the issue is closed."

That was the last straw. My job search recently resulted in a job offer from Mellon Bank in Pittsburgh, so I called the manager who interviewed me at Mellon and, over the next few days, we hammered out a deal. Chris and I then contacted a real estate broker and signed a listing agreement to sell our home, the sign to go up at the end of the business day on Friday. Then, on Friday, October 7, I tendered my resignation letter as follows:

October 7, 1977

Mr. Peter S. Frank, Controller

The Edward J. DeBartolo Corporation

7620 Market Street

Youngstown, Ohio 44512

Re: Letter of Resignation

Dear Pete,

After a great deal of deliberation, soul searching and discussion, I am tendering to you my formal resignation as an Assistant Controller of The Edward J. DeBartolo Corporation. I have tentatively scheduled my last day with the Corporation for October 21, 1977. In the event that this is not enough time to train and explain my job responsibilities to my successor, I will extend my final day by up to two weeks.

My reasons in making this decision are purely personal. At the present time I feel that there is little or no opportunity for advancement for me.

My four years with the DeBartolo Corporation have been very rewarding and, I feel, mutually profitable for both the Company and myself. I would like to thank all those who contributed to my professional development during my stay here. In particular, I would like to thank Mr. DeBartolo, whose leadership has inspired me in feeling that I have been a part of his team.

Sincerely,

Thomas F. Rossetti

TFR/dal

cc: Edward J. DeBartolo

Marie Denise DeBartolo

William D. Pfaus

The FOR SALE sign went up in the front yard of my home that evening. As I left the building that Friday night, I couldn't help but think one chapter in my life was closing, but another chapter would soon be opening. Chris and I arrived in Youngstown four years earlier thinking it would be just the next stepping stone in my career. We were thinking two years and it had lasted four. But, I had to grudgingly agree with the old banker, Bill Jayne, who told me I would learn more in one year with "the man across the street" than I would have in 10 years in New York.

The following Monday, I met with my staff and advised them of my resignation. I told them I expected they would be reabsorbed into the DeBartolo General Accounting Department. That afternoon, Edy Arquilla, Mr. DeBartolo's executive secretary called me and asked if I could meet with Mr. DeBartolo at 5:30pm that afternoon. I agreed.

When I walked into Mr. D's office, he instructed me to close the door and sit down. He pointed to a chair in front of his desk and I noted he had my letter in his hand. He sat down and said he was very disappointed to get that letter. He told me he had spoken that day with all three of the track general managers, as well as Walter Zeplien in Toledo and Jack Black* from Cleveland, and they unanimously agreed Mr. D "would be crazy to let me go."

He then read the sentence where I indicated I had little or no opportunity for advancement. He removed his glasses, looked me in the eyes and said "We both know that reason is horseshit. Eddie, Denise and I have been watching your work and we know that you are capable. So, tell me what is really going on."

I had been in the company for nearly four years and this already was the longest conversation I had with Mr. DeBartolo, even if one-sided. I hadn't wanted to burn bridges with my resignation letter and I took the vanilla high road. I thought for a moment before answering and then said to him, "What the hell. You own this company and you have the right to know."

I told him about the Jack Black* situation – the anonymous call, discussions with Lynn Squire and Pete Frank, my request for an internal audit and Pfaus' declining of my request. Then I threw in that I resented Keith Simon being promoted without Pete or anyone consulting with me.

Mr. D then asked if the company had been fair with me financially and pointed out that my salary had gone up 76 percent in four years. I responded the company had been very fair and that "this is not about money." This may have surprised him because he just stared at me for several moments. Apparently, he had been in this position before and expected this could be rectified with money.

When he spoke, he surprised me. "Is this all about who you report to?" It was my turn to stare at him. This was opening a door I wanted to avoid. I had nothing to lose so I decided to answer him honestly.

"I don't think I can work with Pete, and I'm not sure about Pfaus, either." I told him I thought Pete was a fine accountant and man, but his laid-back style didn't work for me. I told him my opinion of Pfaus was that he didn't care for me. If he did, I'd be in his office right now and not Mr. D's. I was trying to be careful about Mr. Pfaus because of the many years he and Mr. D had been together.

Then Mr. DeBartolo said, "If I take care of these issues, will you stay?"

I realized I was in a position I hadn't anticipated. I avoided answering the question because I knew this conversation could cost me big time in the future if I agreed to stay. Having enemies in your own company is a dangerous position to be in– especially if the enemies are higher up the ladder than you. Then, Mr. DeBartolo buzzed Edy and asked her to have Eddie, Jr. join us.

When Eddie came in, Mr. D summarized the discussion he and I just had. He told Eddie he wanted me to stay and they agreed there were plans for me. Then Mr. D asked me why I wouldn't stay. I was flustered and told him I already accepted another job.

He asked me with whom, and I told him Mellon Bank in Pittsburgh. He replied he did a lot of business with Mellon and they would understand. I then told him I signed a contract with Porter & Porter to sell my house, and Eddie, Jr. said he knew them well and it wouldn't be a problem. Then Mr. D said "We'll take care of those matters. If I take care of the other issues, will you stay?" he repeated. He then stood up and extended his hand.

So many things went through my mind. I only really knew Mr. D from this meeting, I was gambling my future based on that meeting, and he was offering me a "Jersey Contract," a handshake of trust that he would keep his word. I slowly stood up, nodded and shook his hand. I thanked Eddie on the way out, and as I walked out of the building I wasn't sure if I had made a good decision or a pact with the devil. It was great he wanted me to stay as badly as he indicated, but I wondered how this would all play out in the future. It wouldn't take long to find out.

When I came into the office the next day, I told nobody about the meeting with Mr. D and Eddie, Jr. and the apparent change of plans. The ball was now in Mr. D's court, although the FOR SALE sign in my yard came down sometime Monday evening.

I had a scheduled visit to Thistledown for meetings with Keith Simon, so I left and met him for lunch. I confided in him that I might be staying, but little else. Later in the afternoon, I met with the Controller at the Holiday Inn to discuss the third quarter financials. While I was in that meeting, Denise DeBartolo called.

Mr. D had met with Bill Pfaus and Pete Frank, and Denise had the minutes of the meeting. Mr. D wanted me to review them and Denise asked if I could meet her that evening. I told her I would be back by 5:30pm to meet with her. The following are excerpts of the meeting as they related to me. Some portions were omitted since they were unrelated to my situation:

Meeting – Tuesday, October 11, 1977

Present: Edward J. DeBartolo

Edward J. DeBartolo, Jr.

M. Denise DeBartolo

William D. Pfaus

Peter S. Frank

Mr. DeBartolo called the meeting for the purpose of discussing Tom Rossetti, in particular, and the accounting department in general....

With regard to Tom Rossetti, Mr. DeBartolo said he met with Rossetti and wanted to keep Mr. Rossetti in the organization. He said that he talked to Rossetti and he has agreed to stay. While Mr. DeBartolo stressed that he has confidence that Pete Frank is doing an excellent job and has total respect for Pete's ability, he feels that Pete has too many things to handle and possibly has not been giving Rossetti proper guidance and answers to problems that Mr. Rossetti would like to get resolved when these situations come up. Mr. Rossetti also mentioned he thought there was no chance for advancement.

Mr. DeBartolo said one of the main reasons for wanting to keep Rossetti is that he has not only done an excellent job handling the racetrack operations, but also the Foreign Trade Zone, Motels, 49ers and Fun-N-Games and that he has been with the organization four years and has finally gained a very good knowledge of all of these operations, particularly racing, and Mr. DeBartolo does not want to take three or four years to break someone else into these complicated operations.

Mr. DeBartolo said eventually, possibly in five or six years, the Company will be more involved as a management organization and will be getting into more diversified investments and that we will need more and more people of the type like Mr. Rossetti to handle these diversified operations.

Mr. Pfaus said he feels this situation about Tom Rossetti will not work—he said you cannot create a job for everyone who isn't satisfied that they aren't moving up. Mr. Pfaus feels that it will fracture the department—he said one person has to monitor and run the department—it has to be coordinated in the department or it won't work. Right now Mr. Pfaus feels the department is functioning well—while there are areas of improvement that we are working on, it is functioning well.

When Mr. DeBartolo, Jr. commented that Tom Rossetti is a very capable person, Mr. Pfaus commented that Rossetti's greatest asset is his personality—he still has a lot of training to go and knows nothing about the shopping center operation. With regard to the job that Rossetti has done with the racetrack operation, Mr. Pfaus said that he didn't do it single-handedly-the whole department has been involved.

Also, Mr. Pfaus feels that if Rossetti is dissatisfied this year when next year comes he will be dissatisfied with something else—in the meantime, we could be training someone else for his job. Mr. DeBartolo said that he would take full responsibility if this situation occurred. In reviewing the matter with Rossetti he was not seeking more money he was just seeking advancement and proper direction and answers to questions concerning operations he handled.

Mr. DeBartolo asked Pete if he didn't think the job is getting so big that he should eliminate some of his responsibilities—he stressed that he is not belittling Pete's efforts. Mr. Pfaus commented that idealistically the person who runs the department should not have to do anything except administrative work, but you have to bring others along to take over this responsibility-he feels Rossetti should have taken over more responsibility on his own without having to be told to do this or that....

Mr. DeBartolo said he made the decision regarding Tom Rossetti-he said he talked to Rossetti this morning. He said he will be put in charge of the operations he has been handling and Mr. Pfaus and Pete Frank are to decide who Rossetti will report to. Mr. Pfaus asked, and was told, there was no insinuation to Rossetti as to who he would report to. Mr. Pfaus said he will have to report to Pete. Mr. DeBartolo instructed Pete that when Rossetti comes up with a problem, Pete should give him a quick answer....

Mr. DeBartolo closed the meeting by again stressing the fact that he is happy with the job Pete Frank is doing and his decision regarding Tom Rossetti is in no way to be construed as belittling Mr. Pfaus or Pete Frank-he also stressed the fact that he takes full responsibility in the event his decision turns out to be a wrong decision.

End of Meeting

I had to read the minutes twice in Denise's office and my first reaction was one of anger. I told Denise the minutes did not reflect what Mr. DeBartolo and I agreed to. Denise told me her father suspected this might be my reaction, and I should wait for some "future developments." I went home that night more confused than ever.

The minutes clearly indicated that Bill Pfaus didn't want me to stay. He belittled my accomplishments and questioned my abilities. Pete's involvement, or lack thereof, didn't surprise me. He never answered any of Mr. D's questions. Instead Bill Pfaus answered them. It also confirmed to me that neither Pfaus nor Pete Frank had any idea what my job had been.

Apparently, Pfaus evaluated an employee's ability and zeal based on the shopping center business. Granted, Mr. D made his millions (or billions) on the mall business, but his comments about the future of moving toward a management company was a telling statement. Most troubling was Mr. D had indicated in the meeting that no insinuations had been made to me as to whom I would report to, and that was really a play on words. He had insinuated I would not report to Pete Frank and the meeting came out with the opposite result. I decided to wait and see how it would play out. I guess this time it was me who was "all in."

The next few days were nerve-wracking. The following Monday, Bill Pfaus called me in and told me he was dividing the accounting department, and henceforth I would be reporting to him. One of my issues was resolved.

But, the other now loomed even bigger. Pfaus wasn't friendly when he told me he was making the Internal Audit Department available for my direction on the "Cleveland matter." Walking out of his office, I was even more nervous. I no longer was reporting to Pete Frank, but now I was reporting to a man who clearly wanted me to go away. I started thinking maybe I had made a serious miscalculation.

The next day, Pfaus issued the following announcement:

MEMORANDUM

October 18, 1977

TO: ALL EXECUTIVES, DEPARTMENT/DIVISION HEADS

FROM: W.D. PFAUS

RE: DIVISION OF ACCOUNTING RESPONSIBILITIES

Effective immediately, controllership of the Accounting Department will be divided into two sections:

(1)Retail Facilities and (2) Diversified Operations.

Pete Frank will continue as Controller-Retail Facilities and will be responsible for the following accounting functions:

Shopping centers

Free-standing retail, industrial and warehouse buildings

Vacant land

Dormant or shell corporations

Internal audit

Taxation

Consolidated statements

Office services

Tom Rossetti is appointed Controller-Diversified Operations and will be responsible for accounting functions of the following divisions:

Motels

Foreign Trade Zone and Toledo Overseas Terminal

Sports Division (horse racing, 49ers, Penguins)

Fun-N-Games

Both Controllers will report to me.

I walked over to Mr. D's office and he was standing by his desk. I pointed to the memo in my hand. He winked at me. The next day, I got the original memo of the announcement given to Edward J. DeBartolo, Jr. At the bottom, he wrote: "Tom Rossetti - See me on Monday!" I also got some congratulatory letters. One of the first came from Jack Black*.

Within the next few days, I sent the Internal Audit people to Cleveland to review systems and controls for the Cleveland Holiday Inns. After a few days, they began looking at the purchase order system at the hotels and to question the roof project. I asked one of the auditors to drive past Jack Black's* home, and the same roofing company was doing work on his roof.

The auditors asked him about it and he said it was a separate contract. They asked for proof and he called me. I told him about the anonymous call and explained it could be cleared up if he provided me with copies of his contract with the roofing company and cancelled checks and bank statements for his payments to the company. He refused to do so and offered to resign. I accepted his resignation and advised Lynn Squire, as well as Bill Pfaus and Mr. DeBartolo. We notified the roofing company and they were only too happy to change our purchase order for roof work. Case closed.

The following Monday, I met with Edward J. DeBartolo, Jr., as directed. He told me he would be getting me more involved in the 49ers operation. It wasn't unusual for Mr. D to walk in on some of Eddie's meetings, and he did so as Eddie informed me I would report jointly to Mr. DeBartolo and himself.

Eddie, Jr. would be doing my annual reviews and salary adjustments and no one else in the company would be involved. He also mentioned there would be no public announcement on this change from Bill

Pfaus' recent memo. Mr. DeBartolo then handed me a letter from him advising me that, retroactive to the first of the year, I would become a partner in the under-development Alderwood Mall in Seattle, Washington. The interest wasn't large – one quarter of one percent -- but Mr. D. advised me it would be worth a great deal of money in the future.

The DeBartolo Corporation never had a pension plan in the entire time I was with the Company. In 1976, the government started and allowed employees without pension plans to set up an Individual Retirement Account, and I took advantage of that and contributed $1,500 into a personal IRA I set up for my future. I heard about these "employee partnerships" the Company had for upper management, but never dreamed they would apply to me so soon. Yet, here I was, a four-year employee and I was already in.

Driving home that evening, I marveled at how Mr. D handled the entire matter my resignation triggered. He kept his promise to me while praising Pete Frank for his job performance and allowing Bill Pfaus to save face and avoid embarrassment. It was like painting yourself in a corner and then finishing the job without stepping on paint. Harry Houdini would have been proud.

Out on the West Coast, the 49ers finally won a game, beating the Detroit Lions, 28 - 7. That started a four-game win streak that ended with a loss to the rival Rams at Candlestick Park, but they bounced back the following week at New Orleans, before ending the season with three losses – by one point to the Vikings, seven to Dallas and two to the Packers in Green Bay. The final record was 5 - 9, but considering the 0 -5 start, it could have been a lot worse.

However, a worrisome trend was underway -- home attendance at Candlestick Park averaged only 42,700 in the 60,000-seat stadium, and excluding the Rams game (56,779} and the Cowboys game (55,848), the average dropped to 37,300. Many season ticket holders abandoned the team and renewals for the 1978 season weren't showing any improvement. The bottom line for the first year showed significant losses.

Back in Youngstown, the fall came and went quietly, and Chris and I hosted Thanksgiving at our home. All my brothers and my sister were there, as well as my Mother and my In-Laws. We had a great weekend and it was sad when everyone left to go home, some to New Jersey and some to Chicago.

Monday afternoon, my sister Pam, who flew from NJ to Illinois to spend time with my mom and two youngest brothers, called from Chicago. My dad suffered an apparent stroke and was in the Northwestern Memorial Hospital in Chicago. He was not expected to live. Pam was crying when she asked me to come quickly.

I told Mr. D what happened and he said, "Go now." Debbie was trying to get me a flight, but the Thanksgiving holiday had filled all the seats on planes to Chicago. I called Chris and told her to start packing for me, stopped home to pick up my luggage and then drove the 403 miles through the night, arriving around one a.m. Central time. The Doctor was still there working on my father and he changed my father's prognosis from a suspected stroke to a brain aneurysm.

The surgeons drained the blood from his brain and were preparing to put a clamp on the artery. Later they would put a stent in to lower the swelling in the brain. I joined my mother, sister and brothers and waited. It was a long night. The top doctor gave us updates during the night and, by morning, the surgeries were done.

My father was in a coma. The doctors didn't know when, if ever, he would regain consciousness and, if he did, whether he would be brain dead or not.

I spent a few days there, but with my dad stabilized, there was nothing any of us could do except pray he would someday wake up. Pam went back to New Jersey, and there was no pressing reason for me to stay in Chicago, so I headed back to Youngstown, stopping at Balmoral in Crete, Illinois along the way. Over the next several weeks, I received updates from my mother, but there was no progress and still no change to my father's status. It wasn't until several months later, I found out from Edy that Mr. DeBartolo had spoken to my dad's doctor several times while I was away, and for several weeks he had her call the hospital daily to get an update on my father's condition.

December had arrived, and the end of the year was usually the slowest time of the year for me. Racing was over, the NFL regular season was ending, and winter had arrived. But, Christmas was coming and, with two young sons at home plus a wife who loves Christmas, it was a great time to be a father and husband. However, with Christmas near, I was about to be dealt another bitter pill.

Remember there were no fax machines or emails in those days. We did have a telecopier at all our tracks that sent a daily P&L to us during the racing season, but it was slow and cumbersome, so we didn't use it for office correspondence. Since Youngstown is so close to Cleveland, and we had so many operations there, the company used a regular courier to deliver and receive mail between the Cleveland operations and Youngstown. The courier also worked at Thistledown, but racing was done for the year, so he just made the trip during the weekdays. This year, he would make a run on Christmas Eve morning.

So, here I was in the office on December 24, 1977, Christmas Eve, and I was called to Mr. DeBartolo's office at eight a.m. He handed me a memo he sent to Keith Simon at Thistledown. It read as follows:

MEMORANDUM

TO: KEITH A. SIMON

FROM: EDWARD J. DEBARTOLO

DATE: DECEMBER 24, 1977

Your position as General Manager of Thistledown has been terminated, effective immediately.

He had initialed it with a big E, as was his method. I was speechless, and I knew Mr. DeBartolo wouldn't joke about something like this, but it was Christmas Eve! Mr. D said to me "You better get going to process him out. Sam (the courier) has already left."

Numbly, I drove the 60-mile trip in record time and arrived before the courier, who stopped at the three hotels prior to the track. Keith was delighted to see me and asked if I had come up to have a holiday drink with him.

It was 9:15 and I would never drink that early in the morning. I said yes. We went into EJD's track office where there was a bar, and he poured both of us a drink. Then we went into Keith's office. Minutes later the courier arrived, and Keith's secretary brought in his mail.

Keith saw the sealed envelope from Mr. D, and joked he must have gotten a holiday E mail from the boss (so-called because Mr. D signed the memos with the E) as he tore it open. Quietly, I told him that was the reason why I was there. Complaints from the union had cost Keith his job.

I had to escort my friend off the premises. I didn't want to leave him alone, so we went to a nearby bar and drank our lunch. I had now seen yet another side of Edward J. DeBartolo, Sr.

CHAPTER 6

1978 – I MOVE INTO PROFESSIONAL SPORTS

I started 1978 with a bit of a heavy heart. My father's coma and Keith's callous firing had me a bit depressed but work quickly took my mind off those issues. On January 1, EJD sent out a memo announcing that Frank J. Liddy was returning to the company to oversee the operations at Thistledown and Balmoral. Liddy, a former F.B.I. agent, had been with the company in the early 70's, primarily at Balmoral. He and Mr. DeBartolo had a professional friendship, but Liddy left abruptly soon after I joined DeBartolo in the fall of 1973.

Additionally, shortly after the New Year, my father finally awakened from his coma, and I took a quick trip to Chicago. My father was out of danger but had severe brain damage that affected his speech, mobility, and memory. He was also having problems with his cognizance, unable to understand what was being said to him. He continued in the hospital in the short-term and then needed several months of physical therapy before anyone would know how much, if any, of his skills would return.

Upon returning from that trip, I had a good meeting with Mr. DeBartolo. We discussed the Simon firing, and I voiced my opinion that we lost a good and loyal employee. Mr. D, who didn't like people questioning his decisions, didn't comment. He did say Simon was let go to make room for Liddy's return. Mr. DeBartolo instructed me to cooperate with Liddy on the management of the two tracks. I would have done so anyway, but I agreed.

Within days, Liddy brought in a new General Manager at Thistledown. George W. Jones, a young body-builder type and a former Chicago City police officer, was appointed to the job. George had a background in racing, having served as Security Director at some of Chicago's biggest racetracks. George was also the first man of color to be appointed to a management position in the DeBartolo organization.

George and I hit it off immediately. George knew I was disappointed in the firing of the person preceding him, and he didn't want that to affect his relationship with me. He admitted he knew nothing about the finances of racing and asked if I would help him in that area. I told him I would be glad to do so provided George would help me improve my understanding of the various operations within the track, which he graciously agreed to do. For the next several months, we averaged meeting once a week mutually improving our skills and understanding. Thistledown was flourishing under George's management and the track's net income improved from $58,000 in 1977 to $408,000 in 1978.

Later in January, I met with Mr. DeBartolo, and he told me it was time for me to get involved with the Pittsburgh Penguins. He told me he bought a one-third interest in the Penguins for $50,000 and lent another $1 million to the team to get them through the season. Now, with the season barely half over, he was being asked to put more money into the franchise. Mr. D told me he asked Vin Bartimo, from Louisiana Downs, to look at the operations, and Bartimo requested I be assigned to Pittsburgh to help him out.

A few days later, I picked up Vin at the Pittsburgh Airport, and we drove to the Penguins office in the Civic Arena in downtown Pittsburgh. We met with Al Savill, one of the three stockholders, who had taken over the responsibility of running the hockey team. Savill introduced us to the Penguins department heads and we all became acquainted. It was agreed that, over the next few weeks, Vin and I would meet with all the department heads individually, review the team's finances, and report the condition of the Penguins back to Mr. DeBartolo.

Bartimo still had Louisiana Downs to run, so he came and went over the weeks. I would work a day or two in Pittsburgh, commuting from Youngstown, as my schedule would permit. By mid-February, it was becoming clear Savill wasn't doing a very good job running the ship. Most of the department heads were qualified, but there was nobody giving them direction. Bartimo's early report to Mr. DeBartolo was to "run, do not walk, to the nearest exit." But, Mr. DeBartolo would wait until the full reports were in.

It was on one of Bartimo's trips that I picked him up in my five-year-old Dodge Charger, and Vince commented on the car. He asked me why I didn't have a company car since I drove so much on DeBartolo business. I told him I had never really thought about it. Two weeks later, Mr. D told me he was approving me for a company car, and a week later I had a new Pontiac.

In mid-March, both the Penguins reports were in – Bartimo's on the operations and mine on the financial condition of the company. Both were equally bad: Bartimo said "in all the years of my experience in business and in sports, I have never seen an operation so poorly operated." My financial report was much more specific, but equally as critical. Tens of thousands of dollars were being wasted over the lack of direction, communications and poor policies. I also reported that Mr. DeBartolo and Otto Frenzel, an Indiana banker and the third owner, responded to the capital call and put their money into the team, but Mr. Savill, who requested the monies, did not contribute his share. Further, I commented that two Penguin loans with Equibank, a Pittsburgh bank, were in default.

A shareholder meeting was called and scheduled for March 31. DeBartolo and Frenzel were present. Savill was not. He sent a proxy representative. Bartimo and I were there, as were a raft of lawyers. My report was presented first and reviewed by the stockholders. My report concluded the Penguins were projected to lose more than $2.2 million for the season just ending. I also noted the team would need an additional $1.25 million between now and the opening of the next season in October.

The shareholders had several questions about the contents of my report, especially Mr. DeBartolo who asked who was running the business affairs of the team. Mr. Frenzel responded it was Mr. Savill. Other questions were answered to the shareholders' satisfaction.

Mr. DeBartolo then moved my report be accepted, but Mr. Savill's representative, Mr. Callard objected on the basis the report was unofficial since it was not done by an officer or employee of the company. He asked for my credentials. I outlined my background and advised the books and records of the Penguins would reflect the contents of my report. Mr. DeBartolo stated he requested the review of the Penguins. At that point, Mr. Frenzel stated he was satisfied, and he seconded the motion. The motion carried by a 2-1 vote with Mr. Callard dissenting.

Bartimo then reviewed his report in more detail and concluded Savill failed to do his duty as the managing partner. Mr. DeBartolo made the motion to accept the report and Mr. Frenzel seconded the motion. After a brief discussion, Mr. Bartimo's report was accepted with a 2-1 vote with Mr. Callard dissenting. New directors were named to the Board of Directors, unanimously.

Immediately after the shareholders meeting ended, the new Board of Directors met and elected new officers. Vincent J. Bartimo was elected chairman of the board and president. J. Paul Martha, a Pittsburgh lawyer and former football player at the University of Pittsburgh and with the Steelers, was named vice president, and I was elected as secretary and treasurer. Savill was replaced as the Club's representative to the National Hockey League Board of Governors by Martha.

Paul Martha's position and hiring by the new Penguins board was an excellent public relations move. Paul was a respected and well-liked sports figure in Pittsburgh. The Penguins front office was off to a good start under the new management. Five days later, on April 5, the team had a new owner. The Edward J. DeBartolo Corporation acquired 100 percent of the Penguin stock. The franchise that went through two bankruptcies in its short lifespan finally had stable ownership.

But, before Mr. DeBartolo agreed to let his company take over the Penguins, he met with officials of Equibank concerning the notes in default. I sat in on the first meeting with Tony Liberati, an Equibank vice president. Liberati told Mr. DeBartolo that Equibank certainly didn't want the Penguins back, and Mr. DeBartolo was reluctant to assume the Equibank loans currently in default. A second meeting took place between Liberati and DeBartolo privately, and the result was DeBartolo's corporation would assume the larger loan, which financed Penguins operations, but not the smaller loan which was used to add some Super Boxes and increase general seating at the city-owned Civic Arena.

Out in San Francisco, the 49ers made headlines when they traded with the Buffalo Bills to acquire one of the greatest running backs in NFL history, OJ Simpson. The March 24 acquisition had a high price tag

(5 draft choices) but, in the days following the OJ trade, the 49ers sold nearly 10,000 season tickets, and enthusiasm was high.

Unfortunately, enthusiasm only went so far – the team lost its first four games, won at home against the Bengals and then dropped nine in a row before a 6-3 win over the lowly Tampa Bay Buccaneers. A 33-14 pounding by the Lions in Detroit mercifully ended a 2-14 season on December 17. Simpson injured his shoulder in the tenth game and was done for the season.

I made a couple trips to see the 49ers play that year, including a 24-7 loss to the Browns in the season opener in Cleveland and a home game on November 12 against the St. Louis Cardinals at Candlestick. The Cardinal game was a bit special – I got to watch the game with Eddie, Jr. in the owner's box.

Normally, Eddie traveled in a large entourage of friends, mostly Youngstowners. The faces would change but the make up was always the same. In later years, when the team became a dynasty, the numbers would swell. But now, with the team's record at 1-9, the group lost interest. Eddie was by himself. Before the game, he asked me to join him and I was thrilled.

Just before kickoff, Eddie saw OJ on the sidelines in street clothes, with his arm in a sling. He called down to the field and invited OJ to join us. The three of us watched the game, chatting as the close game went late into the 4th quarter, and OJ returned to the sidelines. The 49ers were down by 6 points, but were marching downfield, ready to get the lead for the first time with time running out. Unfortunately, just when it appeared the team would come from behind to win, 49er quarterback Scott Bull threw an interception at the Cardinals goal line and the game ended 16-10.

Eddie probably hated losing more than anyone I have ever known, but this loss appeared to stun him. He told me he was going to the locker room and then leaving to return to Youngstown, and would see me in a week. I had learned two days before I would be staying on in the Bay area.

When Eddie arrived on Friday, he called me into his office for a chat. "I need you to do something for me," he said. He asked me to extend my trip by another week in San Francisco. He told me to call Chris and have her fly out to San Francisco as soon as possible. Eddie then said he wanted us to take a "vacation," all around the Bay area. He suggested we visit Monterrey and Carmel, tour the whole city, see the sights and maybe even visit Napa.

He wanted us to visit the popular restaurants and bars and talk to people without saying where we lived or who I worked for. Essentially, he wanted to find out how the local natives really felt about him as owner of the 49ers and how they felt about the team. Eddie would pick up the tab for the entire trip and I was to return a week from the following Monday. There was one caveat – I was not to visit the 49ers office and not tell anyone in the 49er organization where I was or what I was doing. Eddie would tell his dad what I was doing, but no one else in the organization, either in San Francisco or Youngstown, was to know.

I did as he asked. I called Chris and she packed some extra clothes for me and flew out of Pittsburgh the following morning, a Saturday. Eddie's office arranged for a first-class ticket for her. After Sunday's game, we started our "vacation." We spent the week touring the city, taking ferries, visiting tourist sites, restaurants and bars, engaging as many locals as possible about the local sports scene in general and the 49ers in particular.

We took special care to avoid places that were, or might be, frequented by 49er people who might know me. On Thursday, when I called in, Eddie changed his mind and instructed me to visit the 49er office on Friday morning "just for an hour or so," and say hello to Joe (Thomas) and his nephew, Larry, Joe's administrative assistant. I was not to tell them the real reason I was still in town or tell them what I was doing.

On previous trips, I had minor dealings with Larry, but had never spoken to Joe Thomas. We had been introduced, but Joe had little to do with the financial end of the business and we never got together. Someone must have leaked that I was still in the Bay area, because when I walked in the door that Friday morning, the receptionist was expecting me and told me Larry wanted to see me. A few minutes later, Joe Thomas joined us. He peppered me with questions, but I just told him my wife and I were vacationing in San Francisco and I just stopped in to say hello. They clearly didn't believe me, but there was nothing else they could do. Chris and I drove to the Napa Wine country and enjoyed the rest of the weekend.

When I returned to the office, Eddie, Jr. asked what I found out, and said not to "pull any punches."

"They really hate you," I said. "They blame you for everything, including the coaching carousel (three in 2 years, four if Monte Clark was counted), lack of player talent and a complete breakdown in public relations between the team and the fans and ticket holders."

We had talked to some who were season ticketholders, and many said they weren't planning to renew and they couldn't "give their tickets away."

Eddie just listened and then nodded. "Pretty much as I figured," he said. We talked about how Joe Thomas, whom the people also disliked, managed to avoid the brunt of the public ire. It was obvious most of the problems I heard about were caused by, and the responsibility of, Joe Thomas. Yet, Thomas managed to lay the blame on Eddie, Jr. and the public bought it.

Most sports franchises have a familial identity with the community and its fans and the 49ers were no different. Stories and pictures of past victories, achievements and heroes play a big role in the love affair between fans and their teams, but one of Joe Thomas' first orders was to remove all of the photographic treasures that adorned the walls at the 49er headquarters.

He ignored former players and alumni. These poorly thought-out PR moves were attributed to Eddie, Jr, "the new owner." In fact, Eddie, who took a "hands off" approach while he learned the business was being blamed for everything, the Thomas hiring included. I didn't know it at the time, but very shortly Eddie would make sweeping moves that changed the face of the San Francisco 49ers forever.

Most of the other DeBartolo Diversified Operations were having a "bang-up" year financially. Thistledown would go on to have its second-best year in DeBartolo ownership history. Louisiana Downs finally shed the winter racing dates and secured, with legislative approval, the much more lucrative summer dates, and under Mr. DeBartolo's and Bartimo's direction went from losing money to making millions of dollars a year. The Holiday Inns, under new director Mike Sapara had their most profitable year ever. Fun-N-Games Associates, the family amusement center company, was expanding rapidly under the management eye of Thomas J. Poplar, into nearly all the DeBartolo malls and generated incredible cash flows. Even the Toledo operations were making a steady, if unspectacular increase in profit.

The DeBartolos were pleased with the progress and rewarded me with raises of eight percent on May 31 and another nine percent at the end of the year. In my first five years with the company, my salary had doubled.

I had several meetings with Mr. DeBartolo during the year and, in some of those, I began putting out feelers about rehiring Keith Simon, with whom I stayed in touch. I was having trouble filling the Thistledown controllership position. The track's racing schedule, Wednesday through Sunday, and the length of the racing season (200-220 days per year) guaranteed management would work on the weekend for 40 or more weeks a year. Most viable candidates, particularly those with families, understandably weren't interested in giving up that family time.

On my weekly meetings with George Jones, I could handle some of the job, but with my ever-increasing travel schedule, it was becoming more difficult and I found myself entrusting more responsibilities to the two bookkeepers, who were uncomfortable dealing with the myriad of accounting intricacies.

By late summer, Mr. DeBartolo relented and approved me hiring Keith back to fill the controller position. EJD admitted "he may have made a mistake" letting Simon go. With Keith back at the track, the last piece of the puzzle fell into place.

Chris and I were expecting the birth of our third child in the fall of 1978. Chris was having a difficult pregnancy and her doctor told her this should be her last child. Over the last few weeks, I curtailed my travel to stay close by, including avoiding trips to Pittsburgh, where the Penguins were getting ready to open the 1978-79 season. I needed to meet with management there to review and approve the budget for the season.

On October 2, Chris, who knew I needed to get over to Pittsburgh, told me to plan on going to Pittsburgh the following day. She was showing none of the normal pre-birth signs, other than some headaches, and was confident I could go for the day. She was scheduled to see her doctor the next day for a progress update anyway. She did ask if I could drop off our two-year-old at her parents' house in the North Hills section of Pittsburgh.

The following morning, Chip and I headed out, and I dropped him off and arrived at the Penguins office around 10 a.m. We spent the morning into early afternoon tweaking the budget and were finished around 1:30 p.m.

Paul Sandrock, the Penguin Controller and I stepped out for a quick lunch. When we returned about an hour later, Paul Martha's secretary advised my office called and Chris had gone into labor and was enroute to the hospital. I immediately called Chris' parents, advised them what was happening and asked they take Chip home and pick up Mike, who would be staying with our neighbor. I then headed out on the 80-mile trip to the hospital.

When Chris visited her doctor, he advised her she was ready to give birth and needed to get to the hospital. Chris picked up Mike from school, and then dashed home to pack a few things. Cathy Calo, our next-door neighbor, drove Chris to the hospital. We lived in Boardman, a suburb of Youngstown south of the city.

The hospital was north of the city, necessitating they take a byway around the city before hooking up with Interstate 80 for the last few miles. When Cathy exited the byway onto I-80, they immediately encountered a massive traffic jam. Vehicles were just crawling along the road. Cathy started down the shoulder as Chris began to experience discomfort, but a truck cut her off, not allowing further progress.

Cathy rolled down her window and yelled at the driver that Chris was having a baby. The trucker immediately got on his CB radio and alerted all the truckers ahead of the situation. Then, he told Cathy to follow him. He drove down the shoulder while other truckers halted traffic for them to weave over the bridges to the exit. Then the trucker escorted them directly to the hospital door, blew his horn and waved while Chris was ushered into the building.

Meanwhile, I made the trip from Pittsburgh in record time, miraculously avoiding any speeding tickets. I arrived just as they were prepping Chris to go into the delivery room. I donned my scrubs and witnessed the birth of my third child, another boy. The baby was healthy and thankfully, Chris had no issues with the delivery.

Chris and I had been sure the third child would be a girl and we hadn't considered any boys' names. As we admired our newborn child, Chris said "I guess Lisa Lynn isn't going to cut it!" We discussed boys' names and we agreed we should name our last child after me since Chip, whose real name is Christopher, was named after Chris. Thomas Brent Rossetti joined the family.

In the hours and days that followed, congratulatory good wishes flooded in from all over the country. The DeBartolo Family sent a beautiful floral bouquet. Cards, flowers and fruit poured in from the 49ers, Penguins, George Jones and Keith Simon at Thistledown, Vince Bartimo at Louisiana Downs, Mike Sapara from the Hotel Division and many others, both to Chris' hospital room and our home. OJ Simpson even sent a fruit basket.

Seeing all these impressive shows of congratulations overwhelmed us. Chris' roommate in the hospital asked, "Who are you people?" Chris laughed and said she didn't even know most of the people who sent things.

There is one other noteworthy story from 1978. The DeBartolo family was a major supporter of St. Jude Children's Research Hospital. Each year they hosted a fundraiser for that great cause in Youngstown, so early in the year, Eddie, Jr. hosted a party. Danny Thomas and his daughter, Marlo, attended, as did several athletes and other celebrities, as well as many of Youngstown's wealthiest people. The event raised a tremendous amount of money every year, and this year was no exception. Chris befriended a woman at the party and, as the party was breaking up, the woman asked Chris if we would join them for a nightcap at a late-night club in Austintown, Ohio, a nearby suburb. Chris found me, and I said I was good with it.

A bit later we were sitting at the club with the other couple, who I found out were named Louis and Kathy DeNiro. We were sharing stories and, unbeknownst to me, Eddie, Jr. and his friends arrived and were sitting at the other end of the room. A few minutes later, a waiter came up to me, handed me a piece of paper, and said he "was delivering a message from Mr. DeBartolo." I read the message, which said we were sitting with a couple that had ties to the mob, and there were three agents from the FBI watching our table. I looked up and Louis was staring at me. I told Chris we had to get going and I started to apologize to the DeNiro's. Louis stopped me. "I understand," was all he said.

The following Monday, Eddie, Jr. called me in and told me Louis DeNiro was the son of a former mob boss named Vince DeNiro, who was blown up in a Youngstown car bombing in 1961, a crime that was never solved. To the best of my knowledge, Louis was never actually accused of being in the mob, but in those days, it was "guilt by association," so Eddie advised me to keep my distance from him.

So, a great 1978 went into the record books.

CHAPTER 7

1979 – BASEBALL INTERESTS CAUSE MY STOCK TO SOAR

1979 was hectic right from the start. With the recent addition to our family, we had outgrown the three-bedroom ranch we built in 1975, so Chris and I were in the market for a new home. We focused on new construction, which was booming around Boardman, Ohio, where the DeBartolo offices were located, and we spent the January weekends looking at homes under construction.

In San Francisco, Edward J. DeBartolo, Jr. lowered the boom. Joe and Larry Thomas were let go and, when Steve Williams, the 49ers' business manager, voiced his support of the Thomases, he was let go as well. On January 9, Eddie announced Stanford's Bill Walsh would take over as head coach and, later that month, Walsh also assumed the duties of general manager.

While that was going on, I was dispatched to New Orleans by EJD, Sr. for the possible acquisition of a Major League baseball team. Mr. DeBartolo and Vince Bartimo had discussions with Charles Finley about buying the Oakland Athletics. The plan included a probable move of the team to New Orleans to play in the newly-built Super Dome. My trip to New Orleans was to meet with officials of the Hyatt Management Corporation, operations manager of the Super Dome, to discuss lease terms so I could prepare a pro-forma for Mr. DeBartolo on the possible deal.

I spent the second weekend of January in New Orleans and negotiated preliminary lease terms with the Hyatt officials. Denzil Skinner, the President of Hyatt Management told me the State of Louisiana, with significant support from Governor Edwin Edwards, was ready to offer significant enticements to lure a baseball team. Monday, I flew to Shreveport to prepare and review my preliminary proposal with Bartimo. We agreed our proposal and interest would be contingent on a review of the Athletics' books and records, particularly player contracts, as well as Finley's ability to cancel his team's lease in Oakland.

I notified Skinner of our continued interest and he pledged to arrange a meeting with Finley in Chicago the next day. Unfortunately, Skinner and I had to cancel the meeting when a snowstorm closed O'Hare Airport in Chicago, and I returned to Youngstown. I later spoke with Finley by telephone to reschedule the meeting and he asked why I wanted to meet with him, anyway. I told him I needed to review his books to determine what we were buying. He responded a meeting wasn't necessary. "Tell your boss that he is buying some soggy baseballs and washed up ballplayers" was his message to Mr. D. We never did have the meeting, despite a great deal of nationwide press coverage, and the proposed deal quietly died.

Chris and I continued our home search and found a few homes we were interested in, including one from a builder who was a friend of Eddie's. In one of my meetings with Eddie, Jr., I mentioned the builder's name and told Eddie we were considering buying one of his homes. I guess I surprised him because his response was unremarkable. The next day, however, Eddie again summoned me to his office. He told me the builder I mentioned had a habit of "cutting corners," and he directed us toward a couple of other builders.

In mid-February, Eddie called me into his office on a Friday and offered me the position of Business Manager of the 49ers. He told me his father had been reluctant to agree to my transfer, but he told Eddie if I wanted the job he would not object. Eddie and I then talked in generalities about money and responsibility, and he told me to take the weekend to talk it over with Chris and let him know by Monday morning.

By this time, Chris and I believed we found the right home for the family. We were ready to make an offer when I got home that evening and told her about the offered position, after our sons had gone to bed. We both knew it was a decent, not great, offer but the opportunity for the future was there. We talked well into the night and then agreed to sleep on it.

The next day, we talked it over thoroughly, weighing the pros and cons. San Francisco was a great city, but extremely liberal. But, moving directly into sports was always one of my dreams. On the other hand, we came to consider Youngstown as home and we were enjoying the mid-west lifestyle. Cost of living was much lower in Ohio, and more than likely my opportunities for advancement would be greater in the parent company. But, most important was the impact on our boys growing up and, with this issue most in mind, we decided to stay put.

On Monday, I met with Eddie, Jr. and gave him our decision. I declined the San Francisco offer, but I told Eddie I had the next best guy for the job – Keith Simon. Eddie didn't personally know Keith, but he did know how I fought with his father to get Keith back in the company. Eddie called Mr. DeBartolo into the meeting and summarized our discussion. Senior told me he was happy I was staying, but he wondered whether Simon was right for the job and, if so, if he would take it. We discussed Keith's strengths and weaknesses and Mr. DeBartolo then instructed me to call Keith and discuss it with him to gauge his interest.

I called Keith at Thistledown and we discussed the opportunity. Since Keith had been fired nearly 14 months earlier, he had divorced, been out of significant work for a lengthy period and settled for low-paying jobs to get by. He was deeply in debt -- $10-12 thousand or so -- and back in Cleveland was slowly paying it off. The 49er salary offered would barely cover the cost of living and paying off the debt would become a bigger problem. I asked, if we could help him with the debt, would he be interested. His response was "Hell, yes!"

I returned to Eddie's office, EJD joined us, and I relayed the discussion Keith and I had. Senior, knowing that EJD, Jr. didn't know Keith well, told me to "get Keith down here and let's see what happens." Two hours later, the four of us were back in Eddie's office and a deal was reached. The Company would pay off Keith's debt and, if Keith worked out in San Francisco, the debt would be forgiven. That evening, Keith and I flew out of Cleveland to San Francisco.

Bill Walsh had been busy since taking over the helm. He released all the coaches except for Mike White, the 49ers' Offensive Line Coach. He brought in John Ralston, a former head coach with the Philadelphia Eagles and Denver Broncos, as vice president of administration; and John McVay, former head coach with the New York Giants, as director of player personnel. He also hired a number of other coaches.

When Keith and I arrived the next morning, we were ushered into Ralston's office for a meeting with him and McVay. We all exchanged backgrounds and a bit later, Bill Walsh poked his head into the meeting and introduced himself before leaving for another meeting. We met all the new arrivals and I introduced Keith to the holdovers.

That night, McVay had us over for a BBQ at his home, where Walsh and Ralston joined us. Several of the assistant coaches stopped in to introduce themselves. The evening was great, Walsh was magnetic, and it became obvious Keith would fit in perfectly in the new organization.

I was impressed with Walsh right off the bat – an admiration that would only grow in the years to come. Moreover, Walsh was a local guy loved in the Bay area, and his appointment started the process of getting the public to accept Eddie DeBartolo, Jr. That issue, too, would begin to improve over the coming months and years until EJD, Jr. was also respected and loved by 49er fans. I flew home the next day leaving Keith to settle in with his staff and felt very comfortable the future of the 49ers was in good hands.

I settled back into my normal routine and Chris and I made an offer on a new home. In late February 27, Eddie called me into his office.

"This is to help you move into the new house," he said as he handed me a personal check for $5,000. It was labeled as a salary advance, but Eddie made it clear it was a gift - not to be repaid.

In early March, Paul Martha and I met with Edward Obstler, an attorney representing the Baltimore Orioles. EJD, Jr. and William D. Moses, another DeBartolo senior vice president joined us for parts of the meeting. Apparently, Mr. DeBartolo, Sr. had some preliminary discussions with the owners of the Orioles, who wondered if Mr. D was interested in buying their team. However, EJD was interested in the Orioles in the context of moving the team to New Orleans, while the Orioles owners wanted a buyer to keep the team in Baltimore. After my report on the meeting to EJD, the issue died.

The 1979 NFL Draft, Bill Walsh's first, was a memorable one but not right away. The 49ers would have drafted first overall, but the pick was traded to Buffalo in the prior year's O.J. Simpson trade. In the second round, the 49ers picked James Owens, a running back from UCLA, who played decently for a couple of years before ending his career in Tampa Bay.

Walsh's second pick, in the third round, was especially noteworthy – Joe Montana from Notre Dame. Walsh wanted a quarterback he could build a team around, and he felt Montana might be the one. Also, an obscure wide receiver from Clemson, Dwight Clark, was selected in the tenth round. As everyone now knows, those two would one day combine for the play forever known in San Francisco as 'The Catch."

In Pittsburgh, the Penguins were wrapping up the first full season under DeBartolo ownership, finishing second in the Norris Division with a record of 36-31-13, only one win short of the team's best season ever. They also qualified for the playoffs and bounced the Buffalo Sabres out of the qualifying round two games to one, before losing four straight to the Boston Bruins in the quarterfinals. The good news, however, was the three home playoff games cut the regular season losses in half. It was a significant improvement on and off the ice.

In May, I made my public speaking debut, addressing the Youngstown Chapter of the National Association of Accountants. I spoke about the DeBartolo Corporation and the sporting entities. I was well accepted and I'm sure they hung on my every word (at least I didn't see anyone sleeping). But the company got some good PR as the Youngstown Vindicator, the local newspaper, reported on the night.

All my other responsibilities – the racetracks, hotels and Toledo operations were operating normally with no significant problems. On August 10, Eddie Jr. sent a memo to his father, concerning the Seattle Mariners Baseball Club. He copied me on the memo as a heads-up for the future.

Mr. DeBartolo also learned a Sheraton was being auctioned off in Aurora, Ohio, a suburb of Cleveland, and the closest hotel to Sea World and Geauga Lake Amusement Park. He wanted to bid on it. I sat with him and he instructed me to bid up to $4 million for the property. I asked one of our attorneys accompany me and he told me to take Art Wolfcale, assistant vice president of legal, and a friend of mine. Art and I went up and participated in the auction. When we hit the $4 million, we quit. I called Mr. D and he was OK with that.

Two weeks later, Mr. DeBartolo called me from the road to tell me he set up a meeting for me in the Catskill Mountains in New York. Mr. D met with the family that owned the Grossinger's Hotel and Resort, and he was thinking about buying the property. Mr. D told me there was the possibility of casino gambling in upstate New York and that fueled his interest. He wanted me to visit the property and give him a report.

I called Mike Sapara, director of our Cleveland hotels, and we flew into New York City and drove the two hours north to the Catskills. We spent parts of two days there examining the physical property, discussing the habits of the clientele, reviewing the operations and examining the financials for the last few years, including part of 1979.

I grew up outside of New York City, and I was familiar with the Catskills and the Grossinger name. I was aware Grossinger's catered to a Jewish clientele. What I didn't know until this trip was Grossinger's was a totally kosher facility.

It was a beautiful late summer day when we arrived, driving through a gorgeous 27-hole golf course that had absolutely nobody playing on it. There were also well-maintained tennis courts and a health club, also completely devoid of activity.

We were greeted by Mark Grossinger Etess, son of one of the owners, and one of two sons involved in the management of the resort. Mark gave us a complete tour. I asked Mark why there were no people playing golf or on the tennis courts and he responded, "Because there is an extra charge for those facilities."

He explained the Resort operated on the Full American Plan, which means meals are included in the room rate, as are certain amenities such as shows in the nightclub with a different show each night. He said the guests generally don't pay for anything not included.

The food was all kosher, prepared under the watchful eyes of a rabbi, and it was pretty bad, devoid of most spices and without flavor. There was no cocktail service in the huge dining room because the patrons "don't order drinks."

Etess had our waitress go down to the lounge and get drinks for us. Afterwards, we went downstairs to the nightclub for the show. There were 1,200 people there – full capacity and only two cocktail waitresses wandering around in case someone wanted to order a drink. There were few takers and the girls were not busy. Just prior to the show ending, Mike and I went into the lounge to see the activity when the show let out. Of the 1,200 people that left the club, only five people stopped for a drink, including Mike and I, even though they had to walk through the lounge on the way out.

Mr. D told me to call him that night at home. Mike would have joined me on the call, except he was suffering from food poisoning from his dinner and was sick in his room. I told Mr. D what we observed and experienced, and he was chuckling as I related our experiences. When I told him Mike was ill in his room from the food, he actually laughed out loud and said "I guess you better come home then. That's the same impression that I had when I visited!" Then it was my turn to laugh.

When I got back to the office, I gave Mr. D a 10-page report on our findings. Mike Sapara also sent his report. We just couldn't imagine a Catholic man named DeBartolo running a kosher resort. After reading our reports, Mr. D was no longer interested.

A week later, I was in the office of the Cleveland Cavaliers of the National Basketball Association. Nick Mileti, the operating partner, had approached Mr. D about the possibility of him buying the team. The NBA was in trouble in those days, and the Cavaliers were really struggling. They had moved into a new arena far south of the city and attendance was awful. So was the team. In what was a recurring theme over the next several years, I recommended we stay away from this one and we did. However, over the years I was sent to visit Mileti a few more times.

The 1979 NFL season started, and the 49ers lost their opening game in Minnesota, as well as their home owner against the Cowboys. Then, they lost to the rival Rams in Los Angeles. But all the games were close – by six to the Vikings, eight to the Cowboys and three to the Rams.

The 49er offense was spotty and couldn't make the necessary big play to turn games around. OJ, playing his final season, could no longer break away for big gains. It would end up being a long first season for Bill Walsh, Eddie and the 49er faithful.

Bank of America was the 49ers bank, where the team banked and held the loan used for the purchase. From the first day I got involved in 49er matters, we had the same two bank representatives – Lorraine Goddard and Mike Anderson. In several of our meetings, Lorraine and Mike hinted the bank would like to expand the relationship to the DeBartolo Corporation.

Bill Pfaus had his own preferred lenders for the malls and wasn't very interested, but I put a package of loan requests together and presented it to B of A. It included a $250,000 loan to a new company Eddie started that would build racquetball clubs.

The first club was opening in Boardman, Ohio, and the loan would be used to finance equipment purchased. We also restructured the 49er loan with a .25 percent drop in the rate, added a new $1 million line of credit for the team, and requested and received a bridge loan for the Sheraton in Ohio we purchased after losing the bidding war. B of A also gave us a commitment to finance an airplane the company was getting, and to refinance the newest Holiday Inn in Cleveland. Mike and Lorraine also mentioned B of A would like to be considered for any new malls that might need financing.

I stayed in San Francisco that week for the 49ers home game against New Orleans. QB Steve DeBerg was intercepted 3 times and lost a fumble in a 30-21 loss. Over the next three weeks (all losses), DeBerg threw 2 more interceptions in each game.

One of those games was in New Jersey on October 4 against the New York Giants. Since it was in the state where I grew up, I decided to visit my old haunts and go to the game. My oldest son Mike, now 7 years old, had taken to the teams I was working with and was an ardent fan of both the 49ers and the Pens.

I decided to get some of the 49ers allocated tickets and take him, my brother and nephew to a game. We drove to New Jersey for the weekend and stayed with my older brother and his family in Elmwood Park. On Saturday, I took Mike and Chip, my nephew Mark

Vincent, and his sister Cheryl, and a friend of Cheryl's to the Giants' Meadowlands Stadium, where we watched from the field as the 49ers practiced.

After the practice, the kids had their picture taken with OJ Simpson and got his autograph, before I took them back home. I then took the family over to Little Italy in New York for dinner.

The next day, the four of us went to the game. I knew the 0-6 49ers didn't have much of a chance to beat the New Yorkers, but Mike didn't see it that way. The partisan New York fans greeted the San Franciscans with a lusty Bronx cheer when they took the field, and then exploded in cheers when their Giants were introduced, which angered Mike.

The 49ers took the opening kickoff and marched down the field. The drive stalled, and they settled for a Ray Wersching 21-yard field goal to go up 3-0. My 7-year-old son jumped up and shouted loudly to the quiet crowd, "What do you think of that, Giant fans! Who's cheering now?"

I was horrified as 70,350 hostile heads turned to look at the two 49er fans sitting among them. The Giants promptly reeled off 29 unanswered points enroute to a convincing 32-16 win. To this day, I firmly believe only that Giant rally kept me from being tossed out of the upper deck that day.

The team's record was now 0-7 going into a much-needed bye week. They finally got a win at home on October 21 over the Falcons. But it was short-lived as they dropped the next six in a row, before splitting the final two. DeBerg started all the games that season. Joe Montana saw some "mop up" work in relief that year in three of the late games, with modest success. With the team's second consecutive 2-14 season in Bill Walsh's inaugural season, the coach knew who the QB of the future would not be (DeBerg). The only question was whether Montana would be the one who would be. It was another miserable season for the 49ers, but it didn't seem as depressing as the previous one.

You may recall my reference to a bridge loan to finance the acquisition of the Sheraton in Ohio for which we were outbid at auction. Apparently, the gentleman who outbid us at the auction was a local banker, who was overheard in a bar bragging he "outbid the master" – Mr. DeBartolo -- and how he now had a property, appraised at $7 million, that he got for $4.1 million.

Somehow, Mr. DeBartolo found out about the story and called Wolfcale and I to his office. His message to us was clear – find out how to get that property. So, we called the owner who was losing the property and learned there was a short window where the property could be bought from the owner before the auction was recorded, subject to ap proval of the existing lender. So, we did it. The loudmouth banker learned a lesson that day.

As Christmas and the end of the year approached, the Penguins were hanging around .500 as the 49ers season came to an end. Eddie, Jr. invited me to his office for a Christmas Eve cocktail. He handed me a check from the 49ers for $260 and told me he was putting me on the 49ers payroll in 1980. He also told me he was approving an upgrade of my company car.

Chris and I planned to take the family on a trip to Florida to visit my wife's parents the day after Christmas and Eddie said the trip was approved, provided I was available to possibly attend a meeting for him. I assumed he meant in Florida, told him it wouldn't be a problem and left him the phone number for my in-laws' place.

CHAPTER 8

1980- "A LITTLE TRIP", THE WHITE SOX & A PROBLEM IN LOUISIANA

Chris and I and the boys left after Christmas and flew into Tampa for the holiday week with my in-laws. I no sooner arrived at their place when the phone rang. It was Eddie, Jr.

"I need you to take a little trip for me," he said. I asked him where. The answer was Seattle. "You've got to be kidding me," was my response. The only place I could be in the continental US that would be farther was Miami.

Eddie wanted me to meet with Kip Horsburg, the Business Manager of the Seattle Mariners Baseball Club the next day. My ticket would be waiting at the Tampa airport. I repacked into a carry bag and headed back to the airport for a flight that would get me to Seattle late that night. In those days, I was unable to sleep on airplanes, despite spending dozens of hours each year in the air. I checked into a hotel after midnight, Seattle time, and got some much-needed sleep.

The next morning, Kip picked me up and we went to the Mariners facility. I met with several of the partners, and then Kip and I got into the finances. I was tired and just wanted to get what I needed and get back on the plane. We accomplished that, and Kip and I had dinner and some drinks, and then he drove me back to the airport for a "red eye" flight back to Florida.

I did my entire report at the airport and on the plane and was finished when we landed in Tampa. I called my secretary, Sue Bissell, had Marty Hamer listen in, and dictated the report to her, instructing the two of them to get it finished and then call me back on the in-laws' phone. A couple of hours later, she called back and read it to me. I told her to initial it for me and send it out. Then, I went to bed and slept for about 10 hours. My "little trip" was over.

Since I moved to Youngstown, January was usually a quiet month. My staff would go to work closing the year-end books of the entities they were responsible for, and I reviewed their work and worked with the on-site controllers finalizing their budgets for the new year. But this January saw me also working on the Mariners deal, which got more convoluted each day.

The Mariners were in dire financial straits, and had several partners as owners, all of whom wanted out. But most of them had tax issues with a sale, some conflicting with other partners. For example, some of the owners wanted out immediately while others were interested in a multi-year take-out, for tax purposes. There were four parcels of debt they wanted us to assume, and Eddie, Jr. and I gave them a verbal proposal to buy the assets of the club and assume the debt.

There were numerous law firms involved as each of the partners wanted his/her lawyers involved in the negotiations and structure of the deal. To further complicate matters, they indicated there was "another group" interested in buying the club. Most of the owners, including the managing partner wanted to sell to us, but others were interested in the "other group."

I called Mike Anderson of Bank of America to arrange a $7.5 million letter of credit we would use to buy the Mariners, and he had indicated it would not be a problem. I spent hours on the telephone with the various attorneys, and it became obvious we were in the middle of a group of feuding owners and their lawyers, who could not, or would not, agree. Mr. DeBartolo, Sr. asked me to summarize our position while Eddie was out of town, and I did so on January 17.

Mr. D then instructed me to advise the Seattle owners they needed to all get on the same page before we would expend any more time on the matter, but our verbal offer was still good. I did as instructed, and we never heard from the Seattle ownership again, although they didn't sell to the "other group," either.

I also spent some time in January working with our insurance broker, Frank B. Hall & Associates, solving a growing problem sports teams were having-getting workers compensation at a reasonable cost for players in the NFL and NHL. The Penguins were paying $180,000 per year for coverage through conventional routes, even though in their worst year they only paid $35,000 in claims.

We explored the concept of organizing an offshore captive insurance company, funded by the company with a "stop-loss" reinsurance contract with a reputable company such as Lloyd's of London. It made sense for us, and we did it. Over the next few months I enlisted the NHL's New York Islanders and Colorado Rockies to join us and, in February we set up Professional Sports Insurance Company (PSIC) out of Bermuda, and immediately cut our costs by two-thirds. I sat on the PSIC Board of Directors, and over the next few years several additional teams in all the major sports signed on. In March, I was asked to present the concept to the other NFL teams at their Tax Counsel Meeting.

In April, Mr. DeBartolo again sent me to Cleveland to explore the possible purchase of the NBA's Cleveland Cavaliers. This time I met with Joe Zingale, another of the owners. The result of that meeting was no different than my previous visit with Nick Mileti. I recommended against the purchase.

April also saw the 49ers have a promising 1980 draft. Bill Walsh's review of the 1979 season made it clear the team had numerous holes to fill and that one or two good players were not going to do it. He began a system of "trading down" a higher draft choice to get two or more choices, and he ended up with two first round choices he used to get Earl Cooper for the offense and Jim Stuckey for the defense. He also added Keena Turner (defense) in the second round, along with several more additions to bolster his defense. Finally, the team acquired a group of free agents, including Lawrence Pillers from the Jets. These players would turn out to be pivotal in the 49ers future.

Finally, April saw the Penguins reach the playoffs again, even though their record was 30-37-13. This time, they drew the Boston Bruins in the best of five preliminary round. The Pens won the opener in Boston and their home opener in Pittsburgh to take a 2-1 lead in the series. Needing to win one of the final two, they lost 8-3 at home and then 6-2 in Boston the next night to exit the playoffs. It looked promising in the beginning, but in the end, the more talented and experienced Bruins prevailed.

The disappointing end to the season seemed to grate on Vince Bartimo, who directed a few derogatory memos toward the Penguin management team, including me, copying the DeBartolos on his messages. I didn't agree with some of Bartimo's allegations and I respectfully told him so. At that point, Mr. DeBartolo got involved and severely chastised me. The message to me was clear – right or wrong, don't disagree with Bartimo.

Thistledown opened for the 1980 season and results were not encouraging. After a very small loss in 1979, the track started on the downside and as the season continued, it never got any better. One of the problems with the facility was its age. Although always clean, the grandstand and clubhouse were quite old, and the track didn't appeal to the younger clientele. The regular patrons of the track were of an aging generation who weren't bothered, and in many cases were happy, with the old facility.

The problem for the track's management was drawing new blood, and the upcoming generations weren't drawn to the sport, with-out many of the amenities they wanted. A few years prior, the DeBarto-lo interests attempted to get a larger part of the handle (the amount bet at the track) so they could begin to remodel the facility and attract younger people. Although the effort resulted in a small concession by the State, it wasn't nearly enough.

A racetrack is a pari-mutuel facility and, in Ohio, was governed by the State and a Racing Board. Of the pool of money bet at a track, 82.5 percent was required to be returned to the bettors, in the form of winnings. Of the remaining 17.5 percent, 6.5 percent was paid to the State of Ohio as a tax, 5.5 percent went to the horsemen in the form of purses, and the remaining 5.5 percent was retained by the track.

The track's share was used to pay wages for approximately 700 employees, repairs and maintenance of the facility, utilities, real estate taxes and all the other costs involved. The 5.5 percent track's retention, in a good year, could net a cash flow, after expenses, of $100,000-300,000, before reinvesting any money back into the facility. A bad year, which 1980 turned out to be, exacerbated by bad weather and the economy, resulted in a cash loss to us of $653,000. At the same time, the State would generate approximately $7 million from the taxes, with minimal expense, and no investment. DeBartolo always chaffed at the fact the State took such a big share while the track owners struggled.

Mr. DeBartolo, Jones and I came up with a plan to remodel the grandstand and clubhouse, put in suites and other amenities for the younger generation and rebuild the barns and facilities for the horsemen. The cost would be upwards of $20 million, clearly not feasible given the present revenue split. Jones and I proposed a tax abatement plan whereby the State would reduce its share to 5.5 percent, until the track had recovered some or all the cost of new improvements. We began to work with lobbyists and had discussions with several Ohio politicians in meetings set up by Mr. DeBartolo. It would turn out to be a long and arduous process.

Things were also getting rocky in Toledo that summer. The Federal government put a huge tariff on the importation of foreign steel that was having a major impact on the operation of the Toledo Overseas Terminal. Revenues dropped sharply and TOT, as it was known, was operating at a loss. It was time for some drastic changes in Toledo.

I drove over to Toledo and met with Walter Zeplien. I advised him we had to renegotiate the leases with the Toledo Port Authority and cut down our rental costs at the facility. We also needed to review the budgets to eliminate any excess expenses. The alternative was we would have to close the facilities. We hammered the Port Authority before they agreed to reduce rents on the facilities. Then we looked at our in-house spending. Zeplien was skeptical we could put much of a dent in the budget, but, by the time we finished, we had cut nearly $600,000 from the operation, including the rent reduction. The operation was now projected to break even.

On July 30, I got a call from Eddie, Jr. that set me, as well as others, up for five exciting months that ended in heartbreak. Eddie was in Chicago and had just met with Bill Veeck of the Chicago White Sox concerning the DeBartolo organization buying the White Sox. Eddie told me he set up a meeting in Chicago the next day with Veeck and his financial people. I was to meet with Leo Breen, the team's Controller, in Chicago the following afternoon.

I flew to Chicago the next morning and met with Breen in his office at Comiskey Park as scheduled early in the afternoon. It didn't take long for me to realize this was the best baseball opportunity I had seen yet. The Sox were for sale and the deal included the land and stadium, including several acres of parking. The team was in a great market in Chicago and the price was remarkably affordable.

We had recently taken over the concessions at Louisiana Downs and knew how profitable they could be, and I was surprised to find out the concessionaire contract at Comiskey only had a short time left. I poured over the figures with Breen and my head was swimming with possibilities. Veeck indicated to Breen he wanted to meet me when we were winding up.

On the way over to Veeck's office, Breen told me Veeck didn't care for "bean counters" so I shouldn't expect to be with him for very long. Breen also advised Veeck had a keg of beer in his office and he would "sip" throughout the day. On days when the Sox would play at night at home, he took a late afternoon nap before mingling with the fans prior to the game. There would be a home game that night.

So, Breen brought me into Bill's office, introduced me and left. To break the ice, the first thing I asked Veeck about was Eddie Gaedel, the "midget" Veeck had sent up to pinch hit in a big-league game in 1951. Veeck got a big smile on his face and said, "you're a baseball fan!" I acknowledged that baseball was my passion as a kid and told him I was born in Brooklyn and still was a Dodger fan. Veeck then said he was hiring an "old Dodger" as a color commentator -- Don Drysdale.

When I told him Drysdale had been one of my childhood heroes, he made a point of introducing me to Big D later that afternoon. That was a treat for me. Veeck and I spent the next half hour or so talking baseball.

Continuing our meeting, we shared a few beers and he asked me about the DeBartolo's. He wanted to know what they were like and if they would be good owners. After we spoke for a while, he said he was satisfied and would recommend our group to the Sox board. Then he took me over to Drysdale's broadcasting booth, and he went back to his office, presumably to take his nap. After a short visit with my former idol, I headed to the airport for the flight home.

The next day, I prepared my report and pro-forma in the same manner I always do. No matter how hard I looked at the deal, I couldn't come up with a scenario that wouldn't be profitable for the company. I recommended to EJD and EJD, Jr. that we move forward.

Eddie would have a problem with the NFL if he owned the team. The NFL in those days prohibited owners being involved in any sport other than the NFL. That hit the front page of the sports in the Chicago newspapers the next day. The article titled "DeBartolo defies Rozelle with Sox bid" went on to quote EJD, Jr and Pete Rozelle, the Commissioner of the National Football League. Eddie allowed that he would work with Rozelle to avoid a problem, but Rozelle said he "would talk to DeBartolo about his dealings with the White Sox."

A few days later, EJD called a meeting to discuss my report and the possibility the company would pursue the purchase of the Sox. There was no dissent among the 10 or so DeBartolo officials in attendance, as to the purchase. The only real discussion was the need to insulate EJD, Jr. from NFL problems. Mr. DeBartolo, Sr. solved the problem quickly. "I've always loved baseball. I will be the owner of the team."

The balance of the meeting was to discuss what we would offer for the team. Initially, the price of $16-18 million was discussed, but in ongoing discussions with Veeck, he made it clear that amount would only be considered if our assumption of approximately $4 million of existing debt was included as well. That brought our offer to $20 million, including the debt assumption, and EJD gave his approval. A formal offer was prepared, and Mr. DeBartolo felt, rather than mail or courier the offer, it should be delivered and discussed with Veeck personally. He tabbed me to make and deliver the offer.

Right about that time, an internal faux pas nearly killed our bid. Vince Bartimo, who, to this point, was not involved in the White Sox deal, was quoted in the New Orleans Times-Picayune earlier as follows, "The Super Dome is our priority. I feel that Mr. DeBartolo, Jr. was misquoted (in an earlier statement that the Sox would be kept in Chicago). It is my judgment...that the DeBartolo Corporation's primary aim is to bring major league baseball to the Super Dome."

The quote was picked up in the Chicago Tribune on August 8 and caused quite an uproar in Chicago. To Bill Veeck's credit, he attempted to deflect the matter, informing the media from every contact he had with DeBartolo personnel, including from Eddie, Jr. and me, he was assured the team would be kept in Chicago. But, by now the media had taken the ball and run with it. Veeck called me and again asked me what our intentions were, and I assured him once again we had no intention of moving the team. I offered to put a clause in our purchase offer to that effect, and Veeck agreed that would be a good idea.

In mid-August, I flew to Chicago and delivered our formal offer to Veeck. The offer included the clause not to move the team. Veeck seemed positive and indicated he would present the offer to his Board by the end of the week. On Friday, August 22, Veeck called me and indicated our offer was tentatively accepted by his Board. Again, the press coverage was significant, and once again Bartimo couldn't resist commenting to the press in Louisiana.

"The DeBartolo Corporation is buying the thing lock, stock and barrel. They anticipate keeping it in Chicago and they plan on keeping it in Chicago, but all the options are open to them," he said. The Chicago press again picked up Bartimo's quote, which fueled speculation as to our true intentions. Our corporate dysfunction was killing us.

Andy McKenna, a respected Chicago businessman, and one of the owners, had been tabbed to head a three-person committee that would review the purchase offers for the 12-man Board of the White Sox. I met McKenna on one of my trips to Chicago to fine tune our final purchase agreement.

McKenna was very likeable, and he and I got along well. McKenna called me to discuss the ongoing issue of our intent to keep the team in Chicago. McKenna also wanted to know what Bartimo's role was in this entire matter. I said I knew Vince well and I felt, politically, Vince had to try and save face in Louisiana after our failed attempt to buy Charlie Finley's A's and move them to the Super Dome.

I assured Andy Vince wasn't involved, Mr. DeBartolo called the shots and the rest of us all felt it would be crazy to desert a great sports town like Chicago. But, Andy was still troubled about our dysfunction, and he indicated that it would be necessary for Mr. DeBartolo to come to Chicago himself to meet with the Sox Board before our offer could be accepted. I said I would see what I could do.

The opposition of The American League and Major League Baseball had been mentioned in several newspaper articles while the entire process was unfolding. With the board tentatively accepting De-Bartolo's bid, it now moved to the forefront.

Veeck and McKenna received a call from Lee McPhail about the league's reservations, and McKenna arranged a meeting with the major league representatives. That meeting took place on September 5, 1980 at the Ramada Inn at Pittsburgh Airport. McKenna represented the White Sox, while Bowie Kuhn, the Commissioner of Baseball, and Lee McPhail, the Commissioner of the American League, represented the baseball establishment.

Mr. D and I flew in from Youngstown in the helio plane and were joined by Paul Martha of the Penguins, who was also an attorney. The following is a memorandum to the file that I wrote after the meeting.

MEMORANDUM

TO: FILE

SEPTEMBER 5, 1980

FROM: THOMAS F. ROSSETTI

SUBJECT: CHICAGO WHITE SOX

The following people attended a meeting at the Ramada Inn – Airport in Pittsburgh, PA at 11:00am this date:

Bowie Kuhn – Commissioner of Baseball

Lee MacPhail – Commissioner of the American League

Andrew McKenna – Chicago White Sox

Edward J. DeBartolo – The Edward J. DeBartolo Corporation

Thomas F. Rossetti – The Edward J. DeBartolo Corporation

J. Paul Martha – The Edward J. DeBartolo Corporation

Mr. McKenna opened with a narrative describing how the Sox became for sale, the negotiations with the DeBartolo Corporation and subsequent approval by the Sox Board of Directors. McKenna then indicated that he had been contacted by McPhail the week before and Kuhn the previous Saturday and that both gentlemen indicated that we would have a problem with approval by the League owners.

MacPhail then stated that there were three issues involved: The League and its owners were against out-of-state ownerships. MacPhail stated that he felt Mr. DeBartolo would not take the interest necessary to make the Club successful since he wouldn't be there daily. He produced an article written by Mike Royko (a Chicago journalist) as evidence of what negativism would result from DeBartolo's ownership.

MacPhail felt that the owners were not convinced that DeBartolo's intention was to keep the Sox in Chicago. Citing quotes made by Vince Bartimo in New Orleans, McPhail questioned our intentions of what we were going to do with the Sox.

MacPhail stated that the Commissioner (Kuhn) had a "real problem" with owners involved with gambling businesses and McPhail then deferred to Kuhn.

Kuhn stated that he felt so strongly about this issue that he has forbidden any owner to even own shares of a public company that might own casinos. He stated that the Oakland sale involved Levi Strauss' part ownership of a California track and that they (Levi Strauss) had agreed to sell their racetrack interests.

Mr. DeBartolo then commented about each of the points. He indicated that George Steinbrenner owned a one-half interest in Florida Downs and that the Galbreath family owned a stable of racehorses and were on the Board of Directors at Churchill Downs.

Mr. DeBartolo indicated that his credentials in racing were impeccable and that he had done a great deal to keep racing alive in the three states. He remarked that he couldn't see how Kuhn could allow Steinbrenner and Galbreath their racing involvements and discriminate against him (DeBartolo).

The next point Mr. DeBartolo addressed concerned the issue of moving the Club. Mr. DeBartolo indicated that Bartimo's quotes arose from a lack of communication. Mr. DeBartolo added that he fell in love with the Chicago area, its market, etc. He indicated that he had no intention of moving the Club.

To show good faith, Mr. DeBartolo offered to put up a $5 million indemnity to guarantee the Club will stay in Chicago. He agreed to forfeit the indemnity if he would move the Club.

The third issue concerned out-of-town ownerships. A discussion ensued in which our performances in San Francisco and Pittsburgh were reviewed. We indicated that, even though we were absentee owners, we did not feel that the fans in those cities would feel that it hurt the Club. We cited newspaper articles from all cities, including Chicago, wherein our reputation was recognized. We outlined our Sports management expertise, closing with the statement that we felt our ownership would be the best thing for the White Sox organization.

MacPhail and Kuhn then stated that they were not there to argue but they felt 99 percent sure that we wouldn't get the League approval and that we wouldn't get the other owners to approve us. They felt that since the Sox had an "alternate solution to the problem" (Farley) that we wouldn't get League approval.

At that point, a somewhat heated discussion ensued in which we refuted all their points without apparent success. Kuhn commented that he could never approve someone with gambling interests as a baseball owner and that he was adamant on that point.

Mr. DeBartolo and Mr. McKenna then left the room to confer.

In their absence, I asked Mr. Kuhn what the League approval process was. He replied that after the Sox shareholders approve the sale, the League owners would vote their approval. Finally, he (Kuhn) had the right to veto any transaction despite these votes.

I then asked Kuhn what his feeling would be if we secured stockholders and owners approval. Kuhn refused comment saying only that he was against absentee ownership and our racetrack involvement. Kuhn reiterated that it was a moot point since we wouldn't be able to get League approval anyhow.

Paul Martha then took strong exception to all of Kuhn's points.

At this point, Messers. DeBartolo and McKenna returned just as I told Mr. Kuhn and Mr. MacPhail that it appeared to me that, since there was no ballclub in Youngstown that we apparently were being shut out of baseball. Mr. Kuhn stated that there was a ballclub in Cleveland.

I then stated to Mr. Kuhn that it appeared as if they didn't want us in baseball. Kuhn's reply was "That's an unfortunate way to put it", and dropped the issue.

Mr. DeBartolo then offered the following solutions:

On the issue of out-of-town ownerships, he indicated that he would put 3 or 4 of the current owners on the Sox Board. Mr. DeBartolo explained why he was unable to allow them to be owners.

On the question of moving the Club, Mr. DeBartolo reiterated that he would put up the $5 million indemnity as a show of his good faith.

On the subject of Mr. DeBartolo's racetrack interests, Mr. DeBartolo offered to remove himself from an ownership position and allow Marie Denise DeBartolo York to be the sole owner.

Mr. Kuhn replied that Mr. DeBartolo's issue of removing himself as an owner would not be sufficient since Kuhn felt the Club would still be run by the DeBartolo people who are also involved in racing. Besides, Mr. McPhail pointed out, even if DeBartolo were to convince the Commissioners, Mr. MacPhail was of the opinion that the other owners could not be swayed. Mr. MacPhail stated that he informally polled all the owners and that only one owner had allowed that he was in favor of DeBartolo as an owner.

Mr. DeBartolo then commented that he has been extremely successful in business through the years and that he has run up against opposition many times before. Mr. DeBartolo advised MacPhail and Kuhn that he would fight and was prepared to spend millions of dollars to resolve this issue. Mr. DeBartolo commented that his personal and corporate reputation was at stake.

Mr. McKenna suggested at that point that perhaps the meeting was losing its true spirit and suggested a recess would be appropriate.

Over lunch, both MacPhail and Kuhn seemed to somewhat soften their position and after some discussion the following was resolved:

The first step toward determining the germaine issues was that DeBartolo still needed shareholder approval. McKenna felt that he had a "fiduciary responsibility" to report the results of this meeting and the problems outlined therein to his Board of Directors. He indicated that a meeting was scheduled on Sunday, 9/7/80 in Chicago for that purpose. Assuming the Board's decision to accept the DeBartolo proposal remained intact, the issue would be brought to stockholder vote.

It was agreed by all that, if and when the Sox shareholders approved the sale, at that time Mr. DeBartolo would contact each of the American League owners and attempt to persuade them to vote affirmatively in support of him. Mr. MacPhail indicated that the September 17 meeting in Chicago might be the appropriate time to contact many of the owners since they would be together at that time.

The meeting broke up at approximately 1:55pm.

After the meeting, Mr. McKenna, Mr. DeBartolo, Mr. Martha and I met briefly. Mr. DeBartolo relayed to McKenna the importance of his presentation to the Sox Board and asked for his continuing support. McKenna indicated that he was still 100 percent in support of the DeBartolo organization.

McKenna also indicated that three American League owners should be contacted and would be crucial to our effort to sway the votes. The owners were:

Bud Selig – Milwaukee Brewers

Mr. Kauffman – Kansas City Royals

Mr. Fetzer – Detroit Tigers

TFR/jhm

Cc: Edward J. DeBartolo
Edward J. DeBartolo, Jr.
Marie Denise DeBartolo
J. Paul Martha
William D. Moses

The main thing to come out of the meeting was that MacPhail and Kuhn intended to do anything in their power to discredit the DeBartolo purchase. We just didn't know to what extent they would go. Unfortunately, we were going to find out.

Just before we parted from McKenna, he took me aside and asked me to see if I could convince DeBartolo to attend the Sox Board Meeting on Sunday. I told him I would try, but not to get his hopes up because it was on such short notice.

So, Mr. D and I got on the plane to fly back to Youngstown that Friday afternoon, and I asked him if he would consider making an appearance at the Sox Board meeting on Sunday evening. I explained Mr. D's lack of presence in Chicago was reported in the media throughout the entire matter and that even members of the Sox Board were questioning as to whether he even cared enough. I told the Boss McKenna had specifically requested Mr. D be there.

Mr. DeBartolo was an extremely private man who did not particularly like dealing with the media, especially in a non-scripted situation. He knew the media would be outside the Sox Board meeting and that, if he went, he would be expected to answer questions not just from the Board, but from the media afterward, as well. So, I was more than a little shocked when he agreed to do so.

He told me to fly to Chicago and he would fly in and meet me on Sunday. He indicated we could leave right after the Sox Board affair and I would fly back with him. I arranged for my flight and to have my car transported to Youngstown airport by a member of my staff. I called McKenna and asked him what time the meeting was and to get us a room at the Hotel where the meeting would be held, so that Mr. D could "freshen up." McKenna made the arrangements and called me back with the details. I notified Mr. DeBartolo's head pilot and he told me what time to meet Mr. D at Meigs Field in downtown Chicago.

I decided to fly out on Saturday to visit and stay with my mother and brothers in Northbrook, and on Sunday, my brother John drove me to Meigs Field and we waited for Mr. D's arrival. Mr. DeBartolo, who had left the 49ers opening game in New Orleans at half-time, arrived right on schedule on the Company's Lear Jet with the 49ers logo on the tail.

I introduced him to John, who then left to go home. Before getting in the limo for the short drive to the hotel, Mr. D and I stopped to use the restroom. It happened that a member of the airport field staff was at the urinal on the left side of me and asked me if I was on the 49ers plane that just landed. I told him that I wasn't on the plane, but that I worked for the owner. He asked me what it was like working for DeBartolo.

"I heard that he's really a bastard to work for" he commented. I responded to him "Oh, he's not that bad," knowing full well Mr. DeBartolo was at the urinal to my right. I heard him quietly chuckle. Talk about an awkward moment.

The 49ers won their game in New Orleans, so the day was already a success. Now, it was show-time for Edward J. DeBartolo, Sr. at the Sox Board meeting. McKenna arranged for us to have rooms at the Whitehall Hotel, which was in front of the Tremont Hotel, where the Sox Board would be meeting. It was kept quiet and there was no press at the Whitehall when we arrived.

McKenna greeted us and told us the Tremont was crawling with media personnel. We would first meet with the Sox Board, meet the members and answer their questions and then the media would be allowed in. McKenna told us the Board would meet shortly to formally accept our offer and then we would be escorted over from the back of the Whitehall to the back of the Tremont, where the media wouldn't see us. There we'd meet and mingle with the Board members at a cocktail party before the media was allowed in. Mr. DeBartolo went to his room to rest. I went to the bar and waited for the show to start.

About an hour and a half later, McKenna called to give me the heads-up and I called Mr. D to tell him that everything was ready. We went over to the Tremont through an alley and entered from the back to avoid the press. The Sox board members were delighted to meet Mr. DeBartolo. Mr. D was very gracious and answered their questions while praising Chicago and its sports fans. He also went out of his way to thank the board members for their support despite the League's reluctance to support his effort. The evening was off to a good start, but the real test was yet to come. It was time to open the event to the media.

The Chicago media was generally supportive of DeBartolo's quest to buy the Sox, but there were some who were not. McKenna opened with an announcement that the Board had unanimously accepted the DeBartolo bid and then he introduced Mr. D to the Chicago media. Mr. DeBartolo spoke a few words about his background and his plans for the White Sox and then opened to questions.

Naturally, the question about a move to New Orleans came up right away. "This club will never be moved under our ownership" he said. He also conveyed his belief that Chicago was a great sports town and he would be crazy to consider moving the team. Asked why he wanted to buy the Sox, he replied "Why does anyone want to do anything? Because you like to move forward and do something exciting in your life." Finally, he pledged, "With the stature of our organization, within a few short years we will make the Sox a winner." Mr. DeBartolo had brought his "A" game and it was a good night.

It was getting late and time for us to meet the plane. The limo took us to Midway Airport and Mr. D paid the driver and sent him home. It was about 11:30 at night and we sat on a bench in an airport hangar. The DeBartolo plane returned to New Orleans after dropping Mr. D off earlier that afternoon. The plane then flew to Memphis to drop off Denise and John York, her husband, before returning to Chicago.

Mr. DeBartolo was happy with how the day unfolded, but he was tired. As soon as he got on the plane, he dozed off. When we landed at Youngstown Airport, he sent the pilots home, telling them I would drive him home. We got in my company-owned Pontiac LeMans and he said "We've got to get you a better car."

He asked me about my brother, John and I gave him some background and told Mr. D that John was hoping to hook up with the White Sox, once we got the team. Mr. DeBartolo told me it would be fine with him since I would be involved with the staffing of the team, anyway. Then we drove the 20 miles or so to his home in Boardman, which was only two or three miles from my house. It was almost four am Monday morning and he said to me "It's pretty late. Why don't you sleep in tomorrow?" Then, as he got out of the car he said, "I'll see you at 7." I wondered what his idea of "sleeping in" was.

The next two days I tried to get caught up on many of the matters that awaited my involvement the last several days. Meetings about the White Sox and trips to Chicago took up a lot of my time, leaving my staff somewhat adrift from my lack of involvement. Nevertheless, Marty and Chris Bilski held everything together.

DeBartolo called a meeting late Monday morning to update all the corporate executives on what transpired over the weekend. He also appointed various corporate officials to use their connections to enlist the support of many owners in the American League. EJD advised me I would be flying with him on Wednesday morning to Detroit to meet with Bud Selig, John Fetzer and Ewing Kauffman, as recommended by Andy McKenna. Paul Martha would also make the trip.

Wednesday, we left in the morning from Youngstown Airport. Eddie had the Lear Jet in San Francisco, so the company leased a King Air for the trip. We arrived at the host hotel at Detroit Metro Airport for the meeting.

John Fetzer, the Detroit owner, Bud Selig, the Milwaukee owner, and Jim Garner, an attorney representing the American League awaited us. Ewing Kauffman, owner of the Kansas City Royals, was not present. Apparently, his plane developed engine problems and he wouldn't make it.

The meeting went very well from our standpoint. Mr. DeBartolo outlined his background and corporate accomplishments and reiterated what transpired in Pittsburgh with Kuhn and McPhail, and his proposed solutions to their objections. He then asked the two owners whether they had objections to his proposed purchase. Garner reiterated MacPhail and Kuhn's objections for the record. Fetzer and Selig asked a few questions generally about Mr. DeBartolo's plans for the Sox.

During a morning break, EJD assigned me to deal with Selig, and Martha to deal with Garner. He worked on Fetzer to try to win his support. Over lunch, Selig and I had meaningful discussions about our plans to improve the White Sox, and Selig acknowledged he was impressed with our credentials. As our meeting ended, I asked Selig if we could count on his support.

"Probably not," was his answer. I responded I was confused with the answer since he acknowledged he was pleased with our credentials. His answer was, "Bowie Kuhn is against you." I asked him to keep an open mind, and he agreed to do so.

Later, on the plane, EJD acknowledged he had a similar exchange with Fetzer, but he was hopeful that Fetzer also might reconsider. Martha's report was less hopeful: Garner, representing MacPhail, was adamant in his opposition. But, MacPhail didn't have a vote.

Meanwhile, Chicago sports reporters conducted their own straw polls with the American League owners and many, citing their discussions with other owners, reported the owners would easily approve DeBartolo. Calvin Griffiths, owner of the Minnesota Twins, rumored to be one of those opposed, vehemently denied his opposition and said he would vote for DeBartolo.

He joined the White Sox, Baltimore, Cleveland, New York, California and Oakland as definitely on the DeBartolo side. Texas, Seattle and Toronto hadn't yet committed. Detroit, Kansas City and Milwaukee were questionable and only Boston's Jean Yawkey was adamantly against DeBartolo, who declined to bid on her franchise after her husband passed away years before.

Also, on Wednesday, September 10, Jerome Holtzman from the Chicago Sun Times broke the story that answered our questions about our attempt to buy the Seattle Mariners. His headline read "KUHN BLOCKED DEBARTOLO IN SEATTLE."

We were perplexed as to why we never heard back from Seattle when we indicated we were interested and made a verbal offer. Contacted in Youngstown, Mr. DeBartolo told Holtzman, "They sat on our offer. After it lay there for two or three weeks, they withdrew."

When he heard Kuhn intervened, Mr. DeBartolo replied, "Hey, that's possible. I never thought of that." Holtzman's feelings with his straw poll was DeBartolo could wind up with a "13-1 or 12-2 majority – this despite the warnings of Commissioner Bowie Kuhn and A.L. President Lee McPhail, who have been insisting the wealthy Ohioan would not gain league approval."

The Chicago press reported that Friday Mr. DeBartolo flew to Kansas City and met with Ewing Kauffman. It didn't happen. Kauffman, already on record as favoring local ownership, spoke with DeBartolo on the phone. Mr. D was cautiously optimistic, but Kauffman was non-committal.

Although the White Sox matter wasn't on the agenda, the American League owners agreed to allow Mr. DeBartolo to address their group at one of baseball's joint meetings in Chicago on Wednesday, September 17. Denise DeBartolo York flew in with him. Martha and I met the plane and we drove over to the Hyatt Regency O'Hare.

It was a closed meeting for owners only and EJD was in there less than 10 minutes. Ewing Kauffman was quoted as saying DeBartolo "made a beautiful speech to the owners" as he outlined his credentials and plans for the team, and pledged the team would not be moved. DeBartolo was surprised there were no questions.

"That was the most emotionless group I've ever talked to," he said. "You'd think that I had killed their grandmothers or something like that. It really makes you feel funny when you ask if they have any questions and nobody says anything."

No vote was expected in that meeting and none occurred. MacPhail promised a vote would be taken during the League Championship Series or the World Series.

So, the emotional roller coaster continued, with the press having a field day and us getting conflicting reports and pledges of support. The American League meeting was scheduled for October 24. Rallies held in Chicago supported DeBartolo, and politicians and giants of industry got involved to support DeBartolo's cause.

Some local sports reporters used the time to reiterate their opposition to our offer. Others rallied to support him and condemn the "character assassination" being caused by MacPhail and Kuhn. Dick Young of the New York Daily News offered that Lee MacPhail was at one point the most vocal against DeBartolo, but now was in favor of him. Young questioned Bowie Kuhn's motives in his opposition.

On October 16, the White Sox shareholders voted overwhelmingly to accept the sale to DeBartolo by a 76,000 to 3,000 vote of shares. Mr. McKenna called DeBartolo and told him, "The ball is in your court, Ed." The only obstacle left was now the vote of the league owners in eight days. Those eight days would prove to be nail-biting as each team owner was constantly polled. We needed 10 votes of the 14 and we already knew at least two (Kansas City and Boston) would vote "no." It appeared we had five firm "yes" votes (Chicago, Cleveland, New York, Baltimore and Oakland), and four likely "yes" votes (Minnesota, California, Seattle and Toronto). That left us needing one vote from either Detroit, Milwaukee or Texas, with Detroit and Milwaukee reportedly leaning toward Bowie Kuhn. It could go either way. It didn't go our way.

The meeting took place at the Hyatt Regency O'Hare and the vote was eight teams in favor and six against. It was a secret vote and we were not told how each of the teams voted. Kuhn, who wasn't expected to attend the American League meeting and didn't, flew into Chicago and stayed at the hotel, reportedly lobbying against DeBartolo, although MacPhail stated "there is no reason to think" that the vote would have been different had Kuhn not lobbied.

But Jerome Holtzman's article summed up the secret vote as follows: "The distinct impression was that MacPhail, and some of the owners, as well, approached the entire DeBartolo controversy with distaste. It was obvious that they were doing the bidding of Kuhn, who had arrived at the Hyatt Regency Thursday night where he set up a command post in an upstairs suite, the better to be certain his 'recruits" would follow orders."

I was in the meeting with Mr. DeBartolo and Denise when Mr. D made his case for acceptance. He was exceptional and answered the dozen or so questions to the apparent satisfaction of the questioners. At one point Charlie Finley, who was in favor of DeBartolo, asked him, "What is it that Kuhn has against you?" When Mr. D answered he had no idea, Finley asked MacPhail to get Kuhn into the meeting.

"Get the Commissioner down here to explain what the charges are against this honorable man," Finley said. MacPhail refused. Holtzman's article in the paper the next day quoted Bill Veeck as saying "MacPhail had secretly met with Jerry Reinsdorf and Bill Farley, who head a Chicago area purchase group which tried to buy the Sox but were rejected in favor of DeBartolo. Reinsdorf and Farley reportedly met with MacPhail and seven or eight 'friendly' owners – friendly toward Kuhn, that is – at the Hyatt Regency Thursday night and again Friday morning, immediately prior to the 11 a.m. league meeting." Veeck also indicated the results were fixed.

Mr. DeBartolo was crestfallen after the vote, but a little buoyed by how close he came. I may be biased, but there was no legitimate reason why he should not have been approved by the league. The whole thing was ridiculous – a secret vote, Bowie Kuhn showing up and going into hiding while he met with owners, Kuhn and several owners slipping out of the hotel after the deed was done, avoiding reporters and leaving everyone to speculate what could possibly be in this man's background that would make him so undesirable an owner.

The media backlash was considerable across the country. From coast to coast, baseball was taken to task. Kuhn's and MacPhail's flimsy excuses were dissected and dismissed. Over 5,000 fans in Chicago, in a Chicago Tribune Poll voted – 94 percent disagreed with the A.L. decision, 94 percent said Bowie Kuhn abused his rights as Commissioner, and only five percent said Kuhn's job performance was excellent or good, while 95 percent rated him as fair (16 percent) or poor (79 percent). Most, if not all respondents, didn't know DeBartolo, but they were smart enough to recognize injustice when they saw it.

In early December, after a great deal of soul-searching and discussion, Mr. DeBartolo decided, if it was necessary to get the White Sox, he would put the racetracks up for sale. He sent a letter to Bowie Kuhn, Lee MacPhail and each of the American League owners advising he would sell his three racetracks, buy a residence in Chicago, and establish 20 percent residence if the White Sox sale were approved.

Kuhn's reply, not surprisingly, was not encouraging. He seized on the 20 percent residency and maintained that would be an insufficient commitment to White Sox business and could hurt the team. He also doubted the pledge to sell the tracks would sway the owners to approve him since it was so close to the December 11 meeting.

We interpreted this response to mean he now knew he had enough votes to stop the purchase and, regardless of what we offered, it wouldn't be enough. We flew to Dallas on Thursday, December 11, and I think we all had a sense of foreboding.

This meeting was at the Loews Anatole Hotel and, once again, we went into the meeting with the owners. Once again, Mr. DeBartolo went through his background and plans for the White Sox. He addressed the reasons cited for the earlier opposition and reiterated he would dispose of the tracks and establish a residence in Chicago, and then he asked if there were any questions.

This time, Mr. DeBartolo was asked point blank, "If we were to vote against approval, will you sue baseball?" Other than the exchange Mr. D had with Bowie Kuhn in Pittsburgh, there had not once been any mention of a lawsuit from anyone in the DeBartolo organization. Mr. DeBartolo asked for a recess before he answered the question.

We had several attorneys with us and we met to discuss how, if at all, Mr. DeBartolo should answer the question. It had been inferred in numerous newspaper articles Mr. DeBartolo might sue baseball or go after its anti-trust exemption if he was unsuccessful in getting the Sox, but we had never been part of the articles or discussed it outside of the inner circle.

The attorneys were mixed on their recommendations. Some felt he should say "yes" and some felt it should be "no." The problem was we hadn't really felt we wouldn't get the team, so we were unprepared for the question.

If Mr. D said "no" than he was giving the League an opening to get rid of him. Sure, he could always change his mind and sue baseball, but he would be going against his word. If he said "yes", or even declined to answer, then he risked the League circling the wagons and not approving him. It was classic entrapment and a no-win situation for Mr. DeBartolo. We went back into the meeting and he told the owners he would not sue. We were then asked to leave the meeting so the owners could discuss the matter and vote. We went up to the DeBartolo suite to wait.

It didn't take very long. Lee MacPhail came in and advised Mr. DeBartolo the owners voted 11 – 3 against the DeBartolo bid. MacPhail apologized to Mr. DeBartolo, who, for the first and only time that I had seen him, was crushed. Mr. D composed himself and went out to face the media.

After thanking the people of Chicago who supported his bid, he lashed out at the baseball establishment, defending his heritage and lambasting all who were inferring he might have ties to the underworld. He didn't name names but I'm sure the guilty parties knew to whom he referred. I was only 32 years old, but I now knew what racism and discrimination felt like. I felt guilty that such an injustice could still take place in the United States of America.

The limo trip to Dallas Airport, where the plane awaited, was short and quiet. The flight to Youngstown was like attending a funeral. Mr. D looked like a beaten puppy and spent the entire two hours staring out the plane's window, apparently lost in his own thoughts. I was also miserable and completely at a loss for words. Try as I might, I couldn't come up with any words I thought were appropriate. I had witnessed an assassination and no words of comfort came to mind. Quietly, we flew through the afternoon sky.

Landing in Youngstown, we disembarked, and I was headed for my car a short distance away, when I felt a hand on my shoulder. It was my boss. “Cheer up” he told me. “We have a lot of other projects to take care of. I’ll see you tomorrow.”

I watched him get in his car with one of the pilots and they drove away, leaving me to marvel at the strength of this wonderful man. Here he just took perhaps the worst beating in his life and he was concerned about my feelings. I had just witnessed still another side of this mysterious man.

That isn’t the end of the story, however. In a discussion I had with Bill Veeck a day or two later, Veeck told me Kuhn called in each American League owner to his suite the night before the Dallas vote, threatened to use every negative thing he had against the owner and called in every chip he had to get them to vote against DeBartolo, and it worked.

In the days to follow, newspapers across the U.S. speculated how this could happen. The Washington Post called it “THE WHITE SOX SCANDAL OF 1980,” taking Kuhn to task for his nefarious activities. The Los Angeles Times, in a commentary taken from a Dallas newspaper alleged “DEBARTOLO’S VISION SCARED BASEBALL”, wondering if DeBartolo’s view of the future of all sports, including cable TV, might be too frightening to the staid baseball establishment. Some politicians spoke out and suggested that baseball’s antitrust exemption should be repealed.

Mr. DeBartolo considered his options, including the one of suing baseball and challenging the sport’s antitrust exemption. But, in the end, he decided to let it drop. One day, I asked him why he wouldn’t go after baseball. His reply was that he was in a position he couldn’t win. If he filed suit, he would be vilified for going back on his word, given to the owners in the December meeting. And, if he filed suit and won, he would forever be known as the man who ruined America's pastime. It's hard to argue with that logic.

Believe it or not, while the White Sox fiasco was going on, I was involved in other matters. As I mentioned earlier, Louisiana Downs was becoming more profitable each day. The track bought out the concessions contract and was totally in control of all revenue areas in the facility. Vince Bartimo, from all our standards, was running a tight, well-oiled operation. Not surprisingly, Bartimo made some enemies, a fact he constantly mentioned in discussions and memos.

One of these enemies was a gentleman named Tom Russell, a horseman from Texas who also claimed to be one of the minority stockholders of Louisiana Downs and owned a periodical known as the Racing Journal. Russell sent many letters to Mr. DeBartolo over the years, alleging improper actions by Bartimo against shareholders and horsemen. DeBartolo normally would discuss these letters with Bartimo, who dismissed them as nonsense, telling Mr. D it was sour grapes because Bartimo would not give Russell stall space at Louisiana Downs.

In early November, Russell sent such a letter to DeBartolo. For some reason, DeBartolo turned this letter over to me and instructed me to contact Russell and arrange for a private, not to be published, meeting to find out what was bothering him. A few days later, I flew to Dallas and met with Russell and his wife. I collected copies of his documents and allegations and flew back to Ohio. I summarized the complaints, alleged wrongdoings and documents and provided them to Mr. DeBartolo, for his review and use.

A few days later, Mr. D called me to his office and told me Bartimo claimed all the information was false and that he did nothing wrong. Mr. D also said Bartimo was furious at me and my disloyalty. I reminded Mr. D he sent me to the meeting and asked how Bartimo knew it was I who reported back to him (Mr. D). EJD told me he sent my report to Bartimo for his comment, and he acknowledged that may have been a mistake.

He told me Bartimo said I was forbidden from setting foot on the Louisiana property from now on. I asked him how I could do my job and Mr. D indicated he would "work it out." A few days later, Senior told me it would be better for me if I sent one of my staff members down there for the time being. I lost Bartimo as a friend and ally.

The racetrack operations were a mixed bag in 1980. Louisiana Downs was a "cash cow" with cash flows in the millions and, during the current recession, DeBartolo financial people would draw down that cash flow to fund other DeBartolo operations.

Balmoral Park, which EJD acquired in the early 70's, was never a money maker. The track was in Crete, IL, south of Chicago. It was formerly known as Lincoln Fields and its claim to fame was it was a hangout for Al Capone and his syndicate. The track originally was a harness track (trotters), which wasn't EJD's cup of tea, but acquiring the track property entitled the owner to run a small racing meet at downtown Chicago's Sportsman's Park, which was lucrative. In fact, in some years the 15-20 day meet at Sportsman's covered the Balmoral losses for the entire year.

Thistledown started off 1980 slowly and never got any better. The track ended the year with a loss of $653,000, a sizeable loss for the aging property. In November, Jones and I testified in Columbus on our proposed tax bill (HB 308). As part of our testimony, we cited our projected losses and the need to get the bill passed so the improvements could begin.

On November 20, the Cleveland Plain Dealer quoted some of my Columbus testimony. "'We are at a crossroads for keeping Thistledown open,' said Thomas Rosetti (sic), controller of sports and diversified operations for Edward J. DeBartolo, Thistledown owner. 'Without relief, we see no way we can earn an equitable return on our investment.' The track has planned a $10 million improvement in the often-criticized backstretch barns in 1981, but Rosetti (sic) hinted the change might not be made without the abatement."

Over the years, the Ohio press in Columbus and the Cleveland/Akron area was brutal toward Mr. DeBartolo. He was arguably the wealthiest man in Ohio, and they never bought into the story that losses could hurt the man. They also often cited the nature of us being a private company, which didn't have to file financial statements publicly. So, when the press heard us saying that we lost money, they didn't believe it included cash losses.

They often alleged our losses were only on paper and that we never "really lost money." DeBartolo was always reluctant for us to quote our numbers, but I asked for permission to do so and he finally relented. The figures I quoted were cash losses. As expected, the press questioned the numbers and accused us of financial chicanery, but this time we were ready.

One member of the press who was particularly skeptical was a sports reporter named Bob Dolgan. Dolgan wasn't the track reporter, who reported race results and other track-only information. He reported on sports in general including the Browns, Indians and Cavaliers. He also reported on other sports matters relating to the Cleveland area. As expected, Dolgan doubted the accuracy of our numbers, and this time I called him on it.

With Mr. DeBartolo's approval, I contacted Dolgan and told him we were ready to open our books and prove our numbers to him. I suggested he get any reputable CPA in the area, and I would sit with them and prove the numbers I quoted were accurate. The only caveat I requested, was the Plain Dealer pay for the CPA if and when I proved him wrong, and that he retract his prior allegations with the same type of headlines that he used to discredit us.

Dolgan was excited about the prospect of getting "behind the scenes" information on the company, and went to get his editor's approval. When the editor balked at the prospect of paying for a CPA, I told him I would open the books to him anyway. I was gambling that Dolgan was intelligent and would be fair in his reporting. In the meantime, the Ohio House defeated the proposed racetrack improvement bill.

We scheduled Dolgan to visit on Christmas Eve and I promised he would also meet Mr. DeBartolo. I walked him through our financial statements explaining everything to him and answered all his questions. I showed him how much we had paid the State ($8.2 million) while we were losing so much money, and I even told him that, included in our losses was a $100,000 salary for Mr. DeBartolo.

Then, I brought him over to our conference room to meet with Mr. DeBartolo. Dolgan interviewed him, and four days later, the headline on the front of the Sports page in the Plain Dealer read "THISTLEDOWN MAY NOT REOPEN IN 1981," and he reported fairly and accurately on our meeting. He quoted Mr. D and me several times, as follows:

"This isn't an abatement bill," said DeBartolo. "it's a survival bill."

"We welcome an inspection of the books by a certified public accountant or the Ohio Racing Commission," he (DeBartolo) said.

"No business in the state is taxed as we are", said DeBartolo, citing the $8.2 million. "It's crazy."

"Just because people bet $120 million a year at Thistledown, everybody thinks it's a bonanza," said DeBartolo. "But it's not. If the state thinks there's so much money in racing, I'm willing to have the state come in and be my partner, split 50-50. If the state doesn't have the brains to pass a new bill and keep getting this kind of money, it's stupid."

He quoted my projection that, without the abatement, we could expect to lose $5.4 million in cash over the next five years. He also quoted me that EJD got a $100 thousand salary.

When Dolgan mentioned that, if DeBartolo closed the track, he would be considered a villain by local racing fans and how would he feel about that, DeBartolo responded. "It would bother me, but people will understand, if the true story is told. We've fought it out here for 18 years, subsidized racing. We kept this track going because 700 people would lose their jobs."

The article came out better than we expected, and it had the desired effect in Columbus. The state eventually took up the issue again and, though it would be a long uphill battle, we eventually got a bill passed. Moreover, we now finally had an ally in the press. Two weeks later, Dolgan wrote another article, this time about the travesty in Chicago.

"GIVE DEBARTOLO A CHANCE, BOWIE," was the title. This prompted Mr. DeBartolo to send a memo to EJD, Jr., Marie Denise, William D Moses and myself. The memo said "We received dividends on the meeting we had with Bob Dolgan, December 24, 1980, on his visit to our office. Attached you will find a copy of the article which appeared in the Plain Dealer today."

Our open book meeting with Dolgan had not only been fruitful but, from that day forward, I considered Dolgan a friend. To his credit however, he always remained fair and honest.

George Jones' and my racing involvement, particularly since we were now some of the faces of the track, uncovered a glaring inconsistency in our corporate structure. It was revealed, despite Jones and I routinely signed racing applications, capital improvements applications, tax rebate applications, numerous correspondences and often appeared at Racing Commission meetings as representatives of our tracks, in fact, neither one of us were officers of any of the corporations.

I noticed it when I was preparing our 1981 racing application. When brought to Mr. DeBartolo's attention, he agreed Jones and I should be named as vice presidents of all the racing entities.

The San Francisco 49ers recently concluded the 1980 season with a 6-10 record. After winning their season opener in New Orleans on the day that EJD and I met the White Sox Board, they also won their next two against the Cardinals at home and against the Jets in New York. The 3-0 start was rudely interrupted by an eight-game losing streak, which saw Steve DeBerg benched after game six, when he threw five interceptions in a 59-14 loss to Dallas.

Montana saw some work in the Game 3 win over the Jets with two touchdowns in six passes, and he started in seven of the 49ers final 10 games, finishing among the top five QBs in the NFL. Walsh was optimistic he may have found his offensive leader, but he still needed a lot of tools to get the 49ers among the elite teams in the league.

The Pittsburgh Penguins started off the season with the hiring of Eddie Johnson as their new head coach. They also took another step in the right direction, signing a minor league affiliation with the Erie Blades to develop future Penguin players. But the team's NHL record at the end of the calendar year, which was nearly mid-season, was 11-19-7, a disappointment.

A few of the players were having great years, though. Rick Kehoe was having, and would have, his best scoring year with 88 points (55 goals and 33 assists) and would win the Lady Byng Trophy for sportsmanship at year's end. Randy Carlyle was also having a great season enroute to being awarded the Norris Trophy winner as the NHL's top defenseman.

There was also an interesting story regarding OJ Simpson that year. OJ retired from the NFL at the end of the 1979 season. In the late spring of 1980, EJD, Jr. called me into his office. Swearing me to secrecy, he told me to request a vacation day and do a "side job" for him.

He wanted me to fly to Los Angeles to meet with Jack Gilardi, a talent agent in Hollywood. Nobody was to know where I was or what I was doing, including my secretary. Eddie would pay me for the day and cover all the expenses, and have another vacation day credited to me later. I was to talk with Gilardi about a potential movie starring OJ Simpson. Eddie would finance and own the movie. If it made sense, he promised me a 10 percent share of the movie.

The next day I flew to Hollywood and met with Gilardi, who was Annette Funicello's husband at the time. He took me to some fancy Hollywood restaurant where all the actors and movie people had "power lunches," and he told me about the movie. It was titled "The Menopause of Henrietta Luck," and was about a bookish white librarian who wanted to be impregnated by a football star and have a "super athlete" son. They would not get married. OJ would be the football star.

I flew home after lunch and read the script on the plane. I had doubts about the story line. OJ was a hero and was beloved by everyone and I didn't think that the role fit him. It was the early 80's and this would have been a shocking movie on its own merits. I was prepared to tell Eddie to reject it. But, somehow EJD, Sr. learned about it.

When I got in the office the next morning, my secretary told me Edy was trying to get in touch with me all day the day before, because Mr. DeBartolo wanted to talk to me. A few minutes later, Bill Moses came to my office and told me that EJD, who had left early this morning, said that I was to "not get anyone involved in what I was doing yesterday."

A little bit later, Eddie, Jr. called me to his office. He asked me about the project and I told him I didn't think that it was a good idea. "My father got to you, didn't he?" he asked. I told him I never spoke to his father but apparently, he knew what I was doing for Eddie. I told him about Edy's calls and Moses' visit. The project was never mentioned again.

In mid-December, Marie Denise DeBartolo York sent me a letter, advising that the Company was inaugurating an Employee Recognition Program, in five-year increments, marking years of continuous service to the Company. I had been there seven years and the Company would recognize my first five years with an award. It was an appropriate ending to a tumultuous year.

CHAPTER 9

1981 - PITTSBURGH EXPANSION & THE 49ERS PUT IT ALL TOGETHER

1981 started out like 1980 ended. Though it appeared to be easing, the country was still in a deep recession, and like all developers, The DeBartolo Corporation was still feeling the pinch. Unlike most other developers in a recession, however, Mr. DeBartolo not only didn't curtail operations, he accelerated them.

This caused cash flow problems within the company that forced us to get "lean and mean" again. Raises were reduced or eliminated, new hires were delayed or cancelled and we found ways, within the departments, to cut costs and weather through the storm. It was this risky strategy that allowed Mr. D's company to stay ahead of his competitors and remain as the largest shopping center developer in the United States.

The Company's Diversified Operations, through Louisiana Downs, was instrumental in helping ease the cash flow problems arising from the ongoing development. But, we also had another "little" operation that contributed to ease the cash crunch.

Eddie, Denise and Bill Moses put together a partnership called Fun-N-Games Associates and opened a "family amusement center" in the Boardman Plaza, a mile or so from the office. They filled it with machines and Bill and Eddie used to empty the machines themselves. It didn't take long for them to realize they had a bonanza on their hands and, with EJD's approval, they hired a manager named Tom Poplar to oversee the expansion of the business.

Poplar hired an assistant named Mike Pacek, who had experience repairing and maintaining the machines, and the expansion began.

Any DeBartolo mall with a vacancy was ripe for a Fun-N-Games game room, and locations were added in non-DeBartolo malls as well. From that small start the operation eventually expanded to 84 locations, grossing nearly $21 million a year with 300 employees.

Fun-N-Games was handled separately from a normal DeBartolo operation, in that I managed all the cash, with one of my staff handling the accounting function. The cash flows were significant, and many were the times when Bill Pfaus (through Harry Wonderly, the assistant treasurer) would come to me for a loan with the big corporation. Eddie, Bill and I often joked on how this "little" entity helped keep the big ship afloat. And during the recession, Fun-N-Games Associates certainly did that.

In early January 1981, DeBartolo was already in the news. Stepping up the pressure on the Ohio General Assembly, DeBartolo offered to open his books at Thistledown for the last five years to prove he had been forthright in his loss claims. We released our cash profits and losses and the net was a loss of $410,000, ranging from a high of a $407,000 profit in 1978 to a low of a $653,000 loss in 1980.

At the same time, the State earned over $40 million on Thistledown alone. DeBartolo made a proposal. "What I would like the racing commission in Ohio to do is to hire an independent auditor to go over the books of all the tracks in the state for the last five years. If they can't afford it, Thistledown and the other tracks will pick up the bill. I'm sure if this is done, the legislature will see the true picture." DeBartolo also hinted he might not open Thistledown on March 6, unless he sensed a receptive mood in Columbus.

In early January, Mr. D had me visit Ted Bonda, a shareholder of the Cleveland Indians baseball club, who wanted to know if Mr. DeBartolo was interested in buying part of the Indians. Although the meeting was done secretly, word was leaked from unknown sources in Cleveland. On the same page as the article about Thistledown, was a small article speculating the Cleveland Indians were interested in selling a partial interest to Mr. DeBartolo, apparently to raise cash.

But, DeBartolo deflected that possibility. "I would want 100 percent of the club," DeBartolo stated. "Of course, (Baseball Commissioner) Bowie Kuhn would have to give me the green light before I make a bid for the Indians."

On February 10, I got a promotion. Eddie, Jr. promoted me to Vice President-Controller of Sports and Diversified Operations. He clarified what had been in effect for the last three years when he stated I would report directly to Edward J. DeBartolo and himself. He also stated that all Diversified Operations divisional controllers would report to me, and I would "continue to work in conjunction with management at all locations." Finally, he gave me a 20 percent raise from the parent corporation and the 49ers and told me that, other than family members, I was the youngest vice president in company history.

In March, we began negotiations with the City of Pittsburgh to take over control of the Civic Arena, home of the Penguins. We also paid a small amount to acquire the dormant Pittsburgh Spirit franchise in the Major Indoor Soccer League, and I was appointed Secretary and Treasurer of that team.

On April 28, at Eddie's suggestion, I flew out to San Francisco to experience the NFL draft from the 49ers draft room in the Redwood City office, and I witnessed history. Bill Walsh had concentrated on his defense in the last draft, and he continued with that focus in 1981. There were two premier defensive backs in the draft that year – Kenny Easley of UCLA and Ronnie Lott from USC. Walsh wanted one or the other and when Easley went as the number four choice to Seattle, he snatched Lott with his first-round pick.

He then drafted four more consecutive defensive players – DT John Harty and CB/S Eric Wright in the second round, safety Carlton Williamson in the third round and CB Lynn Thomas in the fifth round. He didn't realize it at the time, but he had his defensive backfield for the upcoming season, one that would shock the pro football world, and all of us, on January 24, 1982. It was fascinating to watch the wheels spin while the draft was going on, and all the men responsible for the 1981 draft share in the credit.

Back in Pittsburgh, the Penguins made the playoffs with a second consecutive 30-37-13 record. In those days, 16 of the 21 teams made the playoffs, which I thought made the regular season a mockery. But, we were in at number 15 and drew the number two seed St. Louis Blues.

The best of five series opened in St. Louis with the Blues winning game one and the Pens taking game two. Then it was on to Pittsburgh where the Blues won game three and the Pens game four. Back in St. Louis, the deciding game went into double overtime before the Blues poked in the winner to win 4-3, ending Pittsburgh's season.

May also saw me back in Columbus testifying on the impact of HB 330, the new tax abatement bill we brought to the Assembly. DeBartolo had opened at Thistledown when he was told by lawmakers the bill would again be voted on. But, our "open book" policy garnered the support of several Ohio reporters, including Dolgan of the Cleveland Plain Dealer and Akron Beacon Journal reporter Jack Patterson, who found himself in agreement with DeBartolo after years of being critical of him. Dolgan and I had become friendly, after our "open book" policy and his Christmas Eve interview with EJD.

In early June, I was in Montreal for the NHL Annual Meetings and Draft. At Eddie's direction, my wife joined me since I was in the middle of two weeks of business travel, and we got to tour the Old City and enjoy the beauty and elegance of Montreal. I also joined Rick Kehoe and Randy Carlyle, two of the Penguins best players that year, as they accepted their awards.

Later in June, KDKA-TV in Pittsburgh, in anticipation of our taking over the Civic Arena on July 1, and the resumption of Pittsburgh Spirit soccer, televised a five-part Monday to Friday series entitled "The DeBartolo's – The Empire Comes to Pittsburgh."

The series, which covered DeBartolo's contribution to the sporting scene in Pittsburgh, as well as his mall operations in the area, included interviews with EJD, EJD, Jr., Paul Martha and me, discussing various projects we'd been involved in and might be planning. The first day of the series, on June 21, 1981, featured an interview with Martha, who discussed the first few years of DeBartolo's ownership of the Penguins and how the acquisition of the Civic Arena cemented the Penguins future in Pittsburgh.

KDKA then focused on Mr. DeBartolo's background, including his initial foray into sports when he bought Thistledown Racetrack 23 years earlier, later adding the tracks in Chicago and Louisiana. They then focused on the 49ers acquisition in 1977, followed by the Penguins later that year, and our recent acquisition of the Pittsburgh Spirit indoor soccer team just a week before.

The KDKA reporter, Ken Mease asked me, "Why is a group successful in the business world of finance and development drawn to sports?"

I responded, "Sports serves a number of purposes for the DeBartolo family and for our company. It gives us a tremendous amount of exposure. It kind of helps his mall developments and a developer, in particular, when he's trying to attract outside interests to his projects. It gives him national exposure that can only help his other business deals, as well."

Eddie DeBartolo then added, "Sports is a business. I said that in 1977 in San Francisco and they almost ran me out of town on a rail. I think in what we've tried to do with our sports enterprises is to see that they are run by the best possible people that we could choose, and everything is coordinated and it is a long-range plan, because you can't have a short-range plan with a sports franchise. If anybody thinks they can, I think they are sorely mistaken."

Day two of the series brought up the inevitable possibility of DeBartolo someday owning a professional baseball team as well as an NBA franchise. Mr. DeBartolo spoke about the possibility of acquiring the Cleveland Cavaliers, who were having severe financial, attendance and media problems in Cleveland, but he stressed that "nothing of a serious nature" was being considered at the time.

Separately, Mease asked me about the possibility we may acquire the Cavaliers and move them to Pittsburgh, but I assured him that, while we had given basketball some thought, "we don't have a tremendous interest in it at this time."

Mease attempted to pin down Mr. DeBartolo about the possibility of him buying the cash-strapped Pirates baseball team, since the

Chicago White Sox deal was killed, but EJD only replied "John Galbraith (Pirates Owner) is a good friend of mine. We're both Directors of the Thoroughbred Racing Association and, no; we've had no recent talks with them, nor any talks with them."

Mease didn't give up that easily, though persistently asking, "With your new-found involvement in Pittsburgh, would you seriously look at the Pirates?"

Eddie, Jr. interrupted and said, "I would think so, very definitely, if Mr. Galbraith was truly interested in selling."

It was clear Mr. DeBartolo was still smarting from the White Sox fiasco, something Mease addressed in his closing remarks the second day of the series. "So, baseball is on the back burner until time erases the White Sox trauma of this past year. Basketball is on simmer until it's decided whether it's worth the gamble. But there are two very serious DeBartolo sports commitments here: the Penguins and the Spirit, and we'll cover those in our next report."

Day three concentrated on the Penguins and focused on how DeBartolo rescued that oft-bankrupt franchise and finally gave it stability. Even though the Penguins hadn't become dominant under the DeBartolo ownership, the stability of the franchise had begun to bring fans back to the Civic Arena. Also, the Spirit franchise, another rescue, had now brought professional soccer to thousands of soccer starved young fans and kept the Igloo, as it was known in Pittsburgh, humming.

Day four of the series chronicled the history of the DeBartolo Corporation and the enormous success the Company had in the mall development business, and Day five tied it all up nicely as KDKA described all the DeBartolo holdings in Pittsburgh, including the teams, the arena and the malls, and they saluted the DeBartolo's for their investment in Pittsburgh.

It was the kind of exposure that you could not pay too much for to get comparable goodwill. Mr. DeBartolo was very pleased at a showing of the documentary in the conference room at our office. He did comment, however, that I was very "hairy" in my interviews. In those early 80's days, as many of my generation did, I sported fashionably long hair, "mutton-chop" sideburns and a "Fu-Manchu" moustache, and one of my interview clips was outside of the arena on a breezy day. Enough said.

We took over the Civic Arena on July 1, and, as newly-appointed Sr. Vice President of the new Civic Arena Corporation, I was involved in the closing of the transaction. Prior to the closing, the DeBartolo Internal Audit Group moved in and secured the building overnight so nothing disappeared. I spent the night in the Hyatt across from the Arena and at 5:30 a.m., unable to sleep, I went across to the arena to assure all was in order before the agreements would be signed. I suspect I may have surprised a few of our dozing troops, but all was in order and the closing went smoothly.

We not only took over control of the arena, but we assumed control of the concessions business in the Arena, as well. Araserv Corporation handled the concessions up to closing, but our deal with the City of Pittsburgh included that operation as well, so Araserv was gone.

I knew the GM of Araserv at the arena, a young man by the name of Jim Rozes, and we were able to coax him to join our group, thus ensuring a seamless transition. We also hired a few of the former Arena management staff, including the Controller, Edward Walter, who continued with the Arena throughout my tenure. The next few weeks were busy, and I commuted from Youngstown until we had all the DeBartolo policies and procedures implemented and had discarded the more political governmental policies. By the end of July, everything was running smoothly.

By now, I was completely out of any semblance of Accounting and was spending 100 percent of my time in management and research of proposed acquisitions. It was a very hectic first seven months of the year, and it was nice to spend the rest of the summer in Youngstown with the family. I scheduled my vacation from July 27 through August 7 and could unwind a bit. My wife always told me on every vacation the first week we were gone, I was worthless. It took me that long to get out of "work mode."

After my vacation, I moved. Not out of my home, I moved my office across the street from the DeBartolo Building, a move that underscores a good DeBartolo story. Many years ago, long before I moved to Youngstown, steel was the main industry in Youngstown. The numerous mills included U.S. Steel, Republic Steel, and Youngstown Sheet and Tube Company, which also had their home office in Youngstown.

In 1959, The Edward J. DeBartolo Corporation, a much smaller entity, bought a parcel of land in Boardman, Ohio, a Youngstown suburb, with the plan to build a new corporate office at 7620 Market Street, which happened to be directly across the street from the corporate campus of Youngstown Sheet and Tube. Sheet and Tube's campus was enormous with a huge stretch of lawn in front of the main building, set back more than 100 yards from the street. A long winding driveway wound through the park-like lawn to the parking lot. The entrance had large steel gates.

As related to me by Mr. DeBartolo himself, when DeBartolo's company applied for a building permit, Youngstown Sheet and Tube objected to the plan, because they were concerned The Edward J. DeBartolo Corporation (i.e. Mr. DeBartolo) "would not properly maintain his property," negatively affecting the value of the Sheet and Tube campus. Clearly, the Sheet and Tube executives didn't know anything about the meticulous DeBartolo. However, DeBartolo prevailed and got his permit.

I joined DeBartolo in 1973 and, by that time, the erosion of the steel business in Youngstown was well underway, devastating Youngstown's economy. One of the last companies to shutter its doors was Youngstown Sheet and Tube, which closed its mill in Campbell, Ohio, on September 19, 1977. The magnificent campus was deserted shortly thereafter.

Mr. DeBartolo described how one day he stood behind his desk in his office on the 2nd floor of the DeBartolo Building and looked out across Market Street at the magnificent, but now deserted, campus of Youngstown Sheet and Tube Company – and saw nothing but weeds, overgrown shrubbery and dandelions. He called in one of his attorneys and had him call the real estate broker handling the sale for the property, offering to buy it for $6 million. The attorney was expressly told to complain about the lack of maintenance of the property. The broker relayed the information to Sheet and Tube, and it was promptly rejected. A year later, DeBartolo bought the property for $4.2 million. Clearly, Mr. DeBartolo never forgot the slight from 1959.

At any rate, DeBartolo now had the campus and building and a few months before, moved the entire accounting department across the street into the spacious former Sheet & Tube building. That included my department as well as Pete Frank's. Pete also moved, but EJD and EJD,

Jr. didn't want me to leave the main building because of the nature of the work I was doing for them.

This created a logistical problem for me, with my people across the street, especially since my secretary did a lot of their work as well as mine. I was okay with it. I wasn't doing any accounting at all and I could always drive over for meetings whenever I needed, but it wasn't working very well for my secretary. Her name was Jacque and she shared an office with part-time help recruited from time-to-time by Ruby Kelly, DeBartolo's press secretary.

With me travelling extensively, I was unaware of her working conditions all the time; however, in the spring of 1981, it reached a boiling point. One day when I was out of the office, Ruby's department was putting press kits together and three employees were working in an assembly line fashion in the 10-by-12-foot office.

One of the DeBartolo attorneys stopped by to deliver a memo to me. Since I was gone, he tried to get into Jacque's office to give it to her, but with press kits stacked on the floor and the ladies working, he couldn't get to her desk. The noise was horrific. Jacque had to go into my office to answer her phone. She was quite frustrated. When I got back, she handed me a memo detailing all that had gone on in my absence. I read it and sent a copy to EJD, Jr., telling him we needed to do something about the situation.

It wasn't high on my list or his, because I was always on the road, but later that summer, I met with Eddie and convinced him to let me go across the street with my secretary. I scored the winning point when I reminded him my secretary was constantly typing memos of a highly confidential nature on DeBartolo personal matters as well as 49er and Penguin contract matters. The confidentiality issue clinched it. I moved into a larger office across the street with room for a TV, and my secretary was in a large lobby type area, outside of my office door. It worked for everyone.

Summer was coming to an end and, on Labor Day weekend, the 49ers were going to open the 1981 season in Detroit against the Lions. I got tickets to the game and my son, Mike, my brother, Chas and my friend, Mike Davis set out Sunday morning for Detroit, about a five-hour drive. Joe Montana had been named the starting quarterback by Bill Walsh and the game was close throughout. Montana threw a 21-yard touchdown pass to tie the game midway through the fourth quarter, but a late Billy Sims touchdown won it for Detroit, 24-17. So, we drove back to Youngstown with no inkling that 1981 would be much different than the last few years.

A few days later, I was in Columbus, working on a State committee. The Ohio House and Senate had finally passed the long sought capital improvements bill for the racetracks, allowing the tracks to apply for tax rebates for improvements to their facilities. I was asked by the State Auditor, Tom Ferguson, to represent the DeBartolo track in setting up procedures to be followed in applying for the rebate after the work was done. House Bill 308, which we lobbied for, and on behalf of which I had testified in Columbus the previous May, finally passed. The long-promised backstretch improvements to the barns at Thistledown could now proceed.

In the meantime, the 49ers closed out September with a 2-2 record. After the loss to Detroit, they bounced back to beat the Chicago Bears at Candlestick, lost to Atlanta in Georgia and then beat the New Orleans Saints at home. The offense was looking better each week, and the defense was rounding out well, led by Jack "Hacksaw" Reynolds, acquired as a free agent in the offseason, and Ronnie Lott, who returned an interception for a touchdown against New Orleans to help beat the Saints.

Offensively, Montana and veteran Freddie Solomon had hooked up for a touchdown in each of the four games and Joe had also tossed two TD's to tight end Charlie Young, acquired from the Rams in 1980. It was looking like the 49ers might be putting it together.

October changed the word "might" to "were." San Francisco went undefeated in their four games, beating Washington on the road 30-17, and then shocking Dallas and the rest of the NFL, 45-14 at Candlestick in a game as one-sided as the score indicated. They kept their foot on the peddle the following week, smothering Green Bay in Milwaukee, 13-3, before closing out the month at home with a 20-17 win over the rival Los Angeles Rams.

The offense played steady in October, but the defense was outstanding, winning the turnover battle in the four games 12-4, with three defensive touchdowns. Lott had another interception return for a TD, Dwight Hicks recovered a fumble and returned it 80 yards for a TD, and he later intercepted a pass and returned it 32 yards for a TD, both against the Redskins. Quietly, the 49ers had a five-game winning streak and moved atop the NFC West. Thanks to a "state of the art" Earth Station Satellite Dish installed by the corporation at the Youngstown headquarters, I could watch the games in my office with my family on Sundays.

The Penguins opened their season in October and it was much the same as in the past. They closed the month 5-7-2, winning only one road game. The Spirit would open their season in November. But, this was quickly becoming "49er Time."

The 49ers stretched their winning streak to seven, beating the 4-time Super Bowl Champion Pittsburgh Steelers in Pittsburgh 17-14, on a late Walt Easley touchdown on November 1, and the Falcons at Candlestick the next week, 17-14. In the two games, the defense intercepted Steeler great Terry Bradshaw three times and Atlanta QB Steve Bartkowski another three times. The defense also forced and recovered three Steeler fumbles.

But the following week, the streak ended at home against the Cleveland Browns in a sloppy game on a muddy field. The 49ers controlled the game, but the offense was unable to put the ball in the end zone. They settled for four Ray Wershing field goals and led 12-5 in the 4th quarter, but the Browns rallied for a touchdown to tie and then stopped the 49er offense and won on a Matt Bahr field goal with 43 seconds left.

The team got back on track the next week in a 33-31 win over the Rams in LA, with a Lott interception return for a TD and a 92-yard kickoff return, also for a TD. Ray Wershing added another four field goals as the offense again sputtered in the red zone. They closed out November at home against the New York Giants, winning 17-10 with the defense forcing five turnovers.

At 10-3, the 49ers were one win from clinching a playoff spot, with a road game against the powerful Cincinnati Bengals. A mid-season trade for sack specialist Fred Dean solidified a surprising defense that went from one of the worst in 1980 to the NFL's second best in 1981. But now, with the end of the season rapidly approaching, the offense was having problems scoring touchdowns and the team had to go up against the Bengals' prolific offense.

The 49ers picked a good time to put up one of their best all-around games. Joe Montana tossed two first half TDs and ran for a fourth quarter clincher, and the defense forced five turnovers, holding the Bengals to their lowest output of the season in a 21-3 domination. I was at the game. My friend Mike Davis and I, with a couple of associates that owned a motor home, drove down on Saturday for the Sunday game.

We spent the night at a hotel managed by a former GM of one of the DeBartolo hotels. The next day, at the game, I remember Fred Dean sacking Kenny Anderson, the Bengals quarterback and my friend Mike jumping up and shouting "In your face!" Later, on the way home, it dawned on me that, in all the years that I had known Mike, and the number of games that he accompanied me, he never told me which NFL team was his favorite. I suspected it was probably either the Browns or Steelers, since they were the teams closest to Youngstown, and I asked him who was his favorite team.

He stunned me when he said, "the Bengals." "But you just rooted against them today!" I said to him. His answer was classic Mike Davis. "You're paying for the tickets." So much for team loyalty. By the way, that win clinched the 49ers playoff spot and the National Conference Western Division. But, for good measure, the 49ers closed out with two more wins – 21-6 over the Houston Oilers at home and 21-17 over the Saints in New Orleans. The new winning streak was five and Christmas was upon us.

The Penguins were also on a bit of a rebound. After the lukewarm start, they bounced back to 16-15-6 at the end of the year, which was near the middle of their season. The Pittsburgh Spirit were having a good season, winning twice as many games as losses, and the Civic Arena had been busy since we had taken over. Things were looking pretty good on the DeBartolo sports front. I ended the year making plans to fly out to San Francisco for our first ever NFL playoff game in the Eddie DeBartolo-Bill Walsh era. Little did I know that it would be the first of many.

CHAPTER TEN

EARLY 1982- "THE CATCH" AND THEN SUPER BOWL CHAMPIONS!

The week between Christmas and New Year's Day is normally a slow time for many businesses, but that was not the case at our office in late 1981. The 49ers, in the playoffs for the first time since 1972, hosted the New York Giants in an NFC playoff game on January 3, 1982 and the excitement around the Youngstown office was electric.

The Giants lost a close game to the Niners on November 29 and were hell bent on revenge. They ousted the Philadelphia Eagles the previous weekend, 27-21, in the NFC's first round and were hungry. They hadn't been in the playoffs since 1963.

I left on Saturday for the West Coast. It was a breezy and damp 42 degrees at kickoff time for a game that quickly erased any thought it would be a defensive game, similar to the previous meeting. Joe Mon tana led a first quarter drive culminating in an eight-yard-pass to tight end Charlie Young to quickly put San Francisco up 7-0.

Giants quarterback Scott Brunner immediately quieted the Candlestick crowd with a 72-yard tying touchdown to Earnest Gray on a bizarre pass play that saw 49er DB Carlton Williamson whiff on a tackle and Ronnie Lott and Dwight Hicks colliding with each other trying to make the tackle. That tied the score at seven at the end of the first quarter.

The second quarter was all San Francisco. A 22-yard Ray Wershing field goal was followed by a nifty 58-yard TD pass from Montana to Freddie Solomon. Minutes later, after 49er LB Keena Turner's fumble recovery, 49er RB Ricky Patton broke open for a 25-yard run to stretch the 49er lead to 17 points. Giants kicker Joe Danelo kicked a 48-yard field goal to cut San Francisco's lead to 24-10 at the half.

The Giants defense stiffened in the 2nd half, led by their great linebacker Lawrence Taylor, holding the 49ers scoreless in the third quarter. Scott Brunner connected on another bomb - 58 yards to Johnny Perkins for a TD to tighten the score to 24-17 going into the 4th quarter. Ronnie Lott gambled (and lost) on an interception on the play, which allowed the touchdown. The 49ers were hurting themselves with penalties (14 for 145 yards) and defensive lapses. A few minutes later, Danelo, who had been erratic the second half of the year, missed a 21-yard field goal that would have closed the gap to four points.

The Giants seemingly had all the momentum going into the final quarter, but it was time for them to make a mistake. The 49ers offense continued to sputter, and faced a third-and-18 situation on the Giants 41-yard line, clearly out of field goal range, when Giants defenseman Gary Jeter took a swing at a 49er lineman in clear view of the officials.

The penalty gave the 49ers a first down on the 26. From there, the ground game could pound out yards, leading to a three-yard run for the touchdown. A short time later, Lott redeemed himself, intercepting a Brunner pass and returning it 20 yards for a TD to extend the lead to 21 points and put the game out of reach. The Giants scored a meaningless TD at the end for the 38-24 final.

The win over the Giants created a huge rematch between the 49ers and the Dallas Cowboys. After the 49ers embarrassed Dallas in October, the Cowboys promised they would avenge the "fluke," as they called it, "when and if" the 49ers made it to the postseason. The Cowboys went on to a 12-4 record and plastered Tampa Bay, 38-0, in the other NFC Divisional Playoff game.

The Niners hosted the game at Candlestick because of their better record. There was a lot of chatter before the game, but in San Francisco the quote "This is the real Super Bowl!" was heard often. Dallas didn't disagree. Their defense was dominant in completely shutting down Tampa Bay and the offense, let by Tony Dorsett, Danny White and Drew Pearson was as dangerous as any in the NFL. The Las Vegas bookies seemed to agree. Dallas was installed as a three-point favorite.

Chris and I flew out to the Bay Area on Friday, and it was a jubilant atmosphere we encountered. We did some sightseeing on Saturday, before joining everyone at the 49ers hotel near the airport. The team had a Catholic priest that went to the games and travelled with the team. His name was Monsignor Armstrong and he was a true fan.

On Sunday mornings, the Monsignor would host a Catholic Mass, with short homilies, for members of the team and 49ers officials who chose to attend. On this Sunday, Monsignor Armstrong's homily went as follows: "As Catholics, we have been taught not to pray for material things. But, in this case it has been so damn long since the 49ers have won anything significant, that I think God will give us a pass and let us pray for a victory! So, while we pray for that win, we also ask God to keep our players safe."   To this day, I have never heard a homily like the Monsignor's that day.

Keith Simon arranged for me to sit in the coaches box for the big game. Chris would sit in one of Eddie's boxes reserved for the women and other VIP's. Herbie Clark, a friend of Keith's, and a former jockey in Cleveland would be taking care of her. Although Chris had attended other games, she didn't understand the game and I wasn't really tolerant of questions while the game was going on. Herbie basically taught her football that day.

For my part, it would be interesting to see what the coaches do during the game. I experienced the draft part of the business as well as other facets, but seeing how the coaches reacted during action would be a novel experience for me. Just before kickoff, Keith cautioned me not to cheer loudly during the game so as not to distract the coaches from their duties. The coaches all knew me and were not bothered by my presence.

We had the network feed of the nationally televised game, but without the commercials. We could hear the staff in the truck talking to the announcers during the commercial breaks and the replies from the box. That too was fascinating. Vin Scully and Hank Stram would announce the game on CBS. Being a life-long Dodgers fan, I was familiar with listening to Scully, so that seemed like a good omen.

The game started quickly enough with the 49ers driving 63 yards for the first score. Montana was 4 of 5 on the drive for 60 yards, including the eight-yard scoring toss to Freddie Solomon. Dallas countered with a drive into San Francisco territory, but settled for a 44-yard field goal by Rafael Septien and the score was 7-3. Then came the first of nine turnovers in the game. Bill Ring, the 49ers running back, who scored a big TD late in the Giants game, fumbled and Dallas recovered on the 49er 29-yard line. Two plays later, Dallas struck with a 26-yard pass from Danny White to Tony Hill and the Cowboys led 10-7 at the end of the opening quarter.

The 49ers rebounded at the start of the second quarter. Montana concluded a 47-yard, four-play drive with a 20-yard strike to wide receiver Dwight Clark, who put a series of moves on Dallas DB Dennis Thurman, leaving the beleaguered Thurman heading in the opposite direction as Clark snared the ball. On the play, Montana found himself being hounded by Ed "Too Tall" Jones, tossing the ball as he was going down. Later, that scenario would nearly repeat itself.

That score put San Francisco ahead again at 14-10, but the lead wouldn't last long. Danny White started from his own 20, and moved his team to the Dallas 37. He then rifled a pass to Tony Hill on the 49er sideline to the Niners' 47. Walsh was standing right there and insisted Hill was out of bounds, but the call wasn't made. There was no replay in those days, thus the call stood. But, it was going to get worse.

Danny White once again went back to throw and attempted a long pass down the right sideline to Drew Pearson. Ronnie Lott had Pearson covered perfectly and intercepted the pass, but a flag was thrown on the play. The call was interference on Lott, even though TV replays clearly showed it was Pearson who climbed over Lott to attempt to get his hands on the ball. Dallas was given the ball on the 49er 12-yard line. At this point, the normally stoic coaches among whom I sat were shouting and grumbling about the call. A few plays later, Tony Dorsett carried the ball on a five-yard outside sweep and the Cowboys had a 17-14 halftime lead.

It had been a good game up to that point. The coaches, along with the rest of the watching audience saw the replays again during halftime, and there was some more grumbling and cursing in the box. The official who made the interference call, and who apparently saw it later, explained that Lott bumped Pearson 'further upfield," and that was where the penalty occurred. But he had no excuse as to why he threw the flag after the interception and why the ball was spotted on the 12 instead of 15 or 20 yards further up the sideline.

A tense third quarter ensued, with neither offense being able to move effectively. Both teams committed turnovers and untimely penalties that kept the score the same. Then, late in the quarter, 49er linebacker Bobby Leopold intercepted a tipped White pass and set the 49ers up on the Dallas 13-yard line. Three plays later, the 49ers faced a fourth down and one, just outside the Dallas three. Coach Walsh decided to go for it and Dallas jumped offside, giving the Niners a first and goal. 49er fullback Johnny Davis punched it in and the game went to the fourth quarter with the Niners clinging to a four-point lead, 21-17.

The coaches were intense as the game unfolded. Every time Dallas came up with something new, they came up with answers. And every time Dallas came up with solutions to the 49er offense, the coaches came up with a variance. It was fascinating to watch and didn't hamper my enjoyment one bit. Fifteen more minutes to decide who goes to the Super Bowl and who goes home.

The fourth quarter of this game will always be historic, but nobody knew it at the time. The Cowboys struck first with a 22-yard field goal by Septien. It was set up by another Lott interference call that was legitimate. The score was 21-20, San Francisco. On the 49ers next drive, FB Walt Easley fumbled, and Dallas recovered at mid-field. It was San Francisco's sixth turnover of the game, after averaging only one and a half per game over the regular season, and it was costly. Dallas marched downfield, with White tossing a 21-yard pass to Doug Cosbie. Dallas had the lead back, 27-21 with just over 10 minutes left.

Neither team did much over the next few minutes. It appeared Dallas was content to avoid making a mistake, preferring to wait until San Francisco made another one. With just under five minutes left, the Niners found themselves pinned back on their own 11-yard line.

I didn't know it at the time, but apparently Eddie left his box to console his players as they came off the field. But, the coaches around me hadn't given up yet. Dallas helped them out a bit when they went into the infamous "prevent defense." My Dad, who loved to watch football said many times that teams that employ it "only prevent themselves from winning." I'm sure he was right some of the time, and I hoped that this would be one of those times.

An incompletion and a short pass gained six yards, and then Montana passed for another six to Freddie Soloman for a first down on the 23. With Dallas still in the prevent, Walsh called two running plays and got 11 and seven yards from Lenvil Elliott. After Dallas jumped offside, Montana threw a short five-yarder to Earl Cooper at the two-minute warning. The Niners were on their own 46-yard line.

During the stoppage, the offensive coaches were quietly discussing the options with Walsh. Bill mentioned Dallas might be tired and thought a reverse by the speedy Solomon might work and it did – for 14 yards, putting the Niners on Dallas' 40. Montana then hit Dwight Clark along the sidelines for 10, followed by a cross route to Solomon for 12 and San Francisco was on the Dallas 13-yard line. Montana called a time out with 75 seconds left in the game. Both teams were gasping for air, but Dallas seemed to be more exhausted.

Coming out of the time-out, Solomon broke free in the corner of the end zone, but Joe's pass sailed wide and the opportunity was wasted. The coaches grumbled at the inopportune mistake. Walsh called another sweep and Elliott gained seven yards to the six. The 49ers called their second time-out with 58 seconds left. Dallas abandoned the prevent defense and sent in three linebackers.

During the commercial break, the CBS truck was feeding information to Scully and Stram. When the truck advised them the 49ers had turned the ball over six times, Scully commented there was no way San

Francisco could beat Dallas with six turnovers. When they came out of the commercial, Scully announced, as hard as it was to believe, the 49ers had a chance to win with six turnovers. That, to me, was cool to witness.

Everyone knows what happened next. It was third and three for the Niners, and Dallas' full defense was back in. In the coaches' box, we had the sliding window open and an eerie silence settled over Candlestick Park as Montana faded to pass and then rolled toward the right sideline, chased by the massive Too Tall Jones. Nobody was open.

Joe, it appeared, threw the ball away. As it sailed through the end zone, we saw Clark leap high. It was dead silence when I said, "My God. He caught it." A millisecond later, the end zone stands erupted and the official signaled touchdown. Candlestick went crazy! We were all standing in the box high-fiving each other and clapping. Wershing kicked the extra point and the 49ers led 28-27. But, it was short-lived in the box as the coaches sat back down and went back to work. The game wasn't over. There were 51 seconds left on the clock.

After the kickoff, Danny White immediately went to work and hit Pearson on a long pass. Pearson appeared to break free for the score, but cornerback Eric Wright grabbed his jersey from behind and pulled him down. But the play gained 31 yards and Dallas only needed a field goal to win, and they were knocking on the door.

On the next play, White dropped back again just as 49ers defensive end Lawrence Pillars broke free on his rush and sacked White, stripping him of the ball. The other 49ers end, Jim Stuckey, fell on the ball and the 49ers were going to the Super Bowl! For the second time in the last five minutes, Candlestick Park was bedlam as Montana took a knee and the clock ran out. The coaches were congratulating each other and, even in the normally quiet press box next store, the sound level was incredible. Monsignor Armstrong's prayers worked. The Niners were going to the Super Bowl!

Earlier in the day, the Cincinnati Bengals hosted the San Diego Chargers for the right to represent the AFC in the Super Bowl game. The temperature at kickoff in Cincinnati was minus 6 degrees and the wind chill was minus 32. The game was dubbed "The Freezer Bowl" and was the coldest game in NFL history in terms of wind chill.

Although no team could ever be considered "comfortable" in those temperatures, the Bengals had an advantage over the Chargers from sunny southern California. The game was close for a half, but the frozen Chargers turned the ball over four times versus only one for Cincy, which won easily, 27-7. We played the Bengals earlier in the season and knew their offense. We also knew they would be looking to avenge our 21-3 win in Cincinnati. So, while the partying was going on outside, we all got together in Eddie's Candlestick office/party room for a few drinks and a bite to eat, but there was work to be done.

The facility Eddie had at Candlestick had an office for Eddie in the back and a large gathering room in the front, with a bar and eating area and numerous couches and chairs for Eddie's invited guests. Customarily, the guests gathered there before the game for some fellowship, and then after the games, it would be repeated either in celebration of a win or to lament a loss.

Up until 1981, the latter was more the norm. The 49ers weren't as "high profile" in the early years, due to the lack of winning, but in later years it was not unusual to have Huey Lewis & The News, Journey and other musical groups, mingling with politicians, stars of stage and screen and former athletes at these gatherings.

One year, when Chris accompanied me to a game during the early years, I was meeting with EJD, Jr. in his office after the game. Chris was having a cocktail in the party room waiting for me, when an attractive blonde woman sat next to her on the sofa and they struck up a conversation. During the conversation, Chris told the woman about us living in Ohio and her taking care of three boys while I would travel, describing how she would shuttle the kids to school events, Little League games, Boy Scouts, etc.

Our family was the most important thing to both of us, and Chris was laying it on thick. They had "a nice conversation" and the woman eventually got up and left. The girlfriend of the 49ers business manager ran up to Chris and asked her if the woman was as nice as she was beautiful. Chris just shrugged with a puzzled look on her face until the girlfriend told her she had just had a long conversation with Hope Lange, the actress, and a guest at the game. Chris was thrilled at having met Ms. Lange, but somewhat embarrassed when she recalled the conversation.

Trader Vic's, the famous San Francisco restaurant, catered the parties. The waiters all worked at Trader Vic's and were all of Asian descent. They were also rabid 49er fans, especially their leader, an elderly Chinese man named George Sam, who had gotten to know me well since I was always there on the days the team lost while most others didn't come in after those games during the early loss years.

When I walked into the party room after we won the game, George Sam ran up to me and gave me a big hug. "We're going to the Super Bore!" he shouted in his Chinese accent, handing me a Crown Royal on the rocks. He may have had one himself as we toasted the good fortune finally come our way.

Chris and I were scheduled on the "red eye" flight back to Cleveland later that night, and Eddie called a meeting in his office, including Keith Simon and I. Keith, in anticipation of a possible victory, had called the Pittsburgh Steelers the week before and asked for advice on what we could expect in the weeks leading up to the Super Bowl. The Steelers had a lot of experience having won four Super Bowls in the last six years (1975, 1976, 1979 and 1980), and the Pittsburgh business manager told Keith what to expect and how to plan.

There would be a massive number of requests for tickets to the DeBartolo home office, as well as the 49ers offices. There would also be requests for lodging assistance, entertainment in the Super Bowl venue area, rental cars, and any other thing that could be imagined.

Along with Keith's normal routine of getting the players in their rooms, arranging transportation and meals, taking care of the San Francisco car dealers (who provided company cars to 49er VIPs and staff) and the Bay Area press that travelled with the team, there would now be many more tasks. A post Super Bowl party would need to be arranged, win or lose, for the players, staff and their families. The list was endless.

The participant teams would each get 12,000 game tickets and the NFL would get an equal number. The rest would be split among the other NFL teams. The 49ers would have a random drawing to determine which of the 40,000-plus season ticket holders got tickets. The team itself had to exclude enough tickets for their coaches, players and staff and their families, as well as advertisers and other team VIPs.

Eddie decided to take several hundred tickets for DeBartolo Corporation purposes, including department store and other retail VIPs, corporate staff in Youngstown and other family and friends. Eddie immediately told me all calls to the Youngstown office for Super Bowl tickets would be routed through my office and he and I would review the requests and allocate tickets (and choice locations) "as often as necessary" during the week.

The goal was to get the bulk of the tickets out in the mail by the end of the week, so ticket holders could plan for lodging and rental cars. Keith also said the NFL had planned to get two hotels in the Pontiac, Michigan area for the 49ers; the Sheraton Southfield Hotel, where the team and VIPs would stay, and another a few miles away. Keith also asked Eddie if I could help him in Detroit when the team arrived the week before the game. It would be a busy two weeks for me.

Chris and I arrived in Cleveland in the middle of the night, and it was freezing. The entire northern part of the country was locked in a brutal cold front as evidenced by the Cincinnati game the previous day. When I got into the office the next morning, the calls had already started.

I set up a system for my secretary to field the calls, get the information and advise the callers they would be advised of their request status by the end of the week, if not sooner. EJD and EJD, Jr's secretaries added their VIP names to the list. At the end of the day, I met with Eddie, Jr. and we began to allocate tickets. Some were "no brainers" (e.g. tickets requested by EJD and Eddie for their friends and business contacts). These were allocated immediately.

I put in a request for 16 tickets for family and neighbors, and those were approved. We worked through the others, a procedure repeated every day that week. Tickets and invoices were sent out via Fedex throughout the week. By Friday night, those who would not be getting tickets were notified and most others had tickets in hand. I still had 50 or so when I flew up to Detroit on the Monday before the game.

Since the postgame party involved a hotel, I arranged for Mike Sapara, who ran our Cleveland hotels, to join us to help plan the party. We didn't know how many to plan for, so we told the hotel to plan for 500-700 people. Mike set out planning the bar and food locations with the Sheraton Southfield's food and beverage director.

In the meantime, the calls requesting tickets kept coming in - to my office in Youngstown, to my home and finally, some tracked me to my hotel room in the Sheraton. Coaches and players needed some for extra family members and we accommodated them. Of the calls that got through to me, some were legitimate and resulted in tickets, but most were people who "met me once in Montreal" or who were friends with "my brother's sister-in-law's best friend." Those were the type of requests I was getting. By Friday morning, I only had five to 10 tickets left. The Youngstown contingent of my family and friends was in route by car.

The cold I had flown back to two weeks ago hadn't abated, and it was terribly cold and snowy in Detroit. The parking lot at the Sheraton was frozen over and there wasn't a lot to do in the area. We attended a banquet put on by Frank B. Hall & Associates on Friday night hosted by the Pipinos, which was very nice, and on Saturday, I arranged for a bus to transport my family and friends to the Ford Museum, leaving in the morning and returning in the afternoon. But, other than that we stayed indoors and partied. I ended up with a party of 18, including a few friends of my brothers from Chicago. We all had rooms together on the same floor.

When Chris was ready to leave for Detroit on Friday, our youngest son, Tommy, started to vomit. Chalking it up to nerves, she put a bucket in front of him and the caravan of four cars began. He didn't vomit any more on the way. They arrived in late afternoon and Tommy seemed to be OK the next day.

On Sunday morning though, he had a slight fever and was starting to get a rash. I searched out Jim Klint, the 49ers doctor, who agreed to look at Tommy. Klint turned pale when he saw him. "He has roseola (a contagious virus)," he told me. "Have either you or he been around the players?"

I had and told him so as he hurried off to see if any of the players had developed symptoms. Thankfully, I had none and the players didn't either. Tommy would be staying at the hotel with brother Chas' wife, Helen, and their young daughter during the game.

Sunday dragged along. The game was scheduled for 4 p.m. and the players buses would leave around 1:45, with the other buses leaving shortly thereafter. Some players took cabs and left early, but the main bus with Walsh and most of the team onboard left on time.

Unfortunately, bad timing fouled the scheduled 25-minute drive. Vice-President George H. W. Bush's motorcade backed up the interstate and the trip for the players' bus took over an hour. When we left around 2:30, it was an eight-bus caravan from the Sheraton. We drove to the other hotel and added another seven buses. The Michigan State Police held up traffic on the surrounding intersections and the 15 buses went nonstop until the interstate ramp and then came to a dead stop.

The traffic was backed up on the interstate for as far as we could see, and we were still miles from the stadium. I was in the lead bus, and I got out and walked to the State Trooper car that was leading the caravan. "What are we going to do?" I asked him. He looked out at the traffic and said, "Not much we can do." And I looked where he was looking. It didn't look good.

There are times when it is OK to tell a little lie, and this was one of those times. "I have Joe Montana and a few more of the players on that bus behind us," I told him. He looked at me and then looked out at the traffic and told me to get back on the bus and he would do what he could. I went back to the bus and a minute or two later another trooper car came down the ramp and spoke with the trooper in the lead car. That car then went down the ramp on the shoulder and opened a gap in the cars on the interstate. Our bus then followed the lead car across the traffic to the inside shoulder, with the other buses close behind, and we began the trek toward the stadium.

Each time we came to a bridge, the State Troopers had cleared a lane for us to get to the shoulder on the other side. This continued until the stadium ramp, which the troopers cleared, and we sailed up the ramp and into the parking lot. The going was slow, but all our buses got there around 3:30. That night, I gave that trooper's name to Keith Simon and asked that he take care of him. We were seated about 10 minutes before kickoff. Our seats were on the 50-yard line approximately 15 rows behind the 49er bench.

Diana Ross sang the National Anthem, appropriate for the Motor City, and we settled in for the kickoff. The 49ers won the coin toss and elected to receive. The Bengals kicked off to 49er Amos Lawrence, who returned the ball to the 49er 26 and fumbled it over to the Bengals. Kenny Anderson, the Bengals quarterback, quickly went to work and, three plays later, had his team on the 49ers five-yard line, when the 49er defense stiffened.

A stuffed run for no gain was followed by a Jim Stuckey sack of Anderson and the Bengals were back on the 11. Anderson then threw into the middle and 49er DB Dwight Hicks intercepted and returned the ball to the 49er 32-yard line. With the momentum restored, Montana passed the Niners downfield and scored on a quarterback sneak from the 1. It was 7-0, San Francisco, as the first quarter ended.

With the Bengals driving in the second quarter, Anderson threw a pass to Cris Collingsworth, who fumbled while being tackled by 49er DB Eric Wright, and the 49ers recovered on their own 8. Again, Montana went to work. A third down 20-yard pass to Freddie Solomon put the team on its own 31. Joe then scrambled out of the pocket for eight yards and then hit Dwight Clark for 12 yards on third down to the Cincinnati 31.

A few minutes later, Joe found Earl Cooper open inside the five-yard line and Cooper bulled his way into the end zone to open a 14-0 lead. The half appeared to be over when Ray Wersching hit a 22-yard field goal with 15 seconds left, but Wershing's squib kick-off was mishandled by the Bengals and the 49ers recovered on the Bengal four-yard line. With two seconds to go, Wersching kicked another field goal and the half ended with San Francisco in front by 20-0.

But, the Bengals didn't give up. They took the second half kick-off and drove 83 yards with Anderson running in from the five on a keeper. After 3 three and outs, two by the 49ers, Cincinnati set up shop near their own 35-yard line. Anderson connected to Collingsworth for 49 yards to the SF 14-yard line, and three plays later, the Bengals had a first and goal at the San Francisco three. The momentum had shifted to the Bengals.

On first down Pete Johnson, Cincinnati's 250-pound fullback bulled down to the one. Relying on brute strength, Anderson handed again to Johnson, but veteran Jack "Hacksaw" Reynolds and linebacker Dan Bunz stuffed him for no gain. On third down, Anderson tossed to RB Charles Alexander in the flat and it appeared he would score until Bunz stopped him in his tracks six inches from the goal line. Bunz stood him up and dropped him before he could fall forward.

It was fourth and goal and everyone knew what the call would be. The massive Johnson would get the ball. With Alexander leading the way, Johnson surged into the right side of the 49er defensive line. Linebackers Reynolds and Bunz saw him coming and converged with the rest of the 49er defensive line to plug the hole and Johnson came up just short. The noise in the Silverdome was deafening as Archie Reese, the 49er defensive tackle lay on his back pumping his arms and legs. As the third quarter ended, the momentum had shifted back to the 49ers.

Or had it? The now stagnant San Francisco offense had another three and out, and the Bengals quickly scored on an Anderson four-yard pass to Dan Ross. Just like that, it was 20-14 and San Francisco appeared to be in trouble, hoping to hang on with just over 10 minutes to go. On second and 15 from the 49er 22, Montana faked a long pass and tossed a sideline pass to WR Mike Wilson on the 49er 44, and the resulting first down re-energized the team. The 49ers went to a run offense to control the clock and moved down to the Cincinnati 23, where Wershing kicked his third field goal of the game to put San Francisco back up by nine.

With just over five minutes left, the Bengals needed two scores. Anderson went for broke, trying to hit Collingsworth downfield, but Eric

Wright stepped in front of him and returned the interception back to Cincinnati's 25-yard line. The Niners ran three straight times and the Bengals called time out after each one, but SF got the first down. Three more runs gained only four yards, but the clock kept running since the Bengals couldn't stop it. Wersching kicked his fourth field goal and the lead was now 12 with less than two minutes to go. With no time-outs left, Walsh's defense took away the sidelines and forced Anderson to throw in the middle of the field. Anderson did, six times, and marched his team to a three-yard TD pass to Ross, but there were only 16 seconds left on the clock.

When Dwight Clark fell on the ensuing onside kick, the game was over and the Forty Niners accomplished the implausible from 2-14 in 1979, to 6-10 in 1980, to 16-3 and the Super Bowl Champions for 1981. Eddie DeBartolo's nightmares were a distant memory as the celebration began. The Bay Area finally had a championship team. I joined my wife and kids jumping around in glee as Pete Rozelle handed the Vince Lombardi Trophy to Eddie, Jr. and I thanked God for letting me be a small part of this success.

The Super Bowl party at the Sheraton quickly got started that evening, and the hotel was overwhelmed. We expected several hundred people, but thousands showed up. Fortunately, we had a lot of security and could weed out many of the uninvited just wanting to crash the event. But, our lack of experience in this type of event quickly surfaced. Seating was at a premium and the food was going to run out early.

Sapara and I went into the kitchen and instructed the food and beverage manager to cook everything they had and just keep replenishing the buffet lines. As midnight approached, the manager told me they would have to close the bars, due to local liquor laws. I referred that to Keith Simon, who talked to the appropriate people in law enforcement, and that requirement was waived (or ignored), probably at the cost of a few thousand dollars.

The party roared on. Sometime after midnight, Mr. DeBartolo, seeing the uncontrolled drinking and dining, called me over to his table and instructed me to "shut the party down." There were many people we didn't know there, including friends and family of players, coaches and others.

This, of course, was a problem, since we still had thousands of people there. I went over to Eddie's table, and sat down and quietly told him what was going on. Technically, it was Eddie's party, but when Mr. D gave an order, he expected it to be followed. I was in a bad position and Eddie quickly realized it.

"We're not shutting down," he quickly declared. Then, he told me he realized the position I was in and he would take it up with his father. "I have your back", he told me, and he did. I never heard another word about it after that.

Sometime around two a.m. Monday morning, I called it a night and went up to our room. We'd be leaving later that morning, with a long drive back to Youngstown. It would be back to work with the dawn of a new work week. But, 1982 was off to a great start.

The week after the Super Bowl was a whirlwind of celebrations and parties as the sporting world saluted its new football champion. Eddie, Jr. left Detroit and flew to San Francisco, with a stopover in Las Vegas, where rumor had it that he had another big win. The city of San Francisco was having a parade for the team and an estimated 500,000 San Franciscans clogged the streets to salute their team and its owner.

Edward J. DeBartolo, Jr., who only a few years before was reviled and hated, was now one of the most popular personalities in the City by the Bay.

Youngstown also celebrated the good fortune of its famous family. Longtime Steelers and Browns fans joined in the salute to the DeBartolo family, and there were parties and celebrations throughout the area. Upon returning from San Francisco, Eddie called me on Wednesday afternoon and asked me to meet in his office at five p.m. We shared a drink and reminisced over the events of the previous week. Then, Eddie reached into his briefcase and pulled out a bundle of money and put it on the table.

"This is $5,000," he said. "You have a choice – either this or a Super Bowl ring." I didn't hesitate, "The ring is more important to me. I'll take the ring," I told him.

We talked for another few minutes and then Eddie said he had to head home. I got up, we shook hands and I and walked toward the door, when Eddie called out my name. As I turned around, he tossed the money to me. "You gave me the right answer," he said, "You get both."

CHAPTER ELEVEN

THE REST OF 1982 – A TIME TO FORGET

Two days later, reality came back to me with a thud. EJD summoned me to his office on Friday and began to rant about Vince Bartimo. Apparently, a few weeks before, Bartimo was heard at Louisiana Downs telling many of the influential bettors at the racetrack the 49ers would have "no chance" to beat the Cowboys in the NFC Championship. Even worse, DeBartolo was upset Bartimo hadn't called Eddie to offer congratulations for the 49ers Super Bowl Championship. He asked me to recap for him my concerns about Bartimo's running of Louisiana Downs.

I reminded him I was banned from going to Shreveport since the November 1980 meeting with Tom Russell in Dallas. Since that time, I mentioned to Mr. D on more than a few occasions my concerns about the finances at Louisiana Downs. In fact, as recently as December 31, 1981, EJD instructed me to give him a report on Bartimo's contract and his failure to cooperate.

I detailed how we were unable to get answers to our questions about the track's overhead from the track's controller, who referred all my inquiries to Bartimo; who, in turn, steadfastly refused to take or return my calls. My complaints to Mr. DeBartolo always got the same answer –he would handle it. But, the situation never changed. The chain of command was broken. Louisiana Downs would only respond to Senior.

Mr. DeBartolo asked how my concerns could be addressed without me going down there. I told him we could send the Internal Auditors there and I could tell them what to look for. He instructed me to do just that – as soon as possible. We cancelled the Internal Audit Department's schedule and they were sent to Shreveport the following Monday, with instructions to call me later that evening. The results were as I expected. The controller, Tom Donahue, who I hired several years earlier, cooperated with the auditors, but referred some of the requests to Mr. Bartimo, who refused to cooperate, and stated he responded, "only to Mr. DeBartolo."

A day or two later, I had all the information I needed, and I wrote a report with the findings of the audit to Mr. DeBartolo. The report dated February 4, 1982, detailed numerous questionable payments made, unapproved contracts and dealings, and other wasteful expenditures made by Bartimo without any written approval from the Youngstown office.

The report covered several pages and was addressed only to Mr. DeBartolo, who later copied a handful of other corporate executives, including EJD, Jr. and Marie Denise. The following Saturday, Mr. DeBartolo came up with his plan. Bartimo would be summoned to Youngstown for a meeting on Monday morning and, at the same time, a group of DeBartolo vice presidents, including George Jones and several attorneys, would enter the track and take over the management of Louisiana Downs. Eddie, Jr. and I would be available in EJD's office while Mr. DeBartolo and Bartimo met in the conference room. Mr. DeBartolo made it clear that Eddie and I were to enter the meeting only if summoned by him.

Monday morning, Bartimo arrived at the Youngstown office. He called the track after deplaning in Pittsburgh and learned the track had been taken over by "a bunch of DeBartolo goons." He was primed and angry. The meeting was loud and contentious with both men shouting. At one point, Eddie poked his head in, but was waved off by his father.

We put security on standby. A short time later, the door slammed open, and Bartimo stormed out and left the building. Mr. DeBartolo came out, visibly upset and simply stated, "He's through."

At the same time in Louisiana, Rosalind P. Muller, Bartimo's right-hand person was also relieved of her duties at the track, as were a few others. Two days later, DeBartolo filed a lawsuit against Bartimo and Muller for misuse of corporate funds, and he fired Donahue. A Board of Directors meeting was held, and Mr. DeBartolo was named as President, William Pfaus was appointed Vice President and I was named Treasurer.

The management positions at the track were eventually filled internally. Tom Sweeney was named General Manager and David Vance Assistant. I flew down to Shreveport for the first time in 18 months and we hired a new controller – a young man named Kim Russell. In a matter of a few days, the entire management staff was overhauled.

Unfortunately, there was a major breach in our internal security and my audit report was leaked to the press. The Dallas papers had the report word for word, as did KSLA-TV, the CBS affiliate in Dallas, which did a two-day report on March 22 and 23. Tom Russell's Racing Journal also published the full report. It was my opinion that Tom Russell somehow got the report and leaked it to the rest of the press.

DeBartolo hired a private investigator, but he was unable to trace the source of the leak. I worked with him for a while, after he cleared me as a suspect. It was my feeling one of our other executives, perhaps jealous over the amount being paid to Bartimo, leaked the information, but that was never proven.

The winter continued. In Pittsburgh, the Penguins improved slightly, finishing 4-1-2 in their last seven games to finish with a record of 31-36-13 and a fourth-place finish in the Patrick Division. They did qualify for the playoffs and drew the two-time defending champion New York Islanders in the opening round of the best of five series. After one-sided losses of 8-1 and 7-2 in New York, an embarrassed Mr. DeBartolo went public and offered to refund Penguins ticket holders for games three and four in Pittsburgh because the team was so bad.

This possibly disastrous financial move instead fired up the Penguins fans. In a sell-out on my birthday, Saturday, April 10 they were treated to a 2-1 win on a Rick Kehoe goal four minutes into overtime. The next night, another sell-out crowd saw another Penguin win, 5-2, to send the series back to New York for the deciding fifth game. In all, the Penguins refunded six tickets because of DeBartolo's offer.

Tuesday, April 13 saw one of the most heartbreaking ends to a season. The Penguins led New York, 3-1 with less than six minutes left in the game, when an Islander goal closed the gap to one goal. With the Pens still seemingly in control, Penguins all-star defenseman Randy Carlyle went back to clear an Islander pass in his own end with just over two minutes to go. But the puck jumped over his stick on the choppy ice and Islander John Tonelli pounced on it and shot it into the goal for perhaps the biggest goal of his career.

The crestfallen Penguins went into overtime and six minutes later, Tonelli scored again to end the series. The Islanders went on to win the Stanley Cup again that year and the next – four consecutive years. A year later, Joe Dreyer, the Islanders controller, saw me at the NHL Annual Meetings in Montreal and gave me a keychain commemorating the Islanders four consecutive Stanley Cup Championships. "Thanks to the Penguins", he said. My response was not fit for print.

One thing was evident with DeBartolo's refund offer. It was becoming apparent he was now getting impatient with the Penguins. It was now four years with no significant improvement, and the team was losing on the ice, as well as losing money on the bottom line. Mr. DeBartolo was not a loser. He didn't like losing money on a business and he really didn't like losing money and games.

Paul Martha, Baz Bastien, the general manager and Eddie Johnston, the coach, all had to be getting nervous. Management people were responsible for putting a winning team on the ice and drawing people to the arena, and those three were now on the proverbial hot seat.

My job was to manage the finances and keep them under control and I was doing that. It probably didn't help that the 49ers, in its fifth season under DeBartolo ownership, had won a championship, and whether those two would admit it or not, EJD and EJD, Jr. were competing, and Eddie's success had given him the lead.

The Penguins' arena roommates, the Pittsburgh Spirit, in its first year under DeBartolo ownership had a fine year, finishing second in the eastern Division of the MISL with a record of 31-13. However, they lost to Baltimore in the MISL Quarterfinals. Attendance for the season was decent, averaging 6,335 per game. However, many of the tickets were "youth-priced" and the team lost money. At this point we were still gauging whether there was a viable market for professional soccer in Pittsburgh.

There was a new problem brewing with the Penguins affiliate minor league club in Erie. That team was just finishing its first season and there were financial issues. The Erie Blades, under the ownership of Dr. John Caruso, an Erie physician, sought out the Penguins to become the affiliate. It was a natural fit, with Erie only two hours up the interstate from Pittsburgh.

An agreement was reached between the team and Caruso for the Penguins to supply the players and a coach to Erie for the Blades new American League Hockey franchise. The Penguins players would be under contract to the NHL team, who would pay the players' salaries. Erie would pay a set amount for each of those players and the Penguins would pay the balance of the contracts. Caruso, who had some experience from the Blades other minor league teams, forecast rosy attendance figures for Erie fans to come and see players with NHL potential. Caruso would manage the business and would pay operating expenses and the profits or losses would be split evenly.

The attendance numbers were nowhere near Caruso's forecasts, and the financial losses soon started piling up. Caruso projected average paid attendances of 2,600, but the actual came out to about 1,700. In addition, the Penguins had a rash of injuries and had to call up some of the Blades players to fill out the roster. Caruso stopped paying for the Penguin players.

Caruso and the Penguin management clashed, and the relationship soured. Quietly, the Penguins began looking for an alternate location for the next season. I became involved and in early April, I drove to Erie to meet with Caruso and his attorney to see if the relationship could be salvaged. Caruso now owed the Penguins $130,000. The meeting was cordial, and I offered to keep the team in Erie if Caruso would fulfill his obligation and pay the Penguins. We both agreed to keep it quiet, and Caruso promised to get back with me.

The next day, Caruso was quoted in the Erie Times saying there would be no hockey in Erie the following year, and he laid all the blame on the Penguins. I received calls from an Erie reporter, but told him I had no comment. I called Caruso, and he denied speaking to the press and stopped taking my calls.

Lou Angotti, the Erie Blades coach, who worked for the Penguins, sent me the article from Times. I spoke with DeBartolo and he got our legal department involved. An Erie attorney was retained, and a lawsuit was filed. Then, I called the reporter in Erie and told him the true story. It turns out he didn't care for Caruso, and his story was extremely fair to the Penguin side.

The Bartimo trial was set to begin in Shreveport, Louisiana. For the better part of four months, covering 13 trips and 53 days, I was in Louisiana for discovery and depositions. It required me usually flying out of Pittsburgh on Sunday nights or Monday mornings and returning on Friday nights, and it was stressful. The stressful part started a few weeks in when I got a call at the Hyatt in Shreveport, where I was staying. The phone call came in at four a.m. to my room from an anonymous man, who wanted me to meet him "right now."

Obviously, I declined and as I was hanging up, he screamed I would "have my head blown off" the minute I stepped out of my room. I then called the front desk, asking why the front desk clerk would put a call through to my room at that hour. His response was "I didn't. That call had to be from someone inside the hotel!" I asked him to call the Sheriff's office, and I called the Security Department at Louisiana Downs to send a guard over. The guard got the adjacent room and stayed with me the rest of the trip.

The first few weeks of the trial, Bob Schreiber, DeBartolo's chief legal counsel, accompanied me on these trips. But, after the three defendants gave their depositions, he skipped many of the trips while we were in discovery. After the threatening call, I began altering my hotels and flying and staying under different names. Alarmingly, the calls then started going to my house at all hours of day or night, but mostly from reporters asking for my comments, and on a few occasions, those of my wife. Mr. DeBartolo arranged for the local authorities to keep watch on my home.

DeBartolo hired a private investigator and he helped us on the trial preparations. One of the patterns he noticed was Vince Bartimo would fly from Shreveport to Tampa every Monday with just a brief-case, usually returning the same evening. Mondays were one of the track's off days since we ran from Wednesday through Sunday.

There was speculation of money laundering and the names of Carlos Marcello and Santo Trafficante popped up. They were mob bosses in New Orleans and Tampa, respectively. Marcello also had links to a Charles E. Roemer, a Louisiana politician under the Edwin Edwards regime, who was partners with Bartimo in at least one entity that had dealings with Louisiana Downs. This was getting interesting and, also, dangerous.

Bartimo, Muller and Donahue were all deposed in the summer of 1982. Donahue and Muller had little to say, deferring to Bartimo's one-on-one relationship with DeBartolo. I was not aware Donahue was going to be included in the lawsuit until I heard it from our attorneys. I always felt Tom was in a bad position, answering to a powerful man on-site, while supposedly being responsible to me (and The DeBartolo Corporation). When Bartimo instructed Donahue to not divulge Louisiana Downs financial information to me, he was caught between his day-in-day-out boss and his responsibility to the corporate office. When he followed Bartimo's directive, his job fate was evident, but I didn't think he should have been part of the lawsuit.

Bartimo's deposition was a different story. Bartimo ranted and raved and dominated the deposition. Our Louisiana attorneys couldn't control him. Bartimo's defense was he was given complete autonomy by Mr. DeBartolo, who was aware of and had approved of everything that happened at the track. Bob Schreiber and I were present for the depositions and, as we boarded the airplane for the trip back to Youngstown on that Friday, it was evident this trial was going to pit Bartimo versus DeBartolo in a classic "he said, he said" scenario.

It was now summer, and there was a lull in the legal proceedings. Chris and I made plans to take our family on a camping vacation to the Rocky Mountains in Colorado. After the usual harassment from EJD about my taking vacation in the summer, and two weeks at that, we headed out near the end of July.

The trip was great, and I returned recharged for what lay ahead. At the top of my mail was a memo from EJD, Jr., dated August 2, 1982. It read as follows, "Upon your return I want to immediately meet with you and Marty Hamer regarding your failure to bring Marty Hamer up to date on all matters that you are responsible for and for his inability to have information necessary to be put together for various meetings such as my meeting this morning with the Crocker Bank people." He copied EJD and Marie Denise on the memo.

Marty was the first person that I hired for my department. Originally, he handled the accounting for Thistledown and Balmoral racetracks, some of the financial work on the Toledo operations, as well as the Penguins, Arena and Spirit.

With my extensive travel, I delegated him to handle normal situations for me while I was out of town, and he always did a fine job. However, the 49ers were not part of the DeBartolo conglomerate since the team was owned by EJD, Jr. and not the corporation. EJD, Jr. specifically used me for confidential matters he didn't want other Youngstown people to know.

I had a few locked drawers in my office for only Eddie's matters and only my secretary and I had the keys. The matters Eddie needed information on were in those drawers, but Marty was not aware they were there, and since I was driving to Colorado, he couldn't get in touch with me. In addition, Eddie called at eight a.m. on a Monday morning and needed the information for a meeting an hour later.

I reminded Eddie of the confidentiality of those matters and his desires I keep that type of information to myself, and that matter disappeared. Unfortunately, EJD didn't care. There was also a memo from him in the pile, to all department heads, including me. It read; "As long as conditions prevail as they are, no Department Head will be permitted to take a vacation in excess of one (1) week at a time."

Mr. DeBartolo had a habit of bringing in new people, with no specific responsibilities. A year or so before, he brought in George S. Stewart, a former J.C. Penney executive, with a title of Executive Vice President – Corporate Management. I had minimal involvement with Stewart, who seemed like a nice man and didn't have much, if any, involvement in my area.

In October of 1982, EJD brought in Anthony W. Liberati as Senior Vice President – Corporate Planning. Liberati had been the Vice President of Equibank, which held Penguin loans on the team and the super boxes of the Arena. As part of DeBartolo taking over the team, Liberati agreed DeBartolo would assume the team loan, but not the super boxes loan. That issue would soon rear its head again.

At the same time, Richard S. Sokolov was brought in as Vice President – General Counsel, replacing Bob Schreiber at that position. Schreiber, nearing retirement, was reassigned as Vice President of Special Assignments. Finally, at the same time, DeBartolo brought on board Charles Serednesky, Jr. as a Corporate Vice President.

Serednesky was named a Vice President of the Thistledown companies, Balmoral Racing Club, Inc., and Louisiana Downs, Inc., where his title was Vice President/ Business and Finance. This one was a head scratcher. Serednesky had no racing experience or knowledge and the tracks, apart from Balmoral, were stable and doing well.

In September, the Plain Dealer in Cleveland ran an article headlined "DeBartolo has 'definite interest' in Indians." Written by Bob Dolgan, the article quoted DeBartolo as expressing interest, but he would need assurances from Bowie Kuhn he would not block the way. A day or two later, Dolgan followed up with a telephone interview with Kuhn.

Kuhn cited DeBartolo's racetrack holdings as an ongoing concern. Dolgan asked him "Does that mean DeBartolo cannot get into baseball?" Per Dolgan, Kuhn replied carefully "That's what the rule says. That's all I want to say."

Despite Kuhn's comments, Mr. DeBartolo dispatched me to Cleveland, where I met with Gabe Paul, reviewed the Indians' financial records and discussed a purchase price. In fact, I asked Paul to give me a price tag on the team. Paul indicated he would get back to me, but he never did. It was apparent that, since there would still be opposition from Kuhn, Mr. DeBartolo would be reluctant to publicly pursue the Indians and eventually whatever interest he may have had was extinguished.

In late October, Mr. DeBartolo and I were subpoenaed back to Shreveport to give our depositions in the Bartimo lawsuit. EJD, Bob Schreiber and I flew down to Louisiana. My deposition would be first, as the author of the report that resulted in Bartimo's firing.

Bartimo had the Shreveport law firm of Pugh and Pugh representing him. The lead attorney was Robert G. Pugh, who had an annoying habit of mispronouncing our names, probably by design. He pronounced my name "Rahzetti" and I continuously corrected him throughout the deposition. Schreiber was referred to as "Skriber", but Pugh got Mr. DeBartolo's name right.

My deposition lasted a full day into the next day, as Pugh questioned me extensively on my background and experience, the details of my report, including trying to impeach me on some of my conclusions. We quibbled and disagreed on several issues before he called Mr. DeBartolo to testify.

Much of the same took place on Mr. D's deposition, with Mr. DeBartolo maintaining he and Vince had been "very close friends," and he felt betrayed by Bartimo's actions over the past year. Mr. DeBartolo also maintained he had not agreed to, nor was aware of, most of, if not all, the alleged wrongdoings in my report.

Pugh then produced a memorandum I had prepared for Mr. DeBartolo entitled "Synopsis of Management Contract between the Edward J. DeBartolo Corporation, Louisiana Downs, Inc. and Vincent J. Bartimo, Inc." He focused on a portion relating to the possible termination of the agreement, and Pugh disagreed with my conclusion as to the dates and rights of termination. He suggested to Mr. D I had erred, and Mr. DeBartolo agreed that appeared to be the case.

As the deposition went on, Mr. DeBartolo became agitated and impatient. The emotional toll was certainly taking effect on EJD, discussing the termination of his good friend. Our attorneys recommended we break for lunch.

At lunch, Mr. DeBartolo indicated he no longer wanted to pursue the matter. Schreiber and I, along with the Louisiana attorneys were shocked. We all felt our depositions had blunted Bartimo's and that we would prevail. But, Mr. DeBartolo was adamant.

"Tell them that we are dropping the charges" he told the attorneys. And that is what happened when the break was over. The parties agreed to seal the records, and Mr. D and I headed back to the airport to get on the Learjet. Schreiber would stay on to assist on the sign off on the paperwork. On the flight home, I expressed my disappointment with Mr. D's change of heart. He told me he was tired of it and "anyway, someone might get hurt or even killed." When I asked him who it might be, he looked at me and simply said, "You." I didn't ask any more questions.

On November 5, 1982, I received a letter from Robert G. Pugh, who also copied Mr. DeBartolo. He described the discussion during Mr. DeBartolo's deposition in which he and Mr. D concluded I had erred on the termination clause. His letter then stated in part, "Shortly after this exchange, a break occurred, and I again reviewed the document myself and concluded that the information contained in your synopsis was absolutely correct. As you will recall, after this break things moved in a different direction. I therefore failed to apologize to you for this error that I committed. I now do so. I am taking the liberty of sending a copy of this letter to Mr. D in case I led him into believing you had created an error when as a matter of fact, I know of no error that you committed in the various memoranda you prepared concerning these various contracts. Yours very truly, Robert G. Pugh"

While all these legalities were taking place, the NFL season had started and with it, the 49ers defense of their Super Bowl Championship. The 49ers lost their first two games before the League had a Players' strike and games were cancelled for two months. The 49ers ended up 3-6, with 5 of the 6 losses by 6 points or less. But, the problems started before the strike as rumors of drug use among the younger players, particularly the defensive players were rampant. It was a lost season.

It wasn't any better for the Penguins who stumbled coming out of the gate with a first half record of 11-21-6 at December 31. It would only get worse from there and the team finished 18-53-9, the worst record in the NHL. But, there would be a rainbow at the end of the season.

The Pittsburgh Spirit couldn't build on the success of their first season. They never got any continuity going during the 1982-83 season and finished out of the playoffs at 24-24.

The Erie Blades became the Baltimore Skipjacks and the players were all supplied by the Penguins. After the disastrous first season with John Caruso in Erie, the Penguins farm team was now on sound footing. They ended their season 35-36-9, also out of the playoffs.

One morning, Eddie, Jr. called me into his office. Again, he swore me to secrecy and then he told me he loaned a large sum of money to OJ Simpson in 1979, while OJ and his wife, Marguerite, were getting divorced. OJ had called Eddie and asked to borrow some money to pay the settlement to Marguerite. OJ told Eddie he would pay him back once he was eligible to get his deferred compensation from Buffalo. The amount of the loan was $750,000. There was no interest, no note and Eddie hadn't told anyone about the loan.

Eddie attempted to call OJ on several occasions, but OJ hadn't returned the calls. Eddie asked me to see if I could contact OJ and get the money paid back confidentially. I went back to my office and put a call into OJ. OJ's secretary was also named Marguerite and she answered the phone. I told her I was calling on behalf of EJD, Jr. and it was important and that I needed to talk with OJ. She told me he wasn't in, but she would give him the message and have him return the call.

OJ didn't return the call that day or the next, so I called again the third day. Again, Marguerite answered, and I explained I hadn't received OJ's call and I wanted to speak with him. She replied he was "out", but she expected him back later in the day and she would have him call me as soon as he got in. Again, there was no return call.

The next day, I waited until noon, which was nine o'clock in Los Angeles, and placed the call. When Marguerite picked up the phone, I told her to give OJ this message, "If I don't receive a check for the full amount of the loan by Fedex by tomorrow at five p.m. Eastern time, OJ can expect to read his name in the sports pages the next day as a deadbeat." Then I hung up. The next day, I received a Fedex envelope with the $750,000 check.

But the story didn't end there. A week later, Connie Fair, my newest secretary, answered the phone and she excitedly told me "It's OJ Simpson, for you!" I picked up the phone expecting some type of unpleasantness; but was shocked to hear OJ thanking me for the "friendly and diplomatic" way I handled the matter. As I hung up the phone, I felt I may have just spoken to a Jekyll and Hyde individual.

So, 1982 was in the record books. A great start, thanks to the 49ers, but a washout after that (except for my vacation).

CHAPTER TWELVE

1983-A YEAR OF PROBLEMS

I got in trouble right off the bat in 1983. EJD came out with a memo to all department heads there would be no salary increases for 1983. We were in a wage freeze. I sent a memo on January 12 to EJD, with a copy to Eddie and Denise, questioning the wage freeze. I pointed out we had already given out salary increases at Louisiana Downs and other operations, and I didn't see the fairness in treatment of the Youngstown employees. EJD was succinct in his answer. "I set policy in this Co., not you. Please conform."

Nevertheless, Eddie opened negotiations with me on my own salary. After a few memos and discussions, he agreed to give me an increase of $7,000. Unbeknownst to me, EJD cut the increase to $5,000 and nobody told me for three months. The answer to my inquiries to payroll and finally to EJD, Jr. came in the summer. My increase was $5,000 only.

With the way the 49ers, Penguins and Spirit seasons ended, there were no playoffs for us in any sport in the spring of 1983. But there were plenty of other things that could (and would) go wrong in 1983. On March 15, Penguin General Manager Baz Bastien was killed in an auto accident in Pittsburgh. Marty and I drove down to Upper St. Claire, Pennsylvania, to pay our respects. Baz may not have been a great general manager, but he was a nice guy and it was a sad time for the Penguins organization.

Then one Saturday morning in the middle of March, I got a call in the middle of the night at around one a.m. Eddie, Jr. was negotiating with Bill Walsh and needed a copy of Walsh's contract. I got dressed, went to the office, got the contract, and drove over to Eddie's house to deliver it. This scenario played out a few more times as the years went by. My job was turning into a 24 hour a day position.

Prior to that however, there were problems aplenty in our racing division. Charles Serednesky ("Chas") immediately replaced the general manager at Balmoral with one of his cronies from his soccer days, got into numerous clashes with George Jones at Thistledown and antagonized Tom Sweeney at Louisiana Downs. Their inquiries to Mr. D in their daily calls got the same reply as I got - "Work with him."

Chas didn't really bother me in the office. His time with me was mainly spent trying to understand the financial end of horse racing, and I was glad to help him out. But, out on the road he apparently was quite a different person dealing with the general managers.

His problems with Jones, aside from Chas' attitude, began when he told Jones to call him each morning rather than Mr. D. George, knowing Mr. D expected a call from him each morning, told Chas to take a hike. Chas did the same thing with Sweeney in Louisiana, but Tom was a little more diplomatic - he called me and asked what he should do. I told Tom to continue to call Mr. D every day until Mr. D told him not to. It was clear Chas didn't know the "DeBartolo way." He was trying to take over from all the general managers and be the only conduit to Mr. D. Later, he tried the same thing with me.

On April 6, I blew out my knee in a "Youngstown Snowball Softball Tournament" game representing The Edward J. DeBartolo Corporation team. I went to the hospital, and later saw a surgeon who repaired the knee and had me stay home for a week. I had my secretary, Connie, bring work to my home and dictated memos to her from home over the phone.

Connie told me I was getting a lot of calls from Sweeney, Jones and Dan Groth (Balmoral) about problems with Chas. I had been talking with Jones from home and he told me how Chas wanted to spend $10,000 to $20,000 for fireworks for the 4th of July. There were only a couple of problems: (1) Thistledown runs days, and a night fireworks display would have meant patrons would have to wait 2-3 hours after the last race for it to get dark, and (2) fireworks spook the horses and the horsemen would be up in arms. But, Chas had a solution – noiseless fireworks during the day. We had a good laugh over that one. But then the laughs stopped.

The controllers at all three tracks, as well as the general managers, were told all financial matters would henceforth go through Chas rather than to me or any of my staff in Youngstown. That meant I had no control over the accuracy of the daily reports that ended up on EJD's desk, nor would I have any knowledge what was going on financially.

It was a Saturday, and I got out of bed and went into the office on crutches where I found Eddie, Jr. I told Eddie what was going on and asked if I was being pushed out. He told me he had no knowledge of any of this and called his father into the meeting. I repeated everything I was told and asked if he (EJD) was aware of any of it. He was not. EJD then went back to his office and called Sweeney and Jones to verify my account.

Monday morning, I was back in the office after missing the week. There was a sealed memo from Mr. DeBartolo to Serednesky, with a copy to EJD, Jr., Marie Denise and me. "As soon as you get back in town Monday, I want to see you in my office." was all it said. I never saw Chas again. Apparently, when he came after the GM's and me, he went too far. His name was quickly removed as an officer of the various racing entities.

Earlier that spring, the DeBartolos were contemplating acquiring a United States Football League franchise in Pittsburgh. They asked me what I thought. I told them I didn't understand it - they already had an NFL franchise, and a successful one, at that. Why would they go with a new league that would antagonize the NFL and its owners and compete against their own league? The answer was that it would not compete - the league would use cast-off NFL players and play after the Super Bowl, so there would be no competition. They instructed me to do some projections.

Now, Pittsburgh was a good football town, so a USFL franchise could have a reasonable chance of success if it was done as the league originally planned. Using my experience with the 49er finances, I did three separate projections, based on various attendance averages. All of them projected losses, even with attendances of 30,000-35,000. I did not use similar numbers from the 49er budgets - I only used percentages of what we spent in San Francisco.

When I presented the numbers to the DeBartolos, they called for a Saturday meeting among all the Company top executives. They took a straw vote at the start before passing out the projections. All were in favor, except me. Then, they passed out my projections. Everyone looked them over and then EJD, Jr. said; "These numbers are ridiculous. Where did you get this coaches budget number from?"

I told him it was one-quarter what the 49ers spent. We then discussed the numbers and voted again. There were now three or four against, including Bill Moses, one of EJD and EJD, Jr's closest friends. Bill now thought the losses would be prohibitive and that's why he changed his vote. EJD and EJD, Jr. both wanted it and they got it. On April 24, 1983, Edward J. DeBartolo became the owner of the Pittsburgh Maulers USFL football franchise. Moses told me later they were both fuming at me for my pro forma numbers. I projected the most likely loss at $7 million, but I was wrong. We ended up losing $14 million.

The USFL already had problems. The league started in May 1982, and the teams began signing established former NFL coaches and then NFL players, to begin play in February of 1983. The league had a salary cap of $1.8 million per team, but the New Jersey Generals blew that away when they signed the 1982 Heisman Trophy winner, Herschel Walker, out of Georgia, to a three-year, $4.2 million "personal service contract" with owner J. Walter Duncan, an Oklahoma oil mogul. The $1.8 million salary cap was largely ignored, and owners started to loot NFL rosters. This would eventually kill the USFL.

Eddie, Jr. told me, because of my 49ers involvement, they could not publicly have me involved in the Maulers management. That was okay with me, not only because I wasn't in favor of the venture but because Eddie wouldn't be involved either. But, I would be responsible to monitor the finances and the bottom-line. EJD, through Liberati, brought my Controller at Louisiana Downs, Kim Russell, to Pittsburgh as the business manager. The Maulers began building the office staff.

Three Rivers Stadium was owned by the City of Pittsburgh, and the city was excited to have a new tenant. However, the Steelers wanted no part of the USFL and refused to let the Maulers share the locker rooms or the offices that housed the NFL team. This necessitated the construction of a new complex within the stadium to house the two locker rooms, the office complex and the ticket offices. This unbudgeted expense came to more than $8 million. My projections were already blown up.

Donald Trump originally owned the New Jersey franchise but sold to Duncan in 1983. It was rumored Trump may have been involved in the Walker signing. Regardless, Duncan sold the team back to Trump in 1984. DeBartolo, watching how the league was being run, saw the Los Angeles Express sign Brigham Young quarterback Steve Young, to a $40 million contract, then decided he could play that game, as well. He went after the 1983 Heisman Trophy winner, Mike Rozier of Nebraska, and negotiations began.

A few weeks later, the Maulers went out and signed Dallas Cowboys' reserve quarterback Glenn Carano to a contract. If the attempt to sign Rozier was successful, the core of the Maulers backfield would be set. In addition, the "ridiculous" losses that I originally forecast would probably be ridiculously low.

In the fall of 1983, EJD, Jr. called me into his office and told me he wanted me to accompany him to the NFL owners meeting in New York. I agreed and cleared my schedule for the date. Later that day, Eddie called and said he wouldn't be going after all and that Carmen Policy, his Youngstown attorney, would take his place. This was going to be a "dicey" meeting for the DeBartolos, with all the USFL moves being made (including EJD's Maulers activities), and I just assumed he wanted me to support him, and then Policy, by taking notes of the proceedings.

When I arrived in New York on the day of the owners meeting, I called the office from the airport and Connie told me Policy had cancelled and I was the only representative from the 49ers. I'm pretty sure that neither Eddie, Jr. nor Carmen Policy ever intended to be at the meeting.

As expected, the USFL was the main topic of the meeting. I kept my mouth shut, took notes, and just appeared to be interested. As the noon hour approached, the owners took a break and moved to an adjoining room where lunch was set up. There was assigned seating and I was seated next to Art Modell, the owner of the Cleveland Browns. The seat next to me was unassigned, and all the other owners were already seated.

We chatted for a few minutes and suddenly Modell beckoned toward the door. I looked up and Pete Rozelle, the Commissioner of the NFL was in the doorway. He saw Modell and joined our table, in the seat next to me. So, on one side of me was the NFL Commissioner and on the other side was one of his key advisors in Art Modell.

Over the next hour and a half, I was barraged from both sides about Mr. DeBartolo's involvement with the USFL. Clearly, the owners were trying to discern whether Eddie, Jr. had broken any rules. I answered their questions honestly and explained we were keeping the two teams apart from a management standpoint, and EJD wasn't involved in 49er business and EJD, Jr. wasn't involved in Maulers business. I also said I felt the USFL would not survive. The owners liked that opinion and, in all honesty, I felt in my heart that the USFL would not survive. But, talk about being set up - I got it from Eddie, Jr. and the NFL.

The 1983 NFL season began on September 3 with a 49ers loss to Philadelphia at home. The team then won four in a row before slipping at home to the Rams, 10-7. Two more wins were followed by back-to-back home losses to the Jets and Dolphins. The team finished 4-2 after that with wins over the Saints, Buccaneers, Bills and Cowboys and losses to the Falcons and Bears. The 10-6 record was good enough for first place in the Western Division of the National Conference.

In the Divisional Playoff game, the 49ers hosted the Detroit Lions on New Year's Eve at Candlestick. The 49er defense intercepted the Lions' Gary Danielson five times, but the 49er offense had a lackluster day. The Lions kept the game close, even with the turnovers, but a Montana to Freddie Solomon touchdown pass with 1:23 left in the game put the 49ers up, 24-23. The Lions came charging back, however, and with five seconds left, lined up for a 43-yard Eddie Murray field goal. The normally reliable Murray had already missed a 43 yarder earlier in the quarter, and this one also missed, giving the 49ers a narrow win and a berth in the NFC Championship game in early 1984.

The Penguins got off to a horrendous start and as of December 31 were 9-24-5. They would finish the season in dead last, with a record of 16-58-6, the worst record in the history of the franchise. But, as we would learn in 1984, there was a pot of gold at the rainbow's end.

The Pittsburgh Spirit was in the midst of a terrific season and would finish the 1983-84 season with a 32-16 record. But, losses to Cleveland in the playoff quarterfinals ended a promising season.

I experienced the usual harassment during the summer twice by Mr. DeBartolo when I requested vacation (on 7/27/83 he wrote "You should take vacations during slack periods or not at all!"). The problem I had with that statement is that I never had "slack periods", and I'm pretty sure that he knew that.

On November 3, I was the featured speaker at a joint banquet for the Columbiana Little Clippers and the Touchdown Club. My three sons, ages 11, 7 and 5, accompanied me and I showed the 49ers Super Bowl highlight film, gave a 30-minute speech and fielded questions from the audience. We raffled off some footballs and jerseys and each child in attendance received autographed pictures of Joe Montana, Dwight

Clark, Ronnie Lott and Fred Dean. Many people approached me at the end of the night with compliments to the DeBartolo family for their "continued involvement in and support of the community." One gentleman expressed his feelings that "the 49ers scored a lot of points here tonight!"

In December, there were rumors of a rift forming between Bill Walsh and Joe Montana. Why not? And thus, 1983, my tenth year with the DeBartolo Corporation, came to an end.

CHAPTER THIRTEEN

1984-A YEAR OF LOWS AND HIGHS

January began with the expectations of another Super Bowl as the 49ers visited Washington on Sunday, January 8 in the NFC Championship Game. Washington is a five-hour drive from Youngstown, so Chris and I took the family to see the nation's capital and go to the game. There was early excitement on Saturday when we had a tour of the White House scheduled. My oldest son, Mike, who was 11 and a Cub Scout, triggered the metal detectors upon entering and was quickly whisked away by a few huge Secret Service agents. He did not have a gun, however a tube of toothpaste (remember when they were in metal tubes?) was the culprit. It was confiscated and we could enter.

The weekend was a pleasant winter weekend with temperatures in the 50s to 60s. We stayed at the team hotel at the Marriott in downtown DC, near the Potomac. Unfortunately, the hotel fire alarm system went off twice during the night before the game, waking up the entire hotel, including the players. Both were false alarms. Whether it affected the players later in the day was never discussed.

My family went to the Catholic Mass that Monsignor Armstrong had for the team in the hotel and then we went back up to pack. We rested in the room and then headed over to the stadium for the game. When we stepped on the elevator, Bill Walsh was there. Bill knew us and noticed the kids had 49er hats and my middle son, Chip, had a big foam "49ers #1" finger that fit on his hand.

Walsh, deadpanning with the boys, asked where they were going. They told him "to the big game!" Bill then asked, "Is there a game today?" and Chip answered "Yes. The 49ers are playing the Redskins for the Championship!" The elevator arrived at the lobby level and as we were getting off, Walsh said "Wish the 49ers luck for me!" as he walked away. The boys never knew who he was.

The game didn't go as we hoped. We were sitting in the first row on the field behind one of the end zones and the boys marveled at all the adults wearing pig noses in the stands. The offense was sputtering and the Redskins offense gave the 49er defense a steady diet of John Riggins, who ended up with 36 carries for 123 yards. Riggins scored on a four-yard run late in the second quarter for a 7-0 lead at the half. Riggins then scored on a one-yard plunge midway through the third quarter and, with a minute left in the third, Washington QB Joe Theismann connected on a 70-yard TD pass for a comfortable 21-0 lead going into the fourth quarter. It could have been worse for the 49ers - Washington kicker Mark Moseley had missed three field goals on the muddy field.

And then Joe Montana and the 49ers offense woke up. Thirty-three seconds into the fourth quarter, Montana tossed a five-yard touchdown to Mike Wilson. The defense then held and forced a Redskins punt, but the 49er punt returner fumbled and the Redskins recovered. Moseley missed his fourth field goal of the day and on the next play, Montana threw a 78-yard touchdown pass to Freddie Solomon to make the score 21-14. A few minutes later, Montana connected with Wilson again on a 12 yarder to tie the score. In seven minutes, the 49ers had scored three times and there were still seven minutes left in the game.

The noise in the Stadium was deafening and the CBS field camera crew panned the crowd and settled on my wife, Chris. My youngest son, Tommy was fast asleep in her arms. I was told later that Pat Summerall, the game announcer commented, "Apparently, the noise doesn't affect this young fan."

The 49ers kicked off and the Redskins marched 78 yards using up six minutes to set up yet another Moseley field goal attempt. The drive was aided by a 27-yard pass interference call on Eric Wright of the 49ers on a pass to Art Monk which, according to Walsh "could not have been caught by a 10-foot Boston Celtic."

Still, there was time for the 49ers, who stopped the Redskins again, only to see Ronnie Lott get flagged on third down for a phantom holding call away from the ball. From the eight-yard line, the Redskins tried to score the touchdown, but Riggins was stopped three times for no gain and Moseley finally made a kick. The 49ers, out of time outs with less than 40 seconds, tried two passes, the second a "Hail Mary" to Solomon that was picked off, and the game ended. It was revealed after the game that 49er kicker Ray Wersching had been injured on the last 49er kickoff and would not be available for even a mid-range field goal. That explained the "Hail Mary."

The drive back to Youngstown through the dark night with my entire family asleep was miserable. I listened to sports talk radio all the way home and heard the analysts debate the questionable penalties on Wright and Lott. They were universally in agreement – the penalties should not have been called but, even if only one was called, it was likely that the 49ers, with the extra time the Redskins were able to burn off the clock, might very possibly have won the game on the final drive. It just made a bitter loss even more agonizing. We were so close to another Super Bowl.

But Monday morning it was business as usual and, when I opened the Cleveland Plain Dealer, along with the wrap-up of the 49er game there was an article from Bob Dolgan. The article headline read "It's father against son in NFL-USFL warfare," and went on to quote EJD and EJD, Jr. in what appeared to be a "tongue in cheek" article where the two sparred over the potential success of the USFL and ended with Mr. DeBartolo predicting that "in three or four years" there would be a merger of the leagues, with weaker USFL cities being bought out.

That same day, the Maulers agreed to a three-year contract with Rozier for $3.1 million. On the day the signing was finalized, Mr. DeBartolo dispatched me to Melbourne, Florida, site of the Maulers training camp, and had me escort Rozier back to Youngstown. It was neat walking through the Atlanta airport with Rozier, who was recognized by numerous people and signed autographs as we hurried to catch our connecting flight. Rozier met with Mr. DeBartolo, went through a press conference with the local press and returned to Melbourne the next day. The first regular season game was scheduled for February 26, 1984.

In early February, the long awaited new racing bill in Ohio became law. George Jones and I worked feverishly for years with Jack McCarthy, a DeBartolo lobbyist and other politicians and journalists, including Bob Dolgan, to get the bill passed. Numerous horsemen also supported the bill, with the promise of improvements to the backstretch barn area.

The bill would rebate a percentage of a racetrack's taxes for tracks that made capital improvements. Thistledown was sorely in need of the new barn area and other grandstand improvements to make the experience more fan-friendly and, hopefully bring out the younger generation. The key to a track's success was to get the improvements done, get the rebate started and continue other improvements so the rebate would never end. We estimated the initial value to Thistledown would be a savings of approximately $3 million.

I was so happy when the bill passed that, on February 9, I sent a memo to Mr. DeBartolo, entitled "Bonus," and read, "In view of the fact that the new racing bill will save Thistledown more than $3,000,000, I think it would be appropriate for you to give me a bonus equal to 10 percent of that number. What do you think?" I knew I didn't have a snowball's chance in hell of succeeding and his response was right to the point. "Rossetti-Of course politics and my struggle for 25 years had nothing to do with this bill." It was signed with his initial "E". Oh well, it was worth a try.

The Penguins dreadful season was continuing, but there now was a goal. A young Junior Hockey player named Mario Lemieux would be available to be drafted and scouts had already dubbed him as "The Next Gretzky", the marvelous player who currently was the best in the NHL and would end up the best of all time. The unusual thing about Lemieux was he was unanimously referred to as the next "player of a lifetime," and with the Penguins horrible start, it was clear we would be in the hunt for him.

For years, under General Manager Baz Bastien, the Penguins used to trade their draft choices late in the season to get seasoned players that would help get the team in the playoffs at the end of the year. The NHL in those days had 21 teams and 16 made the playoffs at the end of the regular season. It made the regular season meaningless, so long as a team made the playoffs.

For the small market teams, such as Pittsburgh, the playoffs could be a windfall. Most of the teams lost money during the regular season and the Pens were no exception. Despite running a tight ship, losses of $1 million to $1.5 million were common for the Pens during the regular season. But, making the playoffs would result in net profits to the teams, on a per game basis. In other words, the more playoff games a team played in the more money they made. Getting through the first round for the Penguins, and extending the second-round games could result in a dramatic reduction of the losses for the year, and could even result in a breakeven for the team.

So, the weaker teams would sacrifice the future for the present, to cut losses. The more successful teams from New York, Montreal, Toronto, Boston, Chicago and Detroit rarely missed the playoffs and would gladly trade aging players for young draft choices. It was kind of an ongoing situation.

As the Penguins' deplorable season progressed, Mr. DeBartolo summoned Eddie Johnson, the new general manager, Lou Angotti, the current coach and Paul Martha, the Penguin vice president to Youngstown for a meeting in our offices.

DeBartolo, who knew nothing about hockey and had only seen one or two games since he acquired the team, was concerned about the bad record, declining attendances and resulting bottom line losses. He wanted improvement now. Johnson, Angotti and Martha all filled him in on the prospect of getting Lemieux and made the comparison with Gretzky. Although DeBartolo knew little about hockey, he certainly knew who Gretzky was, and his effect on the sports pages.

He backed the three men into a proverbial corner, and they admitted Lemieux was capable of turning the Penguins from a perennial loser to a Stanley Cup contender. It was clear the only way to do it was to assure the Penguins got the first draft pick. "Get it done," said Mr.

DeBartolo and he walked out of the meeting. The message had been sent.

At that point, the Penguins record was around 13-42-5 and New Jersey was right behind them for the worst record. The Pens only won three of their last 20 games and finished three points worse than New Jersey. The first-round pick was clinched. There were rumors that both New Jersey and Pittsburgh were trying not to win to get that first pick, but the company line was the Penguins were just looking at their prospects from the minor league team when the season ended.

The USFL season opened for the Maulers on February 26, with the Maulers dropping a 7-3 game in Oklahoma. They lost the next week in Michigan, 28-24, and returned home for a March 11 game against the Birmingham Stallions. Before a sellout crowd at Three Rivers Stadium, the Maulers dropped another game, 30-18. Things didn't get much better as the season progressed. Rozier had no blockers, Carano had no receivers and the offense was stagnant. Coach Joe Pendry was fired in mid-season after a 2-8 record, but his successor, Ellis Rainsberger (1-7) was even worse.

The team ended up at 3-15 and, after the first game sellout, the attendances dwindled and averaged just fewer than 23,000. The losses were significant. Later that fall, the league voted to go to a fall schedule and DeBartolo, not interested in competing with the Pittsburgh Steelers and more importantly, his son's own league, decided he was done. We flew to Philadelphia to discuss a merger with the Stars, but they were told it would not include DeBartolo. The Stars had no reason to merge. The Maulers quietly folded.

While the Maulers only season was playing out, the Penguins were in negotiations with Mario Lemieux. The Penguins made it clear they would draft him and were trying to work out a contract. Paul Martha and Eddie Johnston were the negotiators for the Penguins, reporting to Mr. DeBartolo, but the sides could not agree on the contract.

DeBartolo called Martha and Johnston to Youngstown for another meeting just prior to the NHL Draft in Montreal. Johnston discussed the areas where the team and Lemieux were apart. It was primarily money. It was clear Johnston was frustrated and he then offered up an alternative. The Quebec Nordiques were desperate to get Lemieux, who had played Junior hockey in the Quebec Major Junior Hockey League and was a native Canadian. Johnson discussed a trade with Quebec, who offered the entire Stasny family (3 brothers who had defected from the Czech Republic) and were all world class players.

There was an uncomfortable silence in the room when Johnston raised the proposal. I said to Johnston "You told us that a player of Lemieux's ability only comes along once in a lifetime and now you want to trade him?" I'm sure we were all thinking about the horrible season just ended. DeBartolo then said since this was only about money, there would be no trade.

"Get the deal done," he told Martha and Johnston. A few days later, on June 9, 1984, the Penguins drafted Lemieux. Mario refused to shake Eddie Johnston's hand and declined the jersey offered him, because the contract hadn't yet been agreed upon. A few days later, he signed and the Penguins had what they hoped would be the savior of the franchise.

The first quarter of the year was when I negotiated my annual raise, and I met with Mr. DeBartolo in mid-February to discuss my status. DeBartolo threw me a curve by having Tony Liberati in the meeting, and after our discussions he instructed me to summarize my position in a memo to Tony. This was a new wrinkle in my employment because, for the last seven years, I reported directly to Mr. DeBartolo and Eddie, Jr. and the two of them always determined my salary.

EJD had often told me I was "most valuable to the Corporation in my present position." By and large I was satisfied in Youngstown, but I was also looking down the road and my future. The corporation did not have a pension plan and, in fact, never had one until I left the company in 1989. I was given small partnership interests in a couple of DeBartolo malls, but the amount of the worth of those interests wasn't easily quantifiable. I was working hard and wanted it to be worthwhile for my family. Moreover, the introduction of Liberati into my relationship with Mr. DeBartolo was troublesome.

Having been exposed to a family business, I considered doing something on my own. For several months, my brother Chas, who worked for the company in Toledo and now was in Youngstown in our computer department, and I had discussed the prospect of owning a restaurant business, preferably in Florida.

In the spring of 1984, Chas and I flew to Denver to interview with a steakhouse chain for a franchise. Our first choice for a franchise was the Merritt Island, Florida area, not far from Cape Canaveral. We were approved for the Mr. Steak franchise and started looking for locations. Knowing that Mr. DeBartolo had so many contacts in Florida, I knew I needed to tell him what we were doing before he found out through other sources. It was not my intention to move to Florida. I would be an absentee owner and Chas would be the managing owner.

I met with Mr. DeBartolo and told him what we were interested in doing. His first question to me was, "Are you going to leave the company?" I assured him I was not planning to leave anytime soon. This would be a family business and I would be the financial partner. He then gave me his blessing and offered whatever assistance I needed.

A few days later, he called me into his office and proposed a business deal. He explained he had a hotel/condominium project in Marco Island, Florida that included plans for a restaurant. The project already had a chickee roof snack bar that serviced the pool and the hotel for outdoor lunches and a bay-front chickee bar that served cocktails not only to the guests, but to island residents, as well. He wanted me to see the project and see if I had an interest.

The next day I flew down to Marco Island with two of our real estate guys and got a tour. I met the managing partner of the resort, a small Cleveland developer named Bob Stakich, and toured the property and discussed the demographics of the area. Stakich said the chickee bar would not be included in my operation, but that the snack bar "could be negotiated."

Marco Island, south of Naples, was highly seasonal with a tourist season of approximately four months from mid-December to mid-April. The rest of the year was quiet. The two Youngstown guys I was with advised me that several chain restaurants had looked at the site and passed due to the "short season." They also agreed that the bar was not available to me. As we left the island and headed to Miami for the flight home, I decided that the project was not for me.

The next morning, Mr. DeBartolo called me over and asked how the trip went. I told him the island was beautiful but I would have to pass on the restaurant, due to the short season. We talked a bit about the overall project and how much it would take to build the restaurant on the present site. The building shell was already built, and the fourth floor was reserved for the restaurant. The third floor would house a banquet area and the second would be the hotel/condominium check-in area. The first floor would be for parking, due to flood restrictions.

Mr. DeBartolo asked what my interest was and again I told him it wouldn't work out for us, due to the short season. I also mentioned the outdoor bar appeared to be popular and would compete onsite with our lounge. Mr. DeBartolo pointed out this type of restaurant project was usually built out by the developer and then leased out to the operator. I told him I still didn't think that it would work for us, but he said to me "make me an offer."

I told him I didn't want to insult him, so I wouldn't make him an offer. Then, he took off his glasses, looked me in the eye and said again "make me an offer!" It was not a request. I told him I needed to give it some thought before I threw out some numbers and he said, "come back at five o' clock."

The rest of the day, I agonized over the upcoming meeting. Mr. DeBartolo needed me to do this deal for his project and we both knew it. How do you negotiate a business deal with your boss, who might be the greatest negotiator of all time? And not only that, he is the only person who can terminate your employment on a whim!

I needed to safeguard myself and he knew it. I put my offer together and went over to his office to review it with him. I proposed my company (Rossetti Enterprises, Inc.) would get an interior designer to design the restaurant. The designer would be paid for by the hotel entity. The hotel would also build and pay for the entire restaurant and lounge, including the banquet facilities, all kitchen equipment, furniture, fixtures, licenses and permits.

REI, through my investment of $40,000, would get all its own licenses and permits, including the liquor license, china, glass and silverware. I would need $100,000 for working capital. REI would pay $2,800 rent per month starting the month after opening. I also asked to include a couple of available condominium units to house members of my family who would be part of my management team. Finally, even though I was told the chickee bar and snack bar were not part of the proposal, my offer was contingent on REI taking over those operations, as well.

Mr. DeBartolo looked over my offer and asked about the chickee bar and snack bar. I told him I was told they were not available to us. After a few minutes of thought, he said, "We have a deal, and it includes all of the food and beverage operations. I'll take care of Stakich." We shook on the deal and I had my own business. We would take over the chickee bar and snack bar immediately and run those while construction on the restaurant was ongoing. Chas and his family would be dispatched immediately and, within a week, another brother, John, who lived in Chicago asked to be included. A couple of weeks later, he also was on his way to Florida.

I was having some of the same problems with Liberati as I had with Bill Pfaus years ago. Tony was now the CFO of the company, but I couldn't get him to give me answers on anything. He never did anything on my raise request and it lingered until July 1, when EJD took care of it.

In March of 1984, Art Wolfcale, the DeBartolo attorney who took care of corporate matters, came to my office and handed me a resolution to make Tony Liberati the CFO of the Penguins. I was secretary and treasurer of the Penguins, so my signature was needed.

I asked Art if Mr. DeBartolo had approved it. He answered that Liberati told him to prepare the resolution. I told him I had to check with Mr. D before I sign it. Later that day, I stopped in Mr. DeBartolo's office to ask him if he approved the change to the Penguins officer structure, and he blew up at me. He didn't know of it and told me that, under no circumstances, were any changes to be made to the Penguin hierarchy unless he told me to make them.

He tore the paper up and headed toward Liberati's office. The next day, I saw Liberati and explained I had to go to Mr. DeBartolo for the approval. I asked Tony not to be angry with me. He looked at me and said "I don't get angry. I get even." Here we go again.

On April 5, after a few months of frustrating requests, I sent a private memo to Liberati. He had not responded to requests for funding in Pittsburgh. The Pittsburgh operations (Civic Arena, Penguins and Spirit) were nearly $1.6 million behind on their bills, and the Maulers were behind by $900,000. For two months, I had been asking for money and didn't get a dime. I finally went to EJD and the funds were transferred. Strike two in my Liberati relationship.

The Cleveland Hotels would eventually be going on the market. For years, the four properties (three Holiday Inns and a Sheraton) struggled. We were experiencing minimal losses when the Pratt Company, owners of Sands Casinos, was brought in to manage the properties. Pratt fired Mike Sapara, a good and loyal manager and brought in their own people. Revenues did not increase, but expenses exploded and the losses quadrupled. A year or two later, we got rid of them, although we did get a good manager in Mike Dowling, who became a friend of mine as well as a loyal employee. With Pratt out of the picture, Dowling reduced expenses and the properties rebounded.

Construction was going on at Thistledown. With the tax bill passage, we quickly began the work on the new barns and started looking at projects to enhance the experience of our patrons. Those plans included enclosing a portion of the grandstand that included the restaurant so patrons would be warmer in the winter and cooler in the summer.

We were also approached by Mitsubishi, who was interested in putting a giant Diamond Vision Board in our infield, so all patrons could watch the races on the big screen. These negotiations were fun. Mitsubishi really wanted to put the boards in our bigger sporting facilities – the Civic Arena and Candlestick Park, but we told them we needed to see how they performed at Thistledown. So, we worked with their sales representative, Mikio Matsubayashi.

We knew the Board, which would cost $3.2 million, would qualify for the Ohio tax credit and the state tax abatement would pay for $2.24 million, leaving us with an out-of-pocket expense of about $1 million. Jones and I expressed reluctance to spend the money, asking for a guarantee on advertising. Mikio eventually agreed to a 10-year deal that guaranteed us $300,000 annually from advertising that Mitsubishi would sell. With tax credits, that gave us a break-even in three years and $300,000 of new revenue in each subsequent year. We agreed to those terms and became the first racetrack in the country to have a giant video board in the infield.

As construction continued at Thistledown, it also did on Marco Island. Mr. DeBartolo decided to put the Marco Bay Resort under my purview, allowing me to keep an eye on his business as well as my own.

Stakich and his General Manager, Bert Hawkins, were none too happy to find out I negotiated the outside bar and snack bar in my lease with Mr. DeBartolo, and I found out why soon enough. Both men had sons who worked at the resort and it seemed everyone had benefits at the bar and snack bar. Hawkins made little effort to be cooperative with John, Chas or I, and Stakich was a bit miffed about losing "his" bar. I told

John and Chas to work with both men and their sons, but nothing but problems surfaced. The Hawkins and Stakich families were not very co-operative as we put our controls in place and made them all accountable for their consumption at the two operations we had just taken over.

The chickee bar was open air and anyone could go behind the bar when it was closed for business. We had locks on the coolers where the beer, wine and mixers were kept, and each night John or Chas would load up a cart with the liquor and transport it to a storage room in the hotel. I observed the procedure and talked to John about getting insurance on the inventory but Stakich said, "You don't need it. There's no crime on the island."

The very next night, someone broke into the chickee storeroom and the snack bar and stole all the liquor and dozens of eggs and pounds of bacon from the snack bar. We contacted the police and filed a report, but there were no suspects. A day or two later, John was walking the property and smelled cooking bacon. A call to the county police resulted in a visit to that unit, and all our liquor and much of the food was recovered. The knuckleheads who robbed us were staying at the hotel! We had inventory insurance before the end of the week.

Our sports teams were getting ready to start their seasons, and we had high hopes for both the 49ers and the Penguins, the latter being rebuilt around the young Lemieux. The 49ers' season opened first on Labor Day weekend, and they took on the Lions in Detroit in a rematch of the 1984 Divisional Playoff game in San Francisco. It was a very close back-and-forth game that saw the Lions score late in the fourth quarter to tie the game. However, Montana led the 49ers downfield and a Ray Wersching 22- yard field goal with 4 seconds left ended it 30-27. The next weekend, the Redskins came to Candlestick with the 49ers seeking revenge for the loss earlier in the year that kept them out of the Super Bowl.

This one was never close. The Niners jumped out to a 27-0 lead, before Moseley made a late first half field goal. Washington mounted a mini-comeback in the third quarter, before the Niners put the game away with 10 points in the fourth quarter. San Francisco pounded out 534 yards in the 37-31 win, which included a late Washington TD to get them as close as they would be all day.

San Francisco reeled off four more wins, to start 6-0, before a lackluster 20-17 loss at Candlestick against the Steelers ended the win streak. The normally reliable Ray Wersching missed a 37-yard field goal that would have sent the game into overtime. It would be several weeks before the enormity of that missed field goal would be truly felt.

In Boston, the Penguins opened the 1984-85 season with Mario Lemieux in the lineup. On Mario's first shift he scored a goal on his first shot in the NHL. Six nights later at home, Lemieux made a perfect pass on his first shift on home ice, setting up a goal less than 56 seconds into the game. Watching him play in his first home game was a treat and he showed all signs of being as good as advertised.

The team finished 5-4-0 for October, but November wasn't good. Opposing teams quickly learned to double-team Lemieux, and his supporting cast couldn't take advantage. The Pens went 1-8-3 and dropped to the bottom of their division. The defense was giving up nearly five goals per game and even Lemieux couldn't top that.

While Penguins fans were watching Lemieux, the San Francisco 49ers were bouncing back from that bitter loss to Pittsburgh's football team - the Steelers. The 49ers beat the Houston Oilers, LA Rams, Cincinnati Bengals, Cleveland Browns, Tampa Bay Bucs, New Orleans

Saints, Atlanta Falcons, Minnesota Vikings, and the Rams again to finish the regular season 15-1, on a nine-game winning streak. A would-be perfect season was marred by that missed field goal.

In Florida, I was experiencing significant frustration trying to get our restaurant opened. Stakich kept reporting one delay after another and a projected November opening was missed. We had hired a master chef and were hiring other staff, and my overhead kept going up. DeBartolo told me to go down there and find out what the problem was.

In early November, I flew to Southwest Florida and showed up in Stakich's office. I sat in his office and listened while he made lunch plans over the phone. It dawned on me that every time I was in Marco Island, he started each day making lunch plans with his friends, talking various alternatives for what seemed like hours. Then, when he got back from lunch, he'd get on the phone and start making plans for where he would have cocktails and dinner.

That day, I waited for him to get off the phone, and then politely asked him about the most recent delay. Stakich said he didn't know. I asked him who was in charge. He said he was. I then suggested if he spent more time working and less time deciding on where and when to have lunch and dinner maybe he could get some work done.

Stakich said "I don't answer to you!" And then I lost my temper, I slammed my hand on his desk and my Super Bowl ring made a noise like a gunshot, and Stakich winced. "You don't answer to me, but you do answer to Ed DeBartolo and he sent me here today to find out what the delay is! Shall we call him right now?" I said.

Stakich turned pale and said he would get the answers. I told him I wanted answers before I left that afternoon. I took my sister-in-law and little niece out for an ice cream cone and quietly stewed.

A few hours later, I returned to Stakich's office and asked for my answer. It was a bunch of BS and I told him so. "When can we open?" I asked him.

"Probably sometime in January," he answered.

I told him that wasn't good enough and I gave him until the middle of December to get the job done.

"I can't guarantee that" he said.

"If you miss that deadline, pack your bags because I will strongly recommend to Mr. DeBartolo that he get rid of you." And I walked out.

John and Chas later told me activity picked up 100 percent after I left. We did a soft opening on December 18. Christine's by the Bay, REI's first-class restaurant was open and operating.

I flew the family to Marco Island for Thanksgiving and my mother and sister came down and we had a nice holiday. Stakich avoided me and I was okay with that. I got done what I needed to get done.

I went to four 49ers games in 1984; in Detroit in September, in Philadelphia three weeks later, in New York on October 8 and in Cleveland on November 11. The Monday night game in New York was noteworthy.

I was due in Bermuda on November 9 for a Board meeting of our captive insurance company, Professional Sports Insurance Company, and so I decided to overnight in New York (actually New Jersey), stay at the team hotel, take in the game and fly out the next morning. This was a Monday night game that made me realize how good the 49ers were.

The Detroit game had been close, The Eagles game was when Montana was injured and didn't play, and the Browns game was, well, it was against Cleveland. But this game was against a rival and it was in

New York. I love New York fans - I was one myself at one time, although I was never a Giants fan. But, for years after that Monday night game, when I talked to Giants fans, they still referred to that game as the "Twenty Minute Game."

The Forty Niners took the opening kickoff and began the drive on their own 27. After five running plays, Joe Montana lofted a 59-yard touchdown pass to Renaldo Nehemiah for a 7-0 lead 2:32 into the game. The Giants went three and out and punted to the 49ers, who took over on their own 25-yard line, and drove 75 yards in six plays culminating in a one-yard pass to tight end John Frank. It was 14-0 with 6:18 gone in the game.

The Giants then went three and out again and punted to 49er Dana McLemore, who returned it 79 yards for a 21-0 lead with 7:33 gone in the game. There was a lot of grumbling in the stands all around me. The fans then got a little bit of hope when the Giants put together an 82-yard drive over nearly six minutes, but they had to settle for a 20-yard field goal. It was 21-3 after the first quarter.

But the 49ers quickly dashed the Giants fans' hopes, when they took the ensuing kickoff and marched 91 yards in 12 plays, capped by Montana's fourth touchdown pass -- an eight yarder to Roger Craig. The game was 20:56 old, it was 28-3, and I was shocked at what happened next. The Giants fans left by the thousands, and I was left sitting there pretty much by myself. It seemed like 90 percent of them left, but it was probably closer to half. And that's when I realized how good the 49ers were. They just toyed with the Giants in the second half, playing defense. They didn't try to roll up the score; they just let the clock run out. It was a pretty impressive performance.

On December 29, I flew out to San Francisco and watched as the Giants got a rematch in the NFC Divisional Playoffs. Again, the Niners scored quickly – two Montana touchdowns in the first 6:48 for a 14-0 lead after one. The Giants came back with a field goal and a Harry Carson interception for a touchdown to close the gap to 14-10. But, Montana connected with Solomon from 29 yards to open the lead up again, 21-10, and that was all she wrote. Walsh turned the game over to his defense and no more points were scored. The Giants totaled only 260 total yards. Next up for the Niners were the Bears in a week in San Francisco in the NFC Championship Game.

By now, the number of companies I was responsible for had grown significantly. Earlier in the year, one of my friends, Tom Poplar, who headed up the Fun-N-Games entity, suggested I update my business card, so we designed a new one. It was bi-folded with my name and title on the face of the card and, when opened, it listed all my titles and entities on the inside. There was a section for all the sports entities that included the 49ers, the Penguins, the Spirit, the Maulers, the Baltimore Skipjacks (Penguins' minor league affiliate), the racetracks and the Civic Arena; as well as the non-sports entities.

When Mr. D and I flew to Philadelphia earlier in the year to meet with the Philadelphia Stars management, I left a business card with the receptionist of the Stars on our arrival. We were ushered into the conference room to meet with the Stars management and I put a few of my cards on the table to pass around when they entered.

Mr. DeBartolo picked up one of my cards, looked inside and put it into his pocket. Later, in the limo on the way to the airport, he took it out of his pocket and said, "You've become pretty powerful in the sports world, haven't you? Maybe I should get a business card, too."

I didn't take the bait. "You don't need a card. Everyone knows who you are and what you do." He just smiled and put the card back into his pocket.

I got one more little surprise at the end of the year. Recognizing my contributions to Louisiana Downs for the year, EJD gave me a $15,000 bonus from that company, and thus ended a good 1984.

CHAPTER FOURTEEN

1985-AN INTERESTING YEAR

The dawn of the New Year featured the excitement of the 1984 NFC Championship Game in San Francisco on January 6. The Chicago Bears were coming to town with Walter Payton and their vaunted defense. The teams last met in 1983 in Chicago and the Bears dominated San Francisco 13-3, on a cold windy day.

Chris was unable to accompany me on this trip out west, so I decided to take my oldest son, Mike, with me. We flew out on Friday and spent Saturday sightseeing Alcatraz, Fisherman's Wharf and the other sites in beautiful San Francisco. We had a fun day. We stayed at the Amfac Hotel, where the team was housed the night before the game.

Sunday morning, we went to Msgr. Armstrong's Mass at the hotel and then had a late breakfast. After killing a couple of hours at the hotel, Mike and I took the short drive over to Candlestick Park to take in the pre-game tailgate festivities before the four p.m. game.

About an hour before the game, we went inside the stadium. We had field passes that allowed us access to all areas of the stadium, so I took him onto the field while some of the players were loosening up. I saw a five-dollar bill blowing by, caught it and gave it to him. We watched the game from one of the boxes. Mike was excited that day, especially when he saw John Madden and Pat Summerall broadcasting from the box on one side of us and the rock group, Journey, in the box on the other side.

The stadium filled up and the Forty Niners kicked off to the Bears, who promptly marched 54 yards to the 49ers 23-yard line. But, the Bears kicker missed the field goal, and it was San Francisco's turn. That drive would be the Bears' best drive of the day. The 49ers marched to Chicago's two-yard line, but Montana fumbled the snap on third down and the Niners settled for a Ray Wersching field goal. A few minutes later, the 49ers intercepted a Steve Fuller pass in Chicago territory. The Niners again marched to the two, and Montana threw an interception in the end zone.

It was much of the same in the second quarter. Midway through the quarter, San Francisco marched 66 yards to the Bears four, but again had to settle for a field goal. But, while the 49ers offense was misfiring, their defense was stifling the Bears. Chicago didn't get a first down in the second quarter.

Halfway through the third quarter, the 49ers marched 35 yards in five running plays culminating in Wendell Tyler's nine-yard touchdown. Then Montana connected with Freddie Solomon early in the fourth quarter for a 10-yard touchdown, ending an eight-play, 88-yard drive. The Bears were toast and the celebration began in the stands. A late Wersching field goal made the final score 23-0. This was a defensive win. The Niners sacked the Bears nine times, held them to 13 first downs and only 186 yards, most of it on the ground. The San Francisco 49ers had punched their ticket for Super Bowl XIX.

Mike and I missed the "red-eye" back to Pittsburgh, when we both fell asleep waiting to go to the airport. He missed a day of school, but I missed a day in the office, and the calls were already coming into Youngstown for Super Bowl tickets. I talked to my secretary, Connie, and the list was already growing quickly. It was going to be a busy two weeks. The Grand Opening of Christine's by the Bay on Marco Island would be on Friday, January 11. Invitations had gone out weeks earlier.

Back in the office on Tuesday, the process of reviewing the ticket requests began. In every Super Bowl, the NFL takes 24.8 percent, the participating teams each get 17.5 percent, the host team receives five percent and the remaining 38.2 percent is distributed among the other teams in the league. As a participating team, as well as the host team (the game was played at Stanford Stadium), San Francisco would receive 22.5 percent, which comes out to approximately 18,900 tickets. These tickets are distributed to the teams in all sections of the stadium, meaning every team gets some preferred tickets, as well as some in less desirable sections.

So, of the 18,900 tickets the 49ers received, there were a percentage in the area between the 40-yard lines, some in the goal line to 40-yard line areas, some in the corners and some in the end zones. Teams also had contractual obligations. The Players' Association contract dictated how many went to participating players for their families as well as for non-participating players. Coaches were entitled to a certain number per their individual contracts. Officials of the teams usually had rights to tickets, and local sponsors usually had a provision in their deals with the teams. The rest of the allocated tickets go to season ticket holders in some sort of raffle. That was generally the system for all the teams.

As the owner of the Forty Niners, Eddie had a few extra ticket obligations. The Edward J. DeBartolo Corporation would take tickets for their key contacts, politicians, chain department store executives, financiers and others. The local Youngstown folks made it on the list this time. Since the team got the extra five percent as the host team, Eddie decided to offer some of those extra tickets to his employees in Youngstown and other local businesses.

We consigned a certain number of tickets to Alice Porter Travel Agency, a local travel agent that handled the DeBartolo account. Porter chartered a plane and secured a bunch of hotel rooms, including some in the Forty Niners hotel. DeBartolo employees received first consideration on the tickets and the plane quickly sold out. It was a great opportunity for the employees to experience the excitement of rooting for the DeBartolo team in a Super Bowl.

The request to Youngstown for tickets numbered in the thousands. Each morning, Eddie and I would meet and he would tell me who would get the best seats, who would get second-best, etc. My department would then Fedex the tickets and invoices to the people. It was hectic, but it worked out in the end.

There were a few times when Fedex returned the tickets, when people decided not to go. This was usually due to problems getting transportation or rooms. I requested, and received, eight tickets for family and friends, plus two for my father, who called and asked if I could get him tickets. His second wife had family in San Francisco and they would stay with them. My Dad was wheelchair-bound and I could get him tickets in a special section for wheelchairs.

Thursday afternoon, Chris, the boys and I flew to Miami for the Grand Opening of Christine's. There were no direct flights to Ft. Myers in those days. Tampa and Miami were the closest big airports. We arrived on Marco late Thursday, and the Grand Opening the following night was a great success. Chas, John and our chef, Tom Leonard, did a great job. Celebrities included the late Ken Venturi, who lived in Southwest Florida, plus many local politicians and VIP's from Naples and Marco Island. It did not include either Mr. DeBartolo or Eddie, both of whom begged off after the 49ers got into the Super Bowl, due to the additional workload that entailed.

We returned to Youngstown on Sunday, and it was a short week for everyone. On Thursday, all five of us were on another airplane, headed to San Francisco and the Super Bowl. The Rooney family, owners of the Pittsburgh Steelers, were on the same plane. We stayed at the Amfac near the airport again, where the team would be housed under heavy security. The hotel had gone all out – there was a huge Super Bowl cake in the lobby, surrounded by stanchions, and there were 49ers pennants and signs everywhere.

There was palpable excitement in the whole area. My brother John came in from Florida, along with some friends from Chicago. Friday and Saturday was more sightseeing, including the San Francisco Zoo. The city was taken over by 49ers fans and Miami Dolphins fans, and evidence of each party's allegiances were evident everywhere we went.

On Friday night, the 49ers hosted all the team owners at a private dinner. Chris and I sat with the Sullivan family, owners of the New England Patriots. The Sullivan's had bid against Eddie, Jr. to buy the rights to the Michael Jackson concert tour and had won the war. They told me they wished they hadn't won, because it had cost them tens of millions of dollars they never recovered. They were nice people and we enjoyed their company.

We woke up on Super Bowl Sunday to dense fog blanketing the Bay area. The fog hung longer than normal around Stanford Stadium and threatened to affect ABC's lighting plans for the game. But, just before three p.m., the fog lifted, and the TV coverage was unaffected.

The Forty Niners were favored by 3.5 points, but pregame hype mostly centered around Dolphin Quarterback Dan Marino, who had set almost every possible single season passing record including most completions in a season, most games with over 300 yards (9), most games over 400 yards (4), most games with at least 4 touchdown passes (6) and 4 consecutive games with at least 4 touchdown passes.

He had thrown for a record 5,084 yards in 1984 and threw 48 touchdown passes, shattering the previous record of 36. He had such a quick release that he had been sacked only 13 times in the 16-game regular season and none in the two post season games. The Dolphins had scored 76 points in their playoff game wins over Seattle and Pittsburgh.

But in the hours leading up to the big game, we had a bit of hilarity. The hotel's pastry chef had baked a beautiful giant cake in the shape of a football field, 5 or 6 feet long, with 22 little football players on the cake. It was a thing of beauty and was blocked off by ropes so nobody got too close and everyone could see it. Late on Saturday afternoon, I was walking through the lobby and saw the hotel's general manager dragging my middle son, Chip, across the lobby.

I went up to him and asked what the problem was. He said he was looking for "the boy's father." When I told him I was the father, he quickly let Chip go, because he knew who I was. Apparently, Chip had gone under the ropes and ran his finger through the icing the length of the field. I suppressed the urge to laugh as I told him I would pay for the "repairs" and took Chip by the hand. I had him apologize to the crestfallen general manager.

The next morning, I brought my family down to the casual restaurant for breakfast. There were no tables available so we sat at the counter. The place was packed. Mr. DeBartolo and Bill Walsh were sitting right behind us at a table and the same hotel manager was behind the counter helping get everyone served. He gave us water and we ordered.

The day before, Chip bought some magic tricks at a store down on Fisherman's Wharf. Unbeknownst to Chris and me, he had brought some of them with him. While we were talking to Mr. D and Coach Walsh, Chip slipped a 'fly in the ice cube" into Chris' water glass. When we turned around, Chris went to take a sip of water, when Chip said, innocently, "Mom, what's in your water?"

Chris looked at it and gave out a loud shriek and the general manager ran over, saw the bug in the glass and quickly took it away, but the damage was done. Chip said, "No no, it's a trick!" and the entire restaurant was laughing, even Mr. DeBartolo. The furious manager couldn't do anything but laugh himself as he picked up the plastic ice cube and gave it back to Chip. But, I think deep down inside he probably wanted to kill the brat. I apologized again. I'm sure when we left the next day, the poor man probably took a well-earned vacation.

The Super Bowl started normally. The 49ers received and after a few first downs punted to Miami, who took over on their 36-yard line. Marino marched his team down the field with pinpoint passing, reaching the San Francisco 23-yard line. But a third down tackle by 49er cornerback, Eric Wright, forced the Dolphins to settle for a field goal and a 3-0 lead.

San Francisco stormed right back with a 78-yard drive in eight plays, the final a 33-yard touchdown pass from Montana to running back Carl Monroe. The 49ers led 7-3, but it didn't last long. Dolphin coach Don Shula went to a no-huddle offense to keep the 49er run defense on the field, and Marino again dissected the 49er defense, finishing with a two-yard pass to his tight end to regain the lead at 10-7 as the first quarter ended.

Bill Walsh was scratching his head and talking to his defensive coaches. The Forty Niners failed to move on the next drive and punted back to the Dolphins, and Walsh made his move. He decided to put his best pass rushers in on first down and went to a dime defense. Miami tried to run against the defense, but was unable to do so, and safety Dwight Hicks broke up two straight Marino passes, forcing Miami to punt from their own 10. The Niners took over on the Dolphins 47-yard line.

A Montana scramble went for 19 yards, and then Joe tossed a 16-yard pass to Dwight Clark to the 12. Wendell Tyler ran for 4 and then Montana tossed an eight-yarder to Roger Craig and the Niners were back in front, 14-10. The 49er defense again shut down the Dolphins, who punted the ball away. 49er returner Dana McLemore returned the ball to the 49er 45-yard line, and the offense again took over.

Two running plays gained 15 yards and two Montana passes to tight end Russ Francis moved the ball to the Miami 11. Craig ran for five yards and then Montana saw a gaping hole in the middle of the Dolphins defense and nearly walked the six yards for the touchdown. San Francisco now led 21-10.

Again, San Francisco's defense shut down the Miami offense and, after another Miami punt, the Niners started on their own 48. This drive took a bit longer and was aided by a questionable call by an official on a fumble ruled an incomplete pass, but it ended with Craig's two-yard run and the lead was now 28-10 with 2:05 left in the half.

Miami answered with a good drive that stalled on the 49er 12-yard line and settled for another field goal with 12 seconds left in the half. A pooch kick was then muffed by San Francisco lineman Guy McIntyre and Miami got another field goal as time expired. The score was 28-16 and Miami had suddenly taken over the momentum. And they would receive the second half kickoff. Marino and company were back in business.

A fired-up Miami team came out for the second half, but the momentum switch didn't last. A Miami run attempt lost a yard and then Marino threw an incompletion. On third and 11, 49er Dwaine Board smothered Marino for a nine-yard sack and the Dolphins punted. The 49ers drove 43 yards, and Ray Wersching kicked a field goal to up the score to 31-16. The 49ers again kicked off and the Dolphins took over. But, Marino was quickly sacked on consecutive downs - by Manu Tuiasosopo, and then on the next play, by Board again. The Dolphins had run out of tricks and out of luck. They punted again.

San Francisco started on its own 30-yard line and Montana went back to work. A 40-yard pass to Tyler was followed by a 14 yarder to Russ Francis. Three plays later, a Montana to Craig pass for 16 yards ended the scoring for the day. It was Craig's third touchdown on the day and the score was 38-16 with 22 minutes left in the game. Marino and the Dolphins had no chance. With the running game abandoned, Marino was forced to run for his life, was sacked once more and threw 2 interceptions. San Francisco was content to work the clock. The game ended 38-16.

The celebrations started, and we learned from our Detroit experience. There were two post game parties scheduled – one at the Velvet Turtle for VIP's, determined by the DeBartolos, and the other about five miles away for many of the other out-of-towners and players' families.

Eddie, Jr., the coaches and players were shuttled between both parties so that all the fans could get autographs.

We were at the Velvet Turtle with my father and his wife. My dad, a huge sports fan, was marveling at all the celebrities at the party. Eddie, Jr. came over to our table and spoke to my dad for a good five minutes. Mr. DeBartolo also came over and met my father. Bill Walsh sat down and spent another five minutes visiting with my dad and the rest of us. My dad wanted to meet OJ, who was a few tables away, so I asked him to stop over when he had a minute and he nodded. But shortly after, OJ left without stopping. Maybe it was in retaliation over the loan incident a year before.

There were other celebrations when we got back to Youngs-town. The whole area again embraced the DeBartolo family as hometown heroes, and the DeBartolos would prove they would contin-ue to give back. It was a great time to be working for the corporation.

I have mentioned this was before the days of cell phones, but there was an exception. In mid-January, George Jones and I each re-ceived a cellular mobile telephone from Hidetake Sho, the president of Diamond Vision, Inc. The letter accompanying the phones asked that we advise them in the future with our comments about the phones. I guess we were kind of a test case. The phones were large, clunky things that needed to be mounted in our cars. I had mine installed in the company car I drove.

I expected to put the phone to good use. In April, the Erie Blades trial was coming up. Erie was the city where the Penguins had the ill-fated one-year minor league affiliation. Our partner, John Caruso, a doctor, refused to pay his share of the losses. He owed the Penguins $130,000. I made several round-trips to Erie that spring.

This would be a boring jury trial with a lot of legalese. Caruso and his main witness (with whom I worked on some of the Blades issues) both lied through their teeth. The witness, the Blades business manager, accused me of threatening him after his testimony, and he complained to the court. That woke up the jury and the judge put me on the stand to respond to the charges. I denied I had threatened him, but admitted I had spoken to him. The judge asked what I had told him.

"I told him he should go to confession tonight," I said.

The jury and courtroom laughed and the judge chastised me, but he was trying not to laugh. The jury found in our favor, but refused to allow us to "pierce the corporate veil." We had tried to get through Caruso's corporation, to him personally, but we failed. He bankrupted his corporation and we were out $130,000, plus legal fees, but we did get our day in court.

It was April and the Penguins, even with Mario Lemieux, had completed another mediocre season. Despite Lemieux scoring 43 goals and 100 points in 73 games, and winning the Calder Memorial Trophy as the league's Rookie of the Year, the Penguins still finished last in the Patrick Division, although they did improve by 15 points over the previous year.

He was a great player, but a great player needs help, and it was evident we still needed to get that help. Attendance however, increased by 46 percent over the prior year, to 10,018 per game, but the Penguins still lost $2.5 million. The franchise was improving, but would it be fast enough for Mr. DeBartolo? That question was yet to be answered.

The Penguins neighbor, the Pittsburgh Spirit had also had a meltdown season, finishing 19-29, a surprise considering the successes they had the three previous years. It was their worst season since 1978-

79, their first season in the Major Indoor Soccer League. Even worse, attendance dropped by six percent, even with deep discounts for children, who often comprised most fans in the stands.

The Spirit losses for the season were $1.7 million, and Mr. DeBartolo's patience had worn thin. The losing seasons by both teams irked him and he called in the executives for both teams. Mr. DeBartolo told them he was "fed up" with losing, both on the fields (or ice) and on the balance sheet. He refused to hear any excuses and demanded the group find a way to improve the teams' performances and reduce the losses, or he would put the teams up for sale. All the Pittsburgh executives left the conference room knowing their jobs were now in serious jeopardy.

One area where the executives felt the losses could be cut was the City of Pittsburgh's 10 percent amusement tax on gross ticket sales. This amounted to between $600,000 to $700,000 a year for the teams. DeBartolo instructed Paul Martha to approach the city to get relief from the exorbitant tax.

Martha met with the city the third week of April and more meetings were scheduled when the news hit the Pittsburgh Post-Gazette. Martha revealed DeBartolo had been approached by a few groups, including some that would buy either or both teams and move them to another city. DeBartolo was also upset because the City had sued him to fulfill the last two years of the Maulers lease, even though the team had folded.

I received a call on Saturday, April 20 from Ed Bouchette, the reporter who wrote the article about the possibility of a sale of one or both teams. Bouchette asked for my comments. I had not been involved in any sales with Mr. DeBartolo and I told him so, but I agreed the lawsuit had bothered DeBartolo and had brought things to a head.

Bouchette said he heard that William Ballard, son of the Toronto Maple Leaf owner, had contacted DeBartolo and was interested in buying the Penguins and moving them to Hamilton, Ontario. I had been traveling and had no discussion with Mr. DeBartolo prior to that call. My comment was "as far as I know, Mr. DeBartolo has not actively put the Penguins up for sale."

In early May, I was in Columbus for the Ohio Racing Commission meeting. I was advised by Gus Rigas, DeBartolo's vice president of construction, the build-out of the barns at Thistledown had been completed, and we had filed an application with the Racing Board for approval to begin receiving the capital improvement tax reduction. The meeting was on a Tuesday and our application was on the agenda. It was a multimillion-dollar project and, even though I hadn't been to Cleveland in weeks, I was assured by our people it was complete.

When the application was brought up by the Racing Commission, the commission chairman asked the State Auditor if the Auditors' office agreed with the application. The Auditor's office was represented by John Blum, the Deputy Auditor, with whom I established a relationship over the last year. The Auditor, Tom Ferguson, had a fundraising golf tournament every spring and we had supported the event.

Blum stood and told the committee "I am requesting that this matter be shelved for further review by the Auditor's office. We have reason to believe that this application may have been fraudulently submitted."

The commission chairman agreed and Blum marched out of the meeting. I was in shock, but I quickly gathered my gear and chased Blum down. My "friend" said, "You lied to me! The construction is still going on." With that, he walked away.

My work in Columbus completed for the day, I got in my car and drove straight to Thistledown in Cleveland, about a two-hour drive. I arrived in the afternoon with intent to go over to the barn area. I didn't need to. From the grandstand, I could see piles of dirt and heavy equipment working the area. The job wasn't completed. It was a non-racing day. I headed back to Youngstown and put a call into Mr. DeBartolo from my new Mitsubishi cell phone, but he was unavailable.

When I got to the office, I went straight to Rigas' office and confronted him for telling me the job was complete. He listened to me and told me that, as far as he was concerned, the job was substantially done. When I told him it had to be complete, he said, "Get the f*** out of my office. I don't report to you."

Ready for some backlash, I headed over to Mr. D's office. He listened to my account and then told Edy to have Rigas come right over. Mr. D asked how much we were going to lose and I was ready. "About $70,000," I answered.

When Rigas walked into the room, Mr. DeBartolo let him have it. "You also told me that the job was done," he said. "And you do report to me."

Rigas, a blowhard and a bully, saw where this was going and kept his mouth shut. DeBartolo then told him that, from now on, when I would ask him for the status on a job, he would provide me with complete details, in writing, with a copy to Mr. DeBartolo, Eddie, Jr. and Denise. If Mr. DeBartolo heard or sensed Rigas wasn't being fully cooperative and honest, he would be replaced. He told him to get the job finished by the weekend. "Now, get out of here," he finished.

He turned to me, “I’m sorry that this happened to you. Put in another application for the June meeting.” I left his office.

I called John Blum and apologized for not being fully aware of the job. We talked about how this could be avoided in the future. We agreed that, before I submitted the application, I would contact Blum’s office so they could do what they needed to do to approve the job in front of the racing commission. Blum agreed it was an honest mistake and apologized for his choice of words in the commission meeting. After that day, we never had another problem with these applications. But, I never believed Rigas after that date. I always double-checked the job myself before applying.

For the last few years, EJD expressed some interest in building a new thoroughbred racetrack in Oklahoma. He was approached by individuals and companies about the prospect and, on a few occasions, I met with people around Oklahoma City and Ardmore, Oklahoma.

In late May, I flew to Oklahoma, at Mr. DeBartolo’s direction, to look at a plot of land near the zoo in Oklahoma City. On June 1, The Oklahoman, OKC’s main newspaper, featured an article about the potential project. I was quoted throughout the article about our interest in Oklahoma City, and the zoo property , and it was well received. We garnered a lot of support throughout Oklahoma City. There would be a great deal of work to do, but eventually we would open a track in Oklahoma.

In mid-June, I could no longer say, “as far as I know, Mr. DeBartolo has not actively put the Penguins up for sale.” Mr. DeBartolo sent me to Toronto to talk to Bill Ballard about his interest in the Penguins. Ballard did indeed intend to move the team to Hamilton, Ontario.

I met Ballard at his office in Toronto and we later had dinner at House of Chan, a popular steakhouse in Toronto. My presence in Toronto was the worst kept secret in town. The NHL meetings and draft were going on there at the same time and, apparently, I was spotted at the airport by one of the Penguins people. A local gossip columnist in Toronto named George Anthony approached our table at the restaurant and asked Ballard who his guest was.

Ballard told him my name was "Tom" and Anthony told him he knew who I was. I refused to answer any of his questions, but the next day he reported in his column the meeting took place, and the cat was out of the bag. It hit the national news the Penguins might be sold and moved to Hamilton.

With that information out, the National Hockey League (NHL) quickly took note. League President John Ziegler contacted Mr. DeBartolo and asked for a meeting in Youngstown. Ziegler was accompanied by an NHL attorney and William Wirtz, the influential owner of the Chicago Blackhawks. Wirtz was also Chairman of the NHL Board of Governors, and he was there representing the other owners in the league.

The meeting started friendly enough with Mr. DeBartolo telling the group he was tired of losing money in Pittsburgh and he was indeed interested in selling the team. We passed out to our "guests" a spreadsheet showing the attendances over the last seven years and a summary of our losses by year. Wirtz, known as a frugal owner, studied the spreadsheet and told Mr. DeBartolo the statement was a tribute to the Penguins front office. "If I had attendances like this, my losses would be three times what yours are," he said.

Ziegler, painfully aware of the tenuous history of the Penguins (the League was actually the owner for a time in the mid-70's and Equibank nearly owned the team later in the decade), was reluctant to let a wealthy owner off the hook, without the blessing of the League. There was also the matter of a major U.S. city losing a sports team. Finally, Hamilton was extremely close to two existing NHL franchises, in Buffalo and Toronto, and both owners apparently had expressed concern to the League. So, Ziegler outlined what Mr. DeBartolo needed to do if he sold the team; and that was to get the approval of the other owners to sell the team first, and then convince them the new owner wouldn't encroach upon the territories of other franchises. It was clear Hamilton would be a hard sell, at best.

Mr. DeBartolo, perhaps reliving in his mind the White Sox fiasco, once again had to bow down to others to do what he wanted to do. Having said that, I was never sure he wanted to sell the team. It was in the back of my mind that perhaps this was a ploy to get the tax relief from the city of Pittsburgh, but I never heard that from him. I did know that the financial losses were grating on him and the lack of success on the ice was an embarrassment to him.

Mr. DeBartolo told his guests he might just sell the team without the owners' approval. Ziegler then advised him that, if he did go that route, "he would have to find teams to play, because the NHL would remove the Penguins from the schedule." It sounds like the meeting was contentious, but it really it was quite cordial. Mr. DeBartolo thanked the men for visiting, and that was pretty much the end of that saga in Penguin history.

While that was going on, Equibank in Pittsburgh subpoenaed me. They were investigating Tony Liberati, who had been with the bank when DeBartolo took over the Penguins in late 1977. The matter of De-

Bartolo assuming Equibank loans was a point of contention that was settled before Mr. DeBartolo took over the team.

There were two meetings with Liberati, one in which I was present, and it was when the subject of the loans was brought up. Mr. DeBartolo initially told Liberati he would not assume the loans as part of his agreement to bail out the team. The other, which included Liberati, DeBartolo and Cal Harvey, attorney for the Penguins and DeBartolo, had been adjoined to a separate room and I was not present.

When that meeting ended, Liberati left and DeBartolo told me he had agreed to assume the larger loan, which had funded Penguin operations, but not the smaller loan, which was used to build the super boxes in the arena and add to the grandstand seating. DeBartolo felt that, since he didn't own the arena, he shouldn't have to pay for the additions to the building. That loan, as I recall, was around $700,000.

Every year after we took over the team, I got a confirmation letter from the auditors who examined Equibank's books, and each time they asked me, as the Treasurer of the Penguins, to confirm that we owed the loans. Both loans were always on the confirmation and, every year I would agree to the larger loan, but state we were not responsible for the super box loan, and I never heard anything from them, or Equibank, about my clarification. For several months, Equibank had been trying to depose me, but we wouldn't agree to it. Finally, they prevailed and Cal Harvey told me I would have to testify.

Equibank wanted me to say Liberati was eventually hired by DeBartolo in repayment for forgiving the loan, and they badgered me throughout the deposition, but they were out of luck. Although I was in nearly all the discussions about the Penguin takeover, the one I was not in was the one that resulted in the agreement we would not assume the smaller loan. So, all they got from me was hearsay. I believe they dropped the action against Tony.

Between San Francisco, Louisiana Downs, Oklahoma racing, Balmoral Park in Crete, Illinois, Thistledown and the hotels in Cleveland, the Pittsburgh operations, the condominium project in Marco Island, having meetings with interested parties throughout the US, going to League meetings and Racing Board meetings, along with new projects, I found I was traveling approximately 50 percent of the year. The DeBartolo Hotel operations were also expanding rapidly, with the additions of a luxury Maxim's Hotel in Palm Springs, California, and equally luxurious Mayfair House Hotel in posh Coconut Grove, Florida, and a new Holiday Inn Crowne Plaza in Orlando.

It was my job to oversee the financials of those operations, which added more to my travel. We had a management company in Palm Springs and that property didn't last long before we sold it, but the Mayfair House had a new DeBartolo employee named Jack Lambert that oversaw the construction and operation of that property. That hotel also experienced large losses and I had to work closely with Lambert.

It also became evident the entire hotel staff at the Marco operation wasn't doing the job, and we ended up cleaning house and bringing in a new management team of DeBartolo people. But that operation was a financial drag, as well. Liberati hired a hotel consulting firm, headquartered in Pittsburgh to review the new operations to see if changes needed to be made. The representative (Herb deMarrais) would also look at the way my family business was being run, as well.

Rossetti Enterprises, Inc. had finished its first full year with the restaurant open, and my worst-case scenario had become reality. The "season" we expected (December through April) never materialized. Instead, it only lasted about six weeks from Valentine's Day through Easter. We now learned Marco Island was different than the rest of Southwest Florida, which experienced the four- to five-month season.

We were expecting a strong 21-week season and only got six weeks. Mr. DeBartolo asked how we were doing every week or two, so he knew we were in financial trouble. In February, he offered to reduce the rent by 50 percent and I took him up on it. But, even with that we were experiencing cash flow problems.

To make matters worse, the hotel decided to offer free breakfast for each guest daily. We were already having difficulty getting people to work that early in the day and the hotel only paid us $5 per person. We also learned the Stakich and Hawkins families regularly referred our hotel guests to competing restaurants in the area, mainly a restaurant called O'Shea's just a mile down the street from us.

When I learned this and confronted Stakich, he just laughed. It was obvious he was just counting the days when he would get the food and beverage operations back from us. But he miscalculated Mr. DeBartolo. When I told him what was going on, he said "Get rid of all of them!" Within three days, they were all terminated and a new team was in place.

Mr. DeBartolo had already cut our rent in half and he now told me he would subsidize our losses. I told him I would let him know about the subsidy in the future. Later that day, Mr. DeBartolo was talking to George Jones from Thistledown and mentioned that I was having problems in Marco Island. Jones, a good friend of mine, had known about the venture and was up to date with the problems I was having.

In that phone call, Mr. DeBartolo told Jones my business venture would not run out of money. "He has a million-dollar line of credit with me," DeBartolo told Jones, who related the story to me the next day. So, when deMarrais showed up on Marco Island, he spent some time with my brother Chas and became aware of the problems we were having.

In a letter to Tony Liberati on March 7 he stated, "The entrepreneur spirit of the Rossetti Brothers is something you don't find too often and I think it is in the best interest of the DeBartolo Corporation to give them some support instead of discontinuing their services." Obviously, Mr. DeBartolo agreed.

Our Cleveland hotels were now being run by a management company out of Dallas, Pratt Hotel Corporation. These properties never made any appreciable profits, even in their best years, and manageable losses were the norm. In 1982, while I was in Louisiana Downs for the lawsuit, this management team was brought in to run the Cleveland operations. Rather than improving the financial picture, the losses increased and by the end of 1984, we lost just under $2 million on those four hotels. I was constantly in disputes with Pratt, and some of our people in Youngstown, and was lobbying to get rid of Pratt. That battle raged, on and off, for four years. Lambert would eventually help me get rid of Pratt.

In June, Edward J. DeBartolo, Jr. flew Chris and I out to San Francisco for the Super Bowl ring ceremony and I received my second ring. It was another great honor for us, as Chris also got a ring that was given to the spouses of the ring recipients.

That euphoria didn't last very long. Upon my return from San Francisco, I met with the Pratt people in Cleveland. They had recommended we upgrade the North Randall Holiday Inn to present Holiday Inn standards and we agreed. They contracted with a Holiday Inn recommended subcontractor from Memphis, who used their own people from Memphis to do the work, and they were not union.

This was in Cleveland in a completely union environment, both at the hotel and at Thistledown across the street. The local Painters Union threatened to strike and picket the hotel. The call from the union to our office came to Mr. DeBartolo, who referred it to me.

The head of the union, a man named Battaglia, threatened to picket while Thistledown hosted Ohio's biggest thoroughbred race, the $500,000 Ohio Derby. Many of the dignitaries attending the race would be at the hotel. He threatened the picket would cover all doors at the hotel and that all the unions at the hotel would join the Painters Union.

He also said, if we didn't use union labor, the strike would spread to Thistledown and could jeopardize the race. When I advised him we had nothing to do with the project since it was being done under the auspices of the Holiday Inn Corporation, he bristled.

"I'll come down there and club you over the head with a bat," he threatened.

I hung up on him and called Mr. DeBartolo and reported the threat. Moments later, Mr. D and I had George Jones on the phone and Jones took over. He called in his union representatives at the track, explained the situation emphasizing we were not involved in the renovation, and the track representatives agreed they would not strike the track in sympathy.

Then, DeBartolo lawyers moved quickly. They got an injunction that limited the picketing to only one door, and we chose to use the employee door not available to the public. Finally, George put in a call to Milton "Mashie" Rockman, who was involved with the Teamsters Union in Cleveland, and he agreed to deal with Battaglia. Reportedly,

Rockman referred to Battaglia as "old line." He was removed from his position, the strike was called off, the renovation continued and the Ohio Derby went off without a hitch.

While I was putting out fires all over the place, I got a confidence boost from an unlikely source. Tony Liberati was reviewing my job performance and, on July 25, he gave his review to Mr. DeBartolo. A month later, Mr. DeBartolo gave me a copy of it, and I was surprised.

Liberati concluded my job performance was "Distinguished," the highest rating available. Of eight categories, he gave me a top rating in six, with second highest in the other two, although he blamed those ratings on "lack of direction" from DeBartolo top management.

Summer was over and the NFL season was beginning. There was a lot of excitement and expectations for a 49ers Super Bowl repeat. The Niners had drafted a relative unknown from Mississippi Valley State in the first round by the name of Jerry Rice, and many in the League thought San Francisco had wasted a first rounder, but Bill Walsh knew better. Rice would go on to win Rookie of The Year honors and set the table for his sensational career.

Unfortunately, the 49ers developed a penchant for losing games in the fourth quarter that cost them in losses to Minnesota, New Orleans and Chicago, and at the end of October found themselves with a 4-4 record. Joe Montana battled nagging injuries all season, but the team rallied down the stretch, winning five of the last six games to finish 10-6, good for second place in the NFC West. Hopes for a Super Bowl repeat ended quickly in New York on December 29 with a 17-3 loss to the Giants.

In Pittsburgh, the Penguins were playing much better with Mario Lemieux scoring at a record pace. The team was 16-18-4 at the end of the year and hopes were strong the team would end the playoff drought. Attendance and excitement was up as the year ended. The Spirit was also competitive, but attendances and revenues were on the decline and there was little enthusiasm. It would turn out to be the last season for the team, but that decision was still a few months away.

CHAPTER FIFTEEN

1986-A YEAR OF TRANSITION

With the 49ers out of the playoffs, I finally had a legitimate "slow time." This meant there would be slightly less travel for a few months. Thistledown and Louisiana Downs didn't race in the dead of winter. For my staff, it was a busier time because they had to close out the books for all the entities and give the results to DeBartolo's CPA firm to be included as part of the consolidated financial statements and tax returns. Part of my job was to review their work before it got to the CPAs. We also used the first quarter of the year to do our budgets for some of those entities.

Since I was in town more in the winter, I spent more Saturdays in the office, and this was when the corporation had the weekly executive meetings. I often skipped the meetings because they largely related to the development and mall management arm of the company, but I would also occasionally go just to keep tabs on what was going on in general.

1986 saw a significant inflation uptick and lenders were increasing interest rates. DeBartolo Corporation, which was heavily leveraged on the mall side, would certainly be affected, and again EJD installed a cost-cutting procedure. This was not unusual as we went through this every few years. In addition, Mr. DeBartolo wanted each officer in the corporation to have a successor in line in the event something happened to each of us. I always had Marty Hamer, my manager of sports and diversified operations, as my man in charge when I was out of town.

I had a great staff of professionals, both in town and in the field. Marty was the first employee that joined me in 1974 and was experienced with the Pittsburgh operations, all the racetracks, the hotels and the family amusement centers. Chris Bilski had been with me for seven years and specialized in the hotels and family amusement centers, while Ed Nosek handled a lot of the day and day accounting on the racetracks.

All the clerical people in the department were diversified to the extent they could jump in and cover duties for each other, if the need arose. The problem was there were times when Mr. DeBartolo and Eddie, Jr. would have me do things for them "nobody else was supposed to know." And, when I was gone and they needed answers on those issues, they used to blow up when nobody but me knew about, or had access to, the information on those projects.

In my discussions with Marty, he made it clear that he didn't want the responsibility, or the travel, my job required. He was a good manager, but would not be my successor. Chris Bilski probably could have handled the job, but was only experienced in certain areas and didn't have any experience in the sports side of the Company. Nosek didn't have the experience.

To fulfill Mr. DeBartolo's edict, I had to go outside of the department. I tabbed Jerry Wiemann, a member of the Internal Audit team, who worked with me before. I brought him on as regional controller of the Southwest Tracks -- Louisiana Downs and the upcoming Remington Park -- initially to learn the racing business. The plan was to then introduce him to the rest of the areas under my management, including the sensitive ones. I reviewed this plan with the DeBartolos and they agreed to it. Jerry wouldn't be ready for a while, but he was on schedule to eventually take over for me, when the time arose.

The winter and spring of 1986 also saw the end of the seasons for the Penguins and Spirit. The Penguins, who had high hopes for making the playoffs in February fell apart in March (3-9-1) and April (1-3-0) and missed the playoffs by two points. The crushing finish even overshadowed a tremendous year for Lemieux, who had 48 goals and 93 assists for 141 points, second-highest scorer in the league. The Spirit finished 23-25, missing out on the playoffs by losing the last game of the season to the Baltimore Blast.

The Cleveland Hotels were still losing money at an alarming rate. The Pratt organization, whom Tony Liberati brought in to improve the operations and bottom line, and sell the hotels, was failing miserably. The losses were approaching $2 million per year and, despite our remodels, there were no buyers. Even in the summer time, when they had always been profitable, we were losing money, and the dysfunction in the Pratt organization was obvious. The only good thing they did was get us a good on-site regional manager, Mike Dowling. At mid-summer, I had lunch with Dowling, and his frustration was rivaling my own. I asked him if he would be interested in staying on if we terminated Pratt, and he readily agreed.

On July 8, I had a major meeting with Mr. DeBartolo and we covered, in depth, 11 different issues, including Pratt. I told Mr. DeBartolo I was totally disgusted with Pratt in Cleveland, and he agreed and told me he advised Liberati to get rid of Pratt. He told me to follow-up with Liberati. He also gave me approval to hire Dowling and get the hotels back on track.

We also discussed Balmoral Park racetrack. Mr. DeBartolo acquired the track in the early 70s, right about the time I started with the company. Balmoral was a harness track about an hour south of Chicago and, along with the actual track, Balmoral was awarded a month of thoroughbred dates at Sportsman's Park in the city of Chicago. The thoroughbred dates were immensely profitable throughout the 70s and, combined with the harness track's losses kept Balmoral at close to a breakeven.

In the early 80s, the Racing Board changed the way dates were awarded, and Balmoral could still get the thoroughbred dates, but only at its own track. That meant we needed to install a thoroughbred racing surface, which we did. The thoroughbred dates were a flop because the track turns were too tight for thoroughbreds, and Balmoral reverted to a harness track and was losing money every year. The best we could do was run the dates to reduce the losses the overhead caused. But, there was so much competition for horse racing in the Chicago area we would never be profitable, due primarily to our location. We agreed Mr. DeBartolo would think about the possibility of selling Balmoral.

Liberati hadn't done anything about Pratt, so in August I advised Pratt formally we were terminating the management contract as of October 31. I installed Dowling to oversee the properties. We took over on November 1, 1986, and we implemented a multi-point program designed to maximize revenue, reduce payrolls, tighten purchasing and bring food and beverage costs into line. A few months later, we sold the Sea World Sheraton and our 1987 losses were reduced to $418,000 (from nearly $2 million). Revenues were up 13 percent and operating expenses were reduced by eight percent. Looking back, I considered that turnaround, and ultimate sale of the hotels, to be one of the more impressive accomplishments in my DeBartolo tenure.

That summer, we also announced the Pittsburgh Spirit operation would be suspended. A few groups came to us with proposals to buy and operate the team, staying in the Civic Arena, but none of them ever materialized. In that meeting, Mr. DeBartolo agreed to a severance package for Chris Wright, who was the General Manager of the team.

We operated the team for five seasons and never made any money. Our only option was to raise ticket prices to cover player salaries, but that would have priced it out of reach for many families, whose children were the driving force to go to the games. The sad fact of the Spirit was that soccer in the United States had not yet garnered the interest of the American public enough to make the professional game popular enough to be profitable.

Down in Florida, Rossetti Enterprises had turned the corner. With more efficient management at the hotel, our business began to flourish. In that July 8 meeting with Mr. DeBartolo, I advised him I didn't think we would need his offered loss subsidy.

"In fact," I told him, "this is for you." And I handed him a check for $10,000 for the first principal payment on my $100,000 loan. He objected, saying it wasn't necessary.

"It is for me, "I replied. I also told him my mother was moving to Florida to be near her family and work in the family business.

We covered other things in that meeting, but those were the highlights. It was one of the most memorable meetings I ever had with the man that I called "Boss."

Thistledown was having a good year. The construction was on schedule and the tax abatement program was contributing to the best bottom line we had in my tenure. George Jones was the best track general manager I ever worked with, and we were having fun together. George and I would talk on the phone every day I was in the office. He handled the unions phenomenally, had a great rapport with the horsemen, and patrons were happy about the changes taking place. Most importantly, Mr. DeBartolo liked him and was very satisfied with how Thistledown was doing, maybe for the first time since I arrived in 1973.

Louisiana Downs was also having a great year. The track was making tens of millions of dollars a year and was one of the greatest success stories in racing. After the dreadful early days in the 70s, Mr. DeBartolo had been able to convince the Racing Board to give Louisiana Downs the more lucrative summer dates. Once they got those dates, they never gave them back. Everyone was making money - the State, the horsemen and the track.

In late summer, Mr. DeBartolo sent me a memo advising he agreed to sell Balmoral Park to Dick Duchossois for $6 million. He wanted to meet with me later in the day, in his office, to discuss the sale. Duchossois was one of the owners of Arlington Park, a successful race track in Elmhurst, a suburb of Chicago.

When I got to Mr. D's office, and he told me what the sale included, I told him bluntly he left some money on the table. I explained Balmoral had a receivable from the State of Illinois in the form of a tax credit of over $400,000, which wasn't reflected on the books. I told him he should have asked for more.

Senior looked at me and said, "See if you can get more, if you are so smart." For me to suggest he may have been trumped in a negotiation was an insult of the highest nature, as Mr. DeBartolo was known as one of the shrewdest negotiators around.

So, I called Duchossois and told him I would be working on the details of the sale with him. Duchossois said there wasn't much to work on since he and Mr. D "already had a deal." I told him I didn't agree with that, but we needed to talk about the State tax credit, which Mr.

DeBartolo wasn't aware of when he talked with Duchossois. There was a silence on the line.

"We have a deal. It is already in the papers," he replied. I told him the deal wasn't finalized and he replied he would get back to me "in a couple of days."

Apparently, the prospect of a sale had been leaked to the newspapers in Chicago, probably by Duchossois, because the next day, Mr. DeBartolo's secretary forwarded a call to me that had come in for Mr. DeBartolo, who was out of town.

The caller was George Steinbrenner, the colorful owner of the New York Yankees. Steinbrenner wanted to know if the Balmoral deal with Duchossois was for real.

"We are in negotiations," I told him. He then explained he was looking for a business for his son-in-law, Steve Swindal.

Steinbrenner said, "Balmoral would be perfect for him." I told George we were very near to a deal with Duchossois, but he was welcome to make a bid. George said he would pay $8 million for the track. I told him I would take the offer to Mr. DeBartolo when he got back in town.

The next day, Duchossois called and said he would agree to pay the extra $400,000. I told him there was another bidder involved now. Again, he said he "had a deal" with Mr. DeBartolo and I answered it was never finalized. I met with Mr. DeBartolo the next morning and he agreed to let me continue negotiations for the track sale.

Over the next two days, I fielded competing offers from both parties, and in the end, Steinbrenner prevailed for $10,000,000, plus whatever operating expenses we would incur until his son-in-law could get licensed and approved by the Illinois Racing Board. I sat down with one of DeBartolo's in-house attorneys and gave him the name of Steinbrenner's attorney and the information on the sale and what would be included. A confirmation letter went out to Steinbrenner's attorney and earnest money was put into escrow. It was now in the lawyers' hands awaiting the approvals of the Racing Board.

Fall arrived and with it, the NFL season. The 49ers were opening on September 7 in Tampa Bay against the Buccaneers and former 49er Steve DeBerg. I flew down to Tampa for the game and surprised my brother, John, to whom I had sent tickets for him and several of our employees to see the game.

The 49ers scored early and late and romped 31-7. Joe Montana completed 32 of 46 passes for 356 yards and a touchdown, and his 49ers teammates roughed up DeBerg, intercepting seven of his passes. But, late in the game Joe had some back pain and he didn't practice the next week. The prognosis was "congenital spinal stenosis associated with acute rupture of the L5-S1 disc."

On September 15, he underwent surgery to widen his spinal canal and remove the ruptured disc, considered a very risky surgery at that time, and very possibly career ending. The 49ers put him on injured reserve and prepared to finish the season without Joe. They lost their first game without him to the Rams, on a last second field goal, and then bowled over the Saints, Dolphins (in Miami) and Colts, before losing to the Vikings in overtime. A tie with the Falcons, again in overtime, then a win over the Packers in Milwaukee and a loss in New Orleans to the Saints on November 2, had the team at 5-3-1.

On November 6, 1986, Edward J. DeBartolo, Jr. turned 40 years old. On that day, a Thursday, his wife Candy took out a full-page ad in USA TODAY. The headline read "Today, The No. 1 49er turns 40." Chris and I were invited to the party, in San Francisco, all expenses paid. We flew out of Pittsburgh, with several dozen others, were escorted to the new Airport Marriott in San Francisco and later, to the Hard Rock Café. The party was one of the most lavish events we had ever been to, with several rock bands, including Journey and Huey Lewis and the News. It was a fantastic event and experience.

To cap off Eddie's party, Joe Montana returned that weekend for the 49ers game against the Cardinals, and the emotion of the week-end carried over to the field with the 49ers winning 43-17. It was a re-markable recovery by Montana, who played nearly the entire game just over seven weeks after that possible "career ending" surgery. As we flew home the following day, I once again marveled at our good fortune in life.

In Pittsburgh, the Penguins opened the 1986-87 season with the goal of getting to the playoffs for the first time since 1981-82. The Pen guins got off to a great start winning their first seven games, the best start in team history. The team cooled off after that start, but had an 8-3 record in October and a 13-8-4 record at the end of November. But only two wins in December left them at 15-15-7. Lemieux injured his knee on December 20, and the team went 0-3-3 as the year ended.

As Christmas approached, I took my family to the Penguin Christmas Party at the Civic Arena. They had a neat party, where the players all brought their families and anyone could skate on the ice be-fore Santa came with Christmas gifts for all the children. The hockey players all loved Christmas and it was a fun event.

One of the Penguins rookies, Rob Brown, was at the party with his girlfriend, Alyssa Milano, the actress. My son Chip, who had a crush for Alyssa, decided he would skate near them and see if she would notice him. As Brown and Milano skated, Chip waited at the Penguins bench. As they approached, Chip hopped out of the bench area and promptly tripped over the threshold and fell flat, skidding across the ice. Without missing a beat, Brown skated over, helped a red-faced Chip to his feet, and said, "Don't worry, kid. I trip a lot, too." Brown was known for losing his balance on his slap shots and sliding across the ice. I'm not sure if Alyssa noticed Chip, but it was funny.

The Forty Niners finished the 1986 season with a record of 10-5-1, tops in the NFC West, and earned a trip to New York to play the Giants in the NFC Playoff on January 4, 1987. This would be a rematch of the December 1 game in San Francisco, when the Niners blew a 17-0 halftime lead, gave up 21 third-quarter points and lost 21-17.

It was a year of transitions. We got rid of the Spirit, fired our hotel management company in Cleveland, sold one of the Cleveland hotels, and got a new coach for the Penguins. We had a deal pending closing on the sale of Balmoral Park. After several years of dramatic growth, suddenly we were heading the other way. Watching the Penguins and their families skate, I wondered if maybe they would be the next to go.

CHAPTER SIXTEEN

1987-UPS AND DOWNS

The year started on an ominous note. The Forty Niners opened the NFC Championship game against the Giants with Joe Montana completing a 50-yard pass to rookie Jerry Rice for an apparent touchdown. However, Rice, running all alone, inexplicably fumbled the ball before crossing the goal line, without being touched. The Giants recovered in the end zone for a touchback and that was the extent of the 49ers highlights for the day.

The Giants defense then took over, holding the 49ers to nine first downs and 184 total net yards in a 49-3 blowout. The Giants intercepted three 49ers passes and forced a fumble. Late in the second quarter, Giant nose tackle Jim Burt blasted in on Montana, as he was throwing a pass. Montana's head bounced off the artificial turf as Lawrence Taylor intercepted the ball and took it 34 yards for a touchdown. Montana was immediately taken to a New York hospital, where he spent the night with a severe concussion. That's how the 49ers season ended.

The Penguins didn't make it to the playoffs, even though they had a better record than two of the teams that did. The Penguins ended up 30-38-12 for 72 points, four points behind the fourth-place Rangers in the Patrick Division of the Prince of Wales Conference. Two teams with worse records, Los Angeles and Toronto did get in, even with fewer points, because they were in the top four of their respective divisions.

The Penguins misfortune was being in a six-team division, while the other three divisions all had five teams in theirs. But, they didn't deserve to win. In January and February, they finished 8-15-3 and in too deep a hole to dig out. It cost Coach Bob Berry his job. On the positive side, however average attendance numbers rose to 14,965 in the 16,033-seat arena, with 26 sellouts. Both were franchise records. Clearly, the fans were embracing the enigmatic Lemieux. We needed to do our job to pay back the fans for their loyalty. On April 13, nine days after the regular season ended, Berry was fired.

January and February were active this year. I bounced around from Cleveland (twice) to Pittsburgh (three times), Miami (twice), Marco Island (twice) and Chicago (twice). The meetings were for budget and takeover plans for several of the DeBartolo properties. All told, I was out of the office 11 of February's 28 days, or more than 55 percent of the working month. The two Chicago trips related to the Balmoral sale. Closing was scheduled for February 16, now that Swindal had garnered Racing Board approval.

I flew into Chicago that afternoon, accompanied by Alden Chevlen, another of the DeBartolo in-house attorneys. We checked into our downtown hotel and then went over to our attorney's office. The Winston & Strawn firm was representing us. The closing would be at six p.m. CST in their office.

Swindal and Leonard Kleinman, who at the time was Steinbrenner's personal attorney, arrived on schedule and we began signing documents. It was time to wire transfer the money and I was looking over the prorations on the closing statement.

"Where is the operating expense reimbursement?" I asked our attorneys. That created a lot of paper shuffling going on by the attorneys. Two days before the closing, I calculated the amount we had incurred between the date our agreement with Steinbrenner was signed and the date of closing, and advised our attorney in Youngstown the amount was around $465,000. It was not reflected on any of the closing papers.

I asked the Winston & Strawn attorneys and they replied they were not advised of that part of the deal. Kleinman shook his head. "If it's not in the agreement, then we don't owe it." At that point in time, the DeBartolo team adjourned to another conference room and I showed the Winston & Strawn attorneys the memo I had given to our Youngstown attorney (it was not Chevlen), to forward to them.

They had never seen it, and it wasn't reflected in the documentation, although reference to it was included in the letter I sent to Steinbrenner accepting his ultimate winning bid. I called Mr. DeBartolo at home. It was about 10 p.m. his time and explained the mix-up to him. He asked how much was involved. I told him $465,000 and Kleinman said it wouldn't be paid. DeBartolo and I then talked about the ramifications and he decided that, if they won't pay, then we should walk away.

When we walked back into the main conference room, I told Kleinman and Swindal we were at an impasse and that we were prepared to walk away. Swindal got George Steinbrenner on the phone at home and explained the situation to him. Steinbrenner asked to speak with me, so I got on the phone.

"Did I agree to that?" he asked me. When I answered that he did, he asked me to put Kleinman on the phone. "Mr. Rossetti and I agreed to the reimbursement of the expenses as part of the deal. Pay these people and let's get this over with!" Winston & Strawn then drafted the necessary documents while I called EJD back and told him what happened.

The rest of the closing then took place and the money was wired into our account. After confirmation of the funds was received,

Swindal suggested we go down to the street level bar and have a celebratory drink and we agreed. During the conversation, I told Swindal and Kleinman I grew up in the New York area and that my impression of George Steinbrenner from the papers was he was a lunatic to deal with, but in our negotiations and discussions, he was a perfect gentleman.

Kleinman replied, "It's pinstripes (referring to the Yankees uniforms). Anything related to the Yankees, he's a completely different person. In all other matters, he's as friendly as you just described."

A few years later, when I announced I would be leaving DeBartolo, I got a nice letter from George on Yankee stationary. It said in part, "I think fondly of our negotiations on various occasions and you were always a fair, honest and straightforward man, and above all, your word was good. If the occasion arises, you may be sure that I will call on you because as I said I was tremendously impressed with not only your acumen but your integrity." It was signed by George M. Steinbrenner III.

March and April saw much of the same, with numerous trips to Pittsburgh and Cleveland, Atlantic City, Baltimore, Palm Beach, Shreveport, Marco Island and then Atlantic City again. Atlantic City was an interesting story. There was a big, successful car dealer named Spitzer in the Cleveland area, and Mr. Spitzer wanted to build a casino in Lorain, Ohio, not too far from Thistledown.

In those days, casinos near racetracks were deadly for the tracks and DeBartolo wanted to stop him. He sent me to Atlantic City to get some negatives on the impact of the casinos in that city. I flew in and spent a couple of days there and found out the average man on the street suffered when the casinos first came in. The jobs promised were all menial, and management jobs were filled from Las Vegas and other gambling areas. Crime soared and taxes rose and many elderly people were forced out of their homes. There were a lot of negatives.

I put a report together and gave it to Mr. DeBartolo. He, in turn, gave it to Bob Schreiber, the DeBartolo attorney, and had him quietly distribute it to the various churches in Lorain and government officials in Columbus. The people rose against it and the referendum failed. Apparently, my report wasn't kept anonymous.

In 1990, after I left DeBartolo, I received a call from Spitzer in Florida. He wanted me to work with him to resurrect the casino. He offered me $25,000. Although it was tempting, I told him I would not be a part of it. Even after I left, I was still loyal to Mr. DeBartolo. It would be more than 20 years before Ohio approved casinos.

April also saw me receive an appointment to the Board of Trustees of my alma mater, Saint Francis College. This came out of the blue. At the start of 1987, Chris and I received a letter with a questionnaire from the College. The school was attempting to raise over $4 million for improvements and was contacting alumni to see if we would participate.

Plans had not yet been finalized. The survey was to determine if the alumni would contribute. We had not heard anything from the school after we graduated in 1970 and 1971. Other than the annual alumni weekends, there were no socials, and no correspondence from them at all. We filled out the survey and I let them know of the irony we were only hearing from them when they needed money. I thought that would be the end of it, but it wasn't.

A few weeks later, I got a phone call in my office from the president of the College, the Rev. Christian R. Oravec. He told me he had seen my comments on the survey, and he asked if he could come to

Youngstown and have lunch with me. I had a break in travel coming up, so I agreed to meet with him. When he arrived, he floated out the offer of me sitting on the Board of Trustees.

The College was, and still is, run by Franciscan priests, many of who are elderly with minimal business and financial experience. Fr. Christian felt, if he increased the presence of lay people on the Board, then perhaps the College could move more into modern times rather than the draconian ways of the past. I told him I would have to run it by Mr. DeBartolo, but I didn't expect it to be an issue.

It wasn't an issue. In fact, Mr. DeBartolo was pleased I was giving back, and he was more than willing to have me sit in on monthly Board meetings in Loretto and contribute to my alma mater. He also agreed to match any contribution I made to the school. So, in early April the school released an announcement in our local paper of my appointment, and I got very nice accolades from all the DeBartolos and a few other people in Youngstown.

With summer approaching, I found the need to be in the office or in Cleveland and Pittsburgh more than in the past. We were working hard to get the Cleveland hotels back under control and the efforts were paying off. Thistledown was also having a banner year as the patrons were responding to the changes made at that track. So, things were looking good in Cleveland.

With the Spirit disbanded, our people in Pittsburgh were actively looking for a new tenant to go with the Penguins, rock concerts, truck pulls, circuses and the like, and up reared the Arena Football League. The Pittsburgh Gladiators became the new tenant in a new four-team league, playing in the summer.

We did not own the team. They were tenants, and were well-supported by the football-hungry Pittsburgh fans. The four home games, including the first-ever Arena Bowl, averaged just under 13,000 fans per game, more than 80 percent of capacity. They finished 4-2 for the season, tied with Denver for first place. The two teams had a playoff game (the Arena Bowl) and Denver prevailed, 45-16. The Gladiators would go on to play three more seasons in Pittsburgh before moving to Tampa.

Louisiana Downs was having still another record-breaking season down in Shreveport. In September, Chris and I flew down there for the Super Derby, the track's richest race. Alysheba, sired by Alydar, was the winning horse. Alydar was famous for losing to Affirmed in all three Triple Crown races in 1978. Alydar lost by 1.5 lengths in the Kentucky Derby, by a neck in the Preakness and by a head in the Belmont. Alydar would go on to earn the title of 'best Thoroughbred to have never won a Triple Crown race." Louisiana Downs had gone from being the track that almost bankrupted DeBartolo in the early 1970s, to one of the most profitable racetracks in the country, with a cash flow of nearly $14 million.

I also spent considerable time in Florida in 1987. Mayfair House in Coconut Grove in Miami was still losing money, and we decided to get a management company to run that high-end property. In late September, we hired the Laventhol & Horwath Company to turn the property around, and Jack Lambert moved to Youngstown to work as an assistant to Mr. DeBartolo, Sr.

Rossetti Enterprises had turned the corner on Marco Island. Mike Dowling and I hired Joe Jiamboi, who had worked for us in Cleveland, to run the Marco property and Jiamboi had turned the property around. We now had group business and the restaurant was booming. In January, I made another principal payment to Mr. DeBartolo in the amount of $40,000, and now I was down to owing him half of the original $100,000.

We made nearly $100,000 profit in 1986 and were on track to exceed that amount in 1987. But, DeBartolo was tired of losing money on Marco and wanted to sell that property. On October 1, I flew to Marco and met with Tom Shea, a Marco restaurateur, and David Bennett, a local businessman, to discuss their interest in buying the property.

In late summer, I had my annual review with Tony Liberati and this year I was given "Distinguished" grades across the board. Apparently, my communications skills had improved. My response was one of gratitude and pride for what we had accomplished, but I cited, with the staff I had built, coupled with the divestitures of some of the entities over which I was responsible, my future with the company might be in question. I stated it was time for us to "discuss my long-range future with the Company." I was ready for more challenges.

In October, Mr. DeBartolo called me into his office. Marco Islanders Shea and Bennett had made an offer to buy the Marco Island property, but there was a caveat. They also wanted the food and beverage department run by Rossetti Enterprises. Mr. DeBartolo said, "the only area making any money is your operation."

I wasn't surprised. Shea owned a restaurant less than a mile from ours and his friendship with Bob Stakich didn't bode well for us. It was rumored Shea would bring back Stakich as his general manager.

The writing was on the wall for Rossetti Enterprises and I know Mr. DeBartolo recognized that as well as I did. He asked me how much I would sell the business to him for, so he could package the entire deal. Again, I was in a tough situation. Without Mr. DeBartolo, we wouldn't even be having this conversation and yet, we did him a favor three years before when we took over and built the restaurant in 1984.

He helped us through the bad times and I still owed him the $50,000 on the loan he gave us to get started. I told him I would send him my financials and accept whatever amount he offered. Once again, I placed my trust in this man who was like a father to me, and once again he didn't disappoint me. Two days later, he offered me $425,000 for the business, plus the inventory. I told him that was fine.

Chris and I invested $140,000 (including the $100,000 loan from Mr. D) and we owned 60 percent of the stock. I gave 10 percent each to John and Chas, who ran the business, and 10 percent to my mother and my sister, Pam, each of whom had put in $2,000. Aside from the fact that Chas and John would be looking for a job, all the shareholders had done well.

Meanwhile, the 1987 NFL season had started. Just prior to the 1987 draft, Bill Walsh made a trade, acquiring Steve Young from the Tampa Bay Buccaneers, for the Niners' second and fourth round picks in the draft. Walsh felt he needed a stronger backup in the event Montana's physical problems continued.

The Forty Niners opened in Pittsburgh on September 13, my oldest son's 15th birthday. He wanted to tailgate for his birthday, so the party was at Three Rivers Stadium. But, it wasn't a happy birthday as the Steelers handled the 49ers in a similar manner as the Giants did in January. Four 49ers turnovers, and the scoreboard read 30-17 at the end, with Pittsburgh on top. That would be the low point of 1987 for San Francisco, however. They reeled off seven straight wins, including a 41-

21 revenge win over the Giants in New Jersey, before losing on a last-minute field goal to New Orleans two months later.

Bouncing back, they then won their next six games, outscoring their opponents 209-53 enroute to a 13-2 record, best in the NFL. Montana had an outstanding season, completing 67 percent of his passes for 3,054 yards and 31 touchdowns, with 13 interceptions; the defense was awesome all year, as was the offense. Next up would be NFC Divisional Game on January 8, 1988.

On November 22, the Forty Niners had played the Buccaneers in Tampa. I flew down to Tampa on the Saturday night before the game and stayed with the team. The next day, I met my brother John and a few of the REI employees at the game. Afterward, we drove back to Marco. It was a subdued group, all of us knowing that in two days we would no longer have the business. The next day, Shea came over and we all took the inventory on the food and beverages that were left. We agreed on the count and Shea paid us without any argument. Rossetti Enterprises was officially out of business.

As that week wound down, it occurred to me that, for the first time since 1977, I had not made even one trip to San Francisco. I had seen the team play in Pittsburgh and in Tampa Bay, but hadn't been out there on Forty Niner business at any time during the year. It dawned on me that was a good thing. We didn't need to do any financing for the team and there were few problems, certainly nothing that required my presence. Again, I started thinking about my future, wondering where I might be in a year or two.

On the downside, Marie DeBartolo, Mr. DeBartolo's wife and the mother of Eddie, Jr. and Marie Denise passed away on August 23. Services were private. I had met Mrs. DeBartolo many times at corporate events, the Ohio Derby, Super Bowls and parties, and she was always nice to me and very gracious. Her death was a loss to everyone who ever met her.

The Penguins were in the midst of the 1987-88 season, as the year ended, and for the first time in our 10 years of owning the team, we had a winning record at the end of the calendar year. The Pens were 16-14-7 and this was a critical year for Paul Martha and Eddie Johnson. Mr. DeBartolo had made it known that our Pittsburgh staff either got "their act together or he would make big changes." So, with that uncertainty looming in the future, the year ended.

CHAPTER SEVENTEEN

1988-DRAMATIC CHANGES THROUGHOUT THE SPORTS DIVISION

Once again, the year was opening with a 49ers playoff game, as the team, with its 13-2 record was the favorite to win the Super Bowl. The wild card games on January 3, saw Minnesota pound New Orleans, 44-10 in the NFC, and Houston nip Seattle in overtime, 23-20 in the AFC. So, Minnesota would visit San Francisco for the late game on Saturday, January 9. Chris was unable to accompany me on the trip, so I decided to take one of my sons. I offered the option to Mike and Chip to either go to the game or I would give them $100 cash. I figured Chip would take the money, but he really wanted to go to the game, so I ended taking both to the game. We flew out on Friday.

When I got there, Eddie, Jr. asked if I would host a group of his guests in one of the super boxes and I agreed. I ended up with the Mahoning County Sheriff and a few of his deputies, who were there as Eddie's guests. My job was to socialize with the guests and make sure the attendants took care of the food and beverage.

It was a gloomy, overcast San Francisco day as the game began. The Vikings scored first, marching down the field on a 15-play, 77-yard drive, but had to settle for a 21-yard field goal. Both teams then sputtered before 49er kicker Ray Wersching tied the game with a 43-yard field goal as the quarter ended. Then, the Vikings stunned the 49ers with a 17-point second quarter, including a "pick-six" on Joe Montana at the midpoint of the quarter. The Forty Niners offense kept backfiring, with the fans growing restless as the first half came to an end. My boys were intently watching and were as restless as the other fans in the stands.

The second half began and the 49er defense got a pick-six of its own as safety Jeff Fuller returned a Wade Wilson pass 48 yards to close the gap to 20-10. But, the Vikings stormed right back, aided by a 30-yard run by Anthony Carter, and scored on a short Wilson pass to Hassan Jones. It was now 27-10 and, when Montana misfired on a pass on the next drive, the boos began at Candlestick, and I couldn't believe my ears.

And then it got worse. The fans began to chant "We want Young!" I couldn't believe the fans had turned on Joe as quickly as they did. Walsh eventually acceded to the fans and put Steve Young in the game, benching Montana for the first time in his San Francisco career.

It appeared the fans might be right as Young quickly finished a 35-yard drive with a five-yard TD, but it wasn't to be. This was Anthony Carter's and Wade Wilson's day. Several times, Wilson threw the ball up for grabs, and the often-well guarded Carter out-jumped everybody for the catch. Carter ended up with ten receptions for 227 yards, added 30 yards on his run, and returned 2 punts for 21 yards. Wilson threw for 290 yards on 20 completions, with 2 touchdowns. Minnesota just out-played the Forty Niners on both sides of scrimmage, in front of a shocked Candlestick crowd.

As the game was ending, even the Mahoning County sheriff and his deputies were depressed. The sheriff came up to me near the end of the game and said, "I've been watching you and your boys. They're depressed, but you seem to be as calm as can be. How can you do that?"

I looked at him as I answered, "I've been dealing with the Pittsburgh Penguins for 10 years. I know how to lose." He chuckled with me as he shook my hand and wished me luck.

It was never fun being at Candlestick after a 49er loss, especially a playoff loss. I took the Youngstown group, and my sons, down to the owner's suite, where VIPs were invited before and after the game. The Sheriff indicated he would like to thank Mr. DeBartolo (Eddie, Jr.) for his hospitality before they took their flight back to Ohio. Eddie had his private office through a short hallway at the back of the room, and I went to get him.

The guards knew me and let me through, and I walked in on a scene that I couldn't believe. There was a young man, obviously drunk, sitting on a chair surrounded by DeBartolo's friends. Eddie's bodyguard, Leo, was restraining the man. One of Eddie's friends told me the fan had "heckled Mr. DeBartolo" after the game and "called him names." The others grabbed him and brought him down to the office so he could be "given a lesson in manners."

I shoved my sons, who had followed me, back out the door and returned and walked up to Eddie. He was quite angry, which was not uncommon after a bitter loss. I asked him for a minute and we walked into the hallway.

"Don't do this," I said to him. "You should be really proud of the season that the 49ers had and it's a shame that it ended this way, but let's not make it worse. The kid is obviously drunk and didn't know what he was saying. Let him go."

Eddie looked at me like he wanted to hit me, as well, but my eyes remained locked on his. After a few seconds, he nodded and I said, "Thank you. The Sheriff and his guys are in the party room and want to thank you before they leave."

I walked back into the office, pushed past Leo and told the inebriated man, "This is your lucky day. Now get out of here fast." He ran out the door.

It didn't take long for 1988 to get worse. For reasons I don't understand to this day, a rift developed between Mr. DeBartolo and George Jones at Thistledown. George's attendance at the track had been erratic for a while. He would take some days off when the track wasn't racing. Although this might be normal, it irked Mr. DeBartolo when he couldn't get Jones when he wanted him. Jones had been tremendously loyal and always spoke well of Mr. D and, although he didn't discuss it with me, it was apparent the two had some recent disagreements. But, the track wasn't racing in the winter and I figured they would work it out.

Rumors were rampant in Cleveland that Jones was on his way out, but neither George nor Mr. DeBartolo said anything to me. On February 12, I was interviewed by Bob Roberts, the racing reporter for the Cleveland Plain Dealer. On the following Sunday, his column was titled "Jones to continue in charge of track" and he quoted me throughout. "Jones is in full charge, "said Tom Rossetti, vice-president/controller for the Edward J. DeBartolo Corp., the track's parent company. "George is in good health and we're looking for him to help Thistledown have a record year."

Roberts then discussed Jones' physical ailments that cost him "considerable work last season." He asked me about that and I responded, "Mr. DeBartolo has expressed concern over the rumors and as to what has been in the newspapers," said Rossetti, who oversees DeBartolo's sports franchises. "However, George has assured that us he's fine."

I spent a lot of time in Pittsburgh that winter, and bounced around in Florida on hotel business, and in Oklahoma City as the opening of the new track approached. The Penguins were snake-bitten again. Despite their first winning record in nine years, they again missed the playoffs due to the division they were in and the NHL system of playoff qualifications. The Penguins had a better record than nine teams in the NHL and five of those teams qualified for the playoffs. Mr. DeBartolo was unimpressed. The season ended on April 3. Mr. DeBartolo demoted Eddie Johnston and Tony Esposito was named general manager on April 14. Esposito fired coach Pierre Creamer and hired Gene Ubriaco as head coach of the Penguins.

In March, I took a couple of days off and went to Myrtle Beach for a weekend of golf. Rick McLaughlin, the business manager of the Penguins, with whom I had struck up a friendship, had a group of friends from his Pittsburgh country club going and they needed another player to fill out the field. Although I received approval to take the vacation days, I knew Mr. DeBartolo wasn't happy that I was away.

On the second morning down there, I called into the office and was told Mr. DeBartolo wanted to talk to me. Carol, my secretary, transferred me to Mr. D's secretary. When Senior got on the line, he didn't say "hello." He just asked me why I didn't copy Tony Liberati on a memo I had sent to EJD, Eddie, Marie Denise and Bill Moses concerning Fun-N-Games Associates, an entity the three of them owned personally. My specific instructions on reports on that entity had been to only copy the owners and Mr. DeBartolo and nobody else.

Mr. DeBartolo shouted into the phone, "You are to copy Liberati on any report that you send out in the future!" I heard laughter in the background, as he slammed the phone down.

Rick McLaughlin, who technically reported to me, and had heard part of the conversation, asked me if everything was okay.

"That call may mark the beginning of the end of my career at EJD Corporation," I answered, putting the phone down. Mr. DeBartolo changed a long-standing policy without telling me, and then shouted at me for not following a policy I knew nothing about.

On May 2, I flew to Atlantic City for a meeting with the Pratt Company, which managed our hotels in Orlando, the Crowne Plaza, and Palm Springs, Maxim's. I flew back to Pittsburgh the next morning, landing around noon, with plenty of time to take the one-hour drive back to the office. I was deep in thought, as I got in my Company car and drove out of the airport.

I drove aimlessly through the Pennsylvania hillsides, off the main highways, looking at and appreciating the sites I had bypassed so many times over the years, without giving them a thought. It became apparent to me I didn't want to go to the office, the first time in my 15 years with DeBartolo, that ever happened. I called Carol, on the car cell phone, told her I didn't feel good and wouldn't be in the office that day, and I drove home. Chris was shocked to see me home that early. We had a long talk.

On May 13, I sent the following memo to EJD, EJD, Jr. and Marie Denise DeBartolo York, titled MY FUTURE WITH THE COMPANY:

I believe that, after fifteen (15) years, I have reached a major crossroads in my career with the Corporation. I would like to share a few thoughts with the three of you – all people that I respect greatly, both professionally and personally.

When I joined the Company in 1973, we were a much smaller company ready to take off. We had little or no financial direction in our fledgling Diversified Operations, which included only Thistledown, the Toledo operations and two Holiday Inns. We were also purchasing Balmoral and building Louisiana Downs and the Wilson Mills Holiday Inn. Fun-N-Games was just getting started.

In 1974, I started taking over the financial controls of those operations. I'd like to think that we greatly improved the controls over those entities at that time.

In 1977, we acquired the Forty Niners and our interest in the Penguins and I was asked to set up their controls and assist in their operations. In 1981, we took over the Civic Arena and bought the Spirit and again I was asked to take over the responsibility over those entities. A few years later, we acquired the Mauler franchise and we operated that ill-fated franchise for a year.

At about that same time, we jumped into bed with the Pratt people, over my strong objections, and I was instructed to cooperate with them in the running of the Cleveland hotels. Crowne Plaza (Orlando) and Maxim's (Palm Springs) followed with Mayfair (Miami) joining the portfolio at about the same time.

During this entire 12-year span, I was very active hiring and firing, setting up cost controls, helping make policy decisions, and generally serving as your eyes and ears in assuring that your best interests were being tended to. I made a conscious decision to build a staff of the best financial people that I could find, always stressing loyalty to the Company and the DeBartolo family. I feel that I succeeded in that goal.

I laughed and cried with you throughout the years. I suffered through the Joe Thomas era and worked closely with Eddie in helping build the new regime. I participated in and celebrated two Super Bowls with you, something that I'll remember for the rest of my life.

I also helped do what had to be done with Vince Bartimo and fought with him all through the bitter lawsuit. I'd like to think that our Company has made millions more at Louisiana Downs just by getting rid of Bartimo.

I suffered with you through the Bowie Kuhn-White Sox indignity and I hurt for you and felt for you as if it had happened to my own family.

There have also been the accomplishments and I'd like to think that I played a major role in:

--The legislative efforts in Ohio that have saved us millions of dollars through the years. Even more important is the fact that we have been lily-clean in our work and have a great rapport with the State Auditor's Office.

--The improved profitability at Louisiana Downs.

--The financial turn-around of the Penguins.

--The success of the Civic Arena.

--The sale of Balmoral at a figure nobody felt we could get.

--The excellent improvement at Mayfair House this year.

--The sale of the Cleveland hotels for a price that far exceeds what they are worth capitalizing their cash flows.
--The two great deals that we negotiated for the Diamond Vision boards at Thistledown and Louisiana Downs.
--Tossing Pratt out of Cleveland and the major financial improvement we've experienced by running the properties ourselves.

I believe that all those issues are a matter of record. In the 15 years that I've been here I feel that I have done my job well. I'm proud of what we've done and feel privileged to have shared in the growth of your great Company.

But, inevitably, times change and the DeBartolo Corporation is no exception. Since so many of the Diversified Operations have lost money, we have taken the approach that they should be abandoned or sold, a policy that I have supported and agreed with. The Spirit and Maulers were abandoned and the Toledo Operations, Balmoral, Anglers Cove, Sheraton Aurora and, hopefully, Cleveland Holiday Inns have been sold. Plans call for Mayfair, Maxim's and Crowne Plaza to be sold as soon as economically feasible.

My goal, conveyed to Mr. D and Tony Liberati in 1984, was to build a very strong department, both here and in the field, to look out for your interests and manage your assets. I feel that I have succeeded.

Jerry Wiemann is doing a fine job overseeing both Louisiana Downs and Remington Park and Gary Todd has given us a good financial mind at Thistledown.

Our corporate people in house, particularly Marty Hamer and Chris Bilski, with their staff, interplay well with the field people. My secretary, Carol Wilhelm, is superb. All have been here a long time, know their jobs, and do outstanding work. Quite frankly, from a financial standpoint, there are no holes.

These days, my involvement with the Forty Niners is next to nil. Because of recent changes in the Penguins and Arena, coupled with the strong financial people on site (Ed Walter and Rick McLaughlin have given you a strong corporate presence in Pittsburgh) my day-to-day involvement in that operation has diminished.

All of which brings me, in a very long-winded way, to the point at hand. Because of this, I don't enjoy coming to work anymore.

I haven't looked for a job and have no desire to do so. After working for such fine people as the DeBartolo family, I cannot see myself working for anyone else. But, because of my feelings for you, I can't continue taking a paycheck when I don't feel that I completely earn it.

As you know, I have certain family problems. My father, who is alone in Florida, is disabled and has nobody to look after him. I tried to get him to move to Youngstown two years ago, but he can't handle the cold weather any longer. My mother, who is also in Florida, is getting up in years. I haven't lived near her since 1972 and I'd like to keep an eye on her, too.

I've had these problems for a few years now, but as long as I felt that I was contributing and was challenged here, I was satisfied to try and keep things together over a long distance. I don't want to do that any longer. I want to put my personal life in order.

I have a great amount of love, respect and loyalty for you, Mr. D, Eddie and Denise. You have made me feel like a part of your family. When I accepted an offer to work here in 1973, I turned down a higher paying job from Westinghouse in Baltimore. It was one of the best decisions I'll ever make in my life.

I'm not wealthy and I'm faced with putting three boys through college, starting in two years. You don't owe me anything but, I'd like to request some consideration for my partnership interests in Alderwood, Treasure Coast and Lakeland. Alderwood requires me to be here 20 years and I've only been here 15. Obviously, if the answer is "No", I fully understand.

I expect that we may sit down and discuss this memo. I haven't discussed this with anyone other than my wife. Further, please don't think that I'm using this as a wedge to get a raise. I believe that you know that I don't operate that way.

I would stay with the Company until you are fully comfortable that all is in order. I would also be available anytime in the future should you need any help on the tracks, sports teams, hotels or whatever.

God bless you all and thank you for allowing me to grow with you through the years.

Eddie, Jr. was the first to reach out to me. He called me into his office and reiterated that he had plans for me when he took over the Company. He would get more involved in sports and entertainment and, in deference to his father's legacy, he would build a mall "every year or so." It would be more of a management company than a development company, and I was the financial guy that he wanted.

Denise was next. She said that her father would meet with me "in a few days", as he was out of town and he felt that we "could work things out." I just went about my business. Chris and I planned and took our vacation – three weeks this time, with not a word of protest from Mr. D. My interactions recently were not as frequent with Mr. DeBartolo as in the past, but we were both busy – Remington Park was due to open on September 1.

In early August, Mr. DeBartolo wanted to meet with me. His agenda included the status of Remington Park, the ongoing problems with Jones, who often could not be contacted, my annual review, and the memo I had sent him more than two months ago. I assured him that Remington was on schedule, all department heads and key employees had been hired. I had sent Jim Rozes and Mike Dowling down there to button up the foodservice matters and Wiemann, Marty Hamer and Ed Nosek from the home office to make sure the financial matters were in order.

He then brought up the issues with Jones and I was forced to admit there were times when I was unable to get in touch with him as well, but it didn't appear the operation was suffering at this time. But, I could see that he was getting impatient with George.

Next, he brought up my annual review, which, since 1982 had been done in August. When I mentioned the memo I sent him, he said, "We'll take care of that," and we proceeded to discuss wages for the new fiscal year. I was taken off guard, but I gave him a number. After all, I hadn't given him a date when I would be leaving.

Mr. D asked for my justification on the number I gave him and I ticked off all the accomplishments I'd had over the last year and the financial impact of those matters to the Company. Mr. DeBartolo agreed that I'd had a good year and offered me exactly $500 less than I asked for. We bantered for a few minutes and then he told me to come back in the morning and we could discuss it further. I didn't know what was going to be discussed that hadn't already been, but I agreed to come back in the morning.

The next morning, I came back and we discussed the same issues and he held fast to his offer. I was getting frustrated - $500 to him was pocket change, and I told him that. Nevertheless, he wouldn't budge. He finally wore me down and I said "OK. Give me the damn paper to sign."

He slid it across his desk and I signed it and slid it back. I was angry. I got up to leave and got to his door that led to the hallway. Turning to him, I asked him, "If you won't pay me the $500, will you give it to me?" He had a big smile on his face as he approached me and handed me $500 from his pocket.

"And you said I didn't challenge you anymore," he said, as he turned away. Score one for the Master Negotiator.

The rift between Mr. DeBartolo and George Jones was getting wider. I told Mr. D I would go up to Thistledown and speak with Jones. On August 28, I drove to Thistledown for the pre-arranged meeting. When I got there, I was told he was out sick. We tried to call him at home, but couldn't reach him. George and I had worked together for more than 11 years and this had never happened before. This was now getting serious.

On August 31, Chris and I flew to Oklahoma City for the official opening of Remington Park the next day. We stayed in the same hotel as Mr. DeBartolo and, on the morning of the opening he called me in my room and asked me to come up to his room. He opened the door and was dressed in slacks and an undershirt. It was the first time in 15 years that I had seen Mr. D in anything other than a suit.

We sat down in his room and he asked me how my meeting went with Jones. Now, a lot of times when DeBartolo asked you a question he already knew the answer, and especially with the Thistledown rumor mill. I had to tell him what happened. And then he said the words that I dreaded to hear, "We have to make a change."

This time, I could not argue with him. I told him George had one year left on his contract, and Mr. D told me to get with our lawyers in Youngstown and see what our options were. I left his room with a heavy heart, knowing that another of the people I had worked with so closely was going to leave us. And George was more than just a co-worker, he was a trusted friend. I called George at Thistledown, but was told he was unavailable, and I knew then this had to change.

The opening of the new, "state of the art" racetrack was a resounding success and Mr. DeBartolo was pleased. There were a few normal glitches among the patrons, but they were mostly due to the fact there were a lot of new racing fans in the park. All-in-all, the opening went well. The next day, we flew back to Youngstown for the rest of the weekend.

On Monday, I reviewed Jones' contract with our in-house counsel and was told we were obligated to pay Jones for the last year on his contract, unless he just walked away or did something so egregious we could find just cause to fire him. George had only missed work for illness and injury and that would not apply.

I told Mr. DeBartolo we had no option other than to pay George if we let him go. I had spoken with George and he sensed what was coming. He referred the calls to his lawyer, Armand Arnson, and I spoke with Arnson at length. It was clear that, if Mr. DeBartolo wanted Jones out, it was either pay him or risk a nasty public battle, most likely fought in the media. Both Art Wolfcale, a long-time DeBartolo lawyer, and I recommended that Mr. D just honor the contract and shake hands with Jones. Mr. DeBartolo said he would take it under consideration.

On September 20, Mr. DeBartolo summoned Jones to his office. George flew into Youngstown and was met by his lawyer, Arnson. The three met in the conference room and I waited in Mr. DeBartolo's office just across the hall, per his instructions. Arnson left first and a few minutes later, Mr. DeBartolo and Jones came out. I offered to drive Jones back to the airport and we stopped for lunch along the way. George was relieved it was over, but we were both sad it had to end. We shook hands and hugged each other. Another big chapter in my life was closing.

By mutual consent, it was determined Jones would stay through October 15. He made the announcement the following Sunday and left as scheduled. Even before he left, the Thistledown rumor mill identified former general manager Mike Mackey as a potential candidate. I was barraged with phone calls from the media, but no agreement had been reached so I had no official comment.

On October 10, I confirmed the worst kept secret in Cleveland history – that Mackey had been hired. At that press conference, I stated Mackey wouldn't arrive until November and I would be running the track until he arrived. The Plain Dealer went on to state, "Rossetti made the announcement of Mackey's hiring with mixed emotions. 'It's bitter-sweet because I have a great deal of respect for George (Jones)," said Rossetti. "George did an excellent job. But, at this juncture, it's best that a change is made."

With Jones gone, somebody had to step up and take the reins until we got a replacement and DeBartolo tabbed me. So, for the five days each week the track was running (Wednesday-Sunday), I did double duty. I spent a few hours in the office and then drove to the track to oversee operations.

I wanted to make a splash and get the media off the Jones story, so I had a department meeting on my first day and asked what the biggest complaint was among our patrons. The answer was unanimous – the people hated the fact the races never went off at post-time. Thistledown was notoriously known as a track who announced times of races that never went off on time. Many patrons felt the big bettors held off betting until past post-time and had an advantage.

I instructed the department heads that, starting on October 20, the races would run as posted. When track announcer Alan Drake made the announcement, Plain Dealer Staff Writer Bob Roberts reported "It was met with sarcastic cheers." Roberts then quoted me, "It's a problem we have decided to address," said Tom Rossetti, vice president/controller for the Edward J. DeBartolo Corp., Thistledown's parent company. "It came up at the meeting that many fans have complained about us not observing post time. Starting next week, we will."

When I left the track that day, several fans approached me and thanked me for making the change. The strategy worked. The Jones story was no longer in the news.

On October 17, we finally sold the Cleveland Hotels, for more money than we planned. That milestone was another check-off on my business bucket list. There was another DeBartolo story that surfaced from the sale.

Ever since the North Randall Holiday Inn was built, there was a suite reserved for Mr. DeBartolo. It was never rented out, but it was cleaned every day, even though Mr. D hadn't used it in years. Mike Dowling told me there were personal items of Mr. DeBartolo's in the room. When the sale was imminent, I went into the room and saw several of Mr. DeBartolo's suits, shirts, ties, cufflinks and other items of clothing.

There were also shoes and some unopened Christmas Gifts left by the Boss. And, there was something that surprised me, a bowling ball in the closet. The next day, I met with EJD, asked what we were to do with the personal items, and he told me to contribute them to charity. Then I mentioned the bowling ball. Mr. D looked off into the distance and said, "So, that's where I left it!" When I asked him when he last bowled, he answered, "Twenty years or so."

The Penguins season had begun, under new ice management. For the first six weeks of the season, they were hovering at .500, with 10 wins and 10 losses. But, starting on November 23, they went on a tear, winning 13 games versus 2 losses and 3 ties and, at the end of the calendar year were 23-12-3. Lemieux was on a record setting pace and he closed out 1988 on New Year's Eve with five goals against the New Jersey Devils, scoring five different ways – even strength, power play, short-handed, penalty shot and empty net. Things were finally looking up in Pittsburgh.

On October 26, I decided to make an unannounced trip to Remington Park. There had been some minor operating problems that had been worked out and I wanted to see for myself. I dressed in blue jeans and cowboy boots and walked in without a briefcase. With my long hair, I fit right in, mingling with the patrons, observing the bars and restaurants and checking on the cleanliness of the facility. I liked what I saw. The track was doing exceptionally well and was profitable. The minor problems we had in September, (which weren't mild to Mr. DeBartolo) had been corrected. I thought to myself, if he were here with me, he would be pleased.

The eighth race was getting ready to go off and I looked at the tote board in the infield. I saw something I had never seen at Thistle-down, Louisiana Downs or even Balmoral. There were nine horses in the race. The program favorite was listed at 3-5 odds and the second favor-ite was 8-1. Every other horse in the race was 25-1 or higher. The bet-ting public was primarily betting on the two favorites.

I walked up to the betting window just at post time and said, "Give me $5 to win on every horse in the race." The woman at the win-dow looked at me strangely and printed out the ticket. She said to me, "We usually say, "Good Luck", but you're going to win no matter what!"

"Only if the two favorites don't," I answered. The horse that won paid 40-1 and I made a quick $160 profit, and never even knew the name of the horse.

In September, Tony Liberati gave me my annual review and, like the others, it was a "distinguished" rating. However, the Company had not made any progress on the concerns I voiced in August. My response to the rating addressed those issues again to EJD, EJD, Jr., Marie Denise and Liberati. I stressed again they needed to decide what they wanted to do with me.

On December 2, Mr. DeBartolo rewarded me with a 0.5 percent partnership interest in Chesapeake Center, a community center the Company was developing next to Chesapeake Square in Virginia. I now had interests in four DeBartolo partnerships.

On December 18, we went to the Penguins' Christmas party. It was also my wife's birthday. The boys had a ball skating with the play-ers, while Chris and I watched from the stands. I didn't realize it then, but that would be the last Penguin Christmas party for us.

I also realized my schedule was so packed I didn't do anything for the 49ers in 1988, and for the first time since we acquired the team, I hadn't gone to even one game. The Niners struggled early as concerns about Joe Montana's health surfaced at the start of the season. Bill Walsh alternated with both Montana and Steve Young sharing the quarterback duties. At mid-season, the team was 6-5 and appeared to be headed nowhere. Then, Walsh decided to go solely with Montana, and the 49ers ended up 10-6, in a three-way tie with New Orleans and the Los Angeles Rams.

The Niners won on a tie-breaker. They would meet the Minnesota Vikings on New Year's Day at Candlestick, the same team that stunned the Niners at Candlestick in January, in the game where the 49er faithful had booed Joe Montana. What a year!

CHAPTER EIGHTEEN

1989-"IT WAS ONE OF THE SADDEST MOMENTS OF MY LIFE"

1989 started the same as nearly every other year in the eighties – with a 49er playoff game. The 49ers once again hosted the Minnesota Vikings in a Divisional Playoff game. But, unlike the prior season's NFC playoff game for San Francisco, this time the Niners thrashed the Vikings 34-9. Minnesota took a 3-0 lead after the opening kickoff, but the 49ers quickly took the lead for good on a short Montana to Jerry Rice TD pass. Rice caught two more TD passes in the second quarter and the Niners had a commanding 21-3 halftime lead.

Minnesota closed the gap on their second half opening drive to 21-9 on a short Wade Wilson pass, but the 49ers defense was dominating and the Vikings scored no more. Roger Craig then took over in the fourth quarter, scoring from four yards out and then scoring on an 80-yard jaunt to close out the scoring and exact sweet revenge for the 49ers.

Next up for San Francisco was the big, bad Chicago Bears at Soldier Field in Chicago on January 8. The Bears were 12-4, tied for the best record in the NFL, and they had visions of a return to the Super Bowl. Because I hadn't seen a live 49ers game all season, I decided this would be the first.

I borrowed a company van and the family and I drove to Chicago on Friday and checked into the Marriott, where the team was staying. We spent Saturday touring the city and museums on a balmy but rainy day, with temperatures in the sixties. The next day, we had plans to meet my brother Bill for brunch and then we would all go to the game.

But weather in Chicago can change quickly and on Saturday night the temperatures plunged and the winds began to blow. I awoke around 7:30 a.m. and listened to the wind whistling outside. I looked out the window and was surprised to see there was ice on the inside of the window. We had brought some cold weather gear that was in the van outside, so I showered, dressed and headed outside to get the coats, boots and gloves, so they would warm up.

The van was in an open lot across the street since it was too tall for the parking garage. I went outside and was hit in the face with a blast of frigid air that took my breath away. It took all the energy I had to walk to the van, get the gear and return to the hotel lobby, and I honestly felt like I might not make it. I ran into Eddie, Jr. in the lobby and he said, "Pretty damn cold, huh?" My teeth were chattering and I told him that might be the coldest weather I ever experienced, as we headed toward the coffee shop.

I truly didn't think we would be able to go to the game, because it would be way too cold and dangerous. Game time was four p.m. and the forecast indicated it would probably be colder. I went back upstairs an hour or so later and told the family we'd probably have to skip the game. The cold weather gear we had wouldn't be enough.

Bill called just before noon and asked if we were "ready for some football?". I told him I didn't think we could make it and he said, "It's all taken care of."

Bill had a friend named Reid Fields, who owned a snowmobiling shop in the suburbs, and was going to the game with us. Over the years, I got Reid tickets for some of the big games, including the Super Bowl. When Reid saw the weather that morning, he immediately called Bill and asked what sizes my family would need. They brought complete snowmobiling outfits for the entire family, from head to toe. We even had the shoes.

After brunch, we all geared up and drove to the stadium. It was too cold for tailgating, at least for us, so we watched the end of the early game on TV in the van, with the heater running. As kickoff neared, we headed into the stadium, surrounded by Bears fans commenting that it was "Bear weather!" and referring to the "California pansies" who wouldn't be able to tolerate the cold.

At kickoff, it was 17 degrees, with a wind chill of minus 26 degrees, and wind gusts up to 30 miles per hour. Only our eyes and a small opening for the mouth were exposed. The wind was blowing right into our faces as we sat down in the stadium. The gear that Fields brought for us was surprisingly effective and three of us (Mike, Chip and I) stayed for the entire game. Chris, a bit less hardy than us, left after halftime with Tommy, our youngest, and watched the second half from the van.

The 49ers came out and several of our big linemen had their arms exposed, not bothering to wear a sweatshirt under their pads. 49er offensive line coach, Bobb McKittrick also came out in short sleeves, but Bill Walsh sent him back in for warmer clothes. The game started out as a defensive struggle with the teams exchanging punts on the first five drives.

My son Chip, who was wearing hard contact lenses, started to complain that his contact lens had frozen to his eye, so I took him into the back of the stands where there were heaters and held him up near one, until it thawed. We were walking back up the ramp, when we heard a little bit of cheering that came from the 49ers section. Montana had thrown a long pass into the wind that Jerry Rice caught in double coverage and completed a 61-yard touchdown, and the 49ers took a 7-0 lead.

The 49ers defense had an outstanding day, holding Bears QB Jim McMahon to only 121 yards and an interception. The Bears offense only penetrated the 49ers 40-yard line twice and could only muster a single 25-yard field goal. Meanwhile Montana added another 27-yard touchdown pass to Rice in the second quarter and a five-yard touchdown pass to John Frank in the third quarter. Tom Rathman, the 49ers fullback, bulled into the end zone from the four-yard line to close out a 28-3 blowout of the Big Bad Bears. The "California pansies" had pasted the home team and their intimidating weather. The Forty Niners were headed to Miami and their third Super Bowl.

Not a whole lot of unusual things took place over the next two weeks. We had the usual requests for Super Bowl tickets and I put in a personal request for a few extra tickets. This year, I was going to take my mother to the game. She lived in Naples, Florida and had never been to any pro football game. A Super Bowl in a warm city would be a novel experience for her.

The family and I flew down a few days early and Mike and I got in a game of golf with my brothers, John and Chas, in Naples. Friday night we drove over to Miami and we used the Mayfair House Hotel in Coconut Grove, one of the DeBartolo hotels, as our base. For the first time, I chose not to stay in the team hotel. Mom had her own luxury suite and she enjoyed the entire weekend.

I arranged for a bus to take us, and others at the Mayfair, to and from the game. One of my family's friends showed up and surprised me on Sunday as the bus was pulling out of the Mayfair. I had no more tickets, so I stopped the bus and ran back into the hotel. I saw Mr. DeBartolo in the lobby and asked him if he had any extra tickets. He had only one left and gave it to me to give to our friend, and then I noticed that Reid Fields was also there. With no more tickets left, Reid and I roamed outside Joe Robbie Stadium, found a scalper and I bought Reid's ticket. All was good.

Super Bowl XXIII turned out to be one of the most exciting Super Bowls of those played to date. The Cincinnati Bengals were coached by a Bill Walsh protégé, Sam Wyche, and the Bengals were prepared for Walsh and Montana. Wyche had been a 49er assistant coach from 1979-1982 and many considered him a vital cog in the development of Joe Montana as a quarterback. He knew the 49er offense, knew Bill Walsh and knew Joe Montana. The Bengals had a pretty good quarterback in Boomer Esiason and, even though the 49ers were favored by a touchdown, many experts expected a close game.

The experts were not wrong. The 49ers defense stymied the Bengals offense for most of the first half and the 49ers offense moved the ball effectively, but mistakes at crucial times kept them out of the end zone. On their second drive of the game, Montana engineered a 73-yard drive from his own three-yard line. But the drive stalled when Mike Wilson, the 49ers opposite side receiver to Jerry Rice, dropped a pass, and the Niners had to settle for a field goal. After stopping the Bengals again, the Niners marched down to the Bengals 10-yard line, but the Bengals held and Mike Cofer, the 49er placekicker, missed the 21-yard field goal, when a bad snap killed the timing.

Again, the 49ers defense shut down the Bengals offense, forcing a punt. And again, Montana drove the team into Bengals territory. But, running back Roger Craig fumbled the ball away to the Bengals, thwarting another opportunity. Later, in the second quarter, the Bengals defense finally shut down the 49er offense, got a great punt return into 49er territory and kicked a field goal to tie the game at 3-3 at the half. It had been a frustrating half for the 49ers, who were dominant, but paid the price for their mistakes.

The Bengals opened the second half with their best drive of the game. Esiason led a 61-yard drive in 12 plays and ate nine minutes off the clock. The defense held for the 49ers and Cincinnati settled for a field goal to take a 6-3 lead and the momentum. The Bengals then held the 49ers offense in check and forced a punt, but again the Niner defense came up big.

Linebacker Bill Romanowski intercepted Esiason and the offense took over on the Cincinnati 23-yard line. Again, a 49er mistake, a dropped pass by Rice, stalled that drive and the Niners were forced to take Cofer's field goal to tie the game. The pattern of 49er mistakes was killing the team, and it wasn't over yet. On the ensuing kickoff, Bengal Stanford Jennings caught the ball on the seven-yard line, found the seam in the 49ers coverage, and raced 93 yards for a touchdown and a 13-6 lead for Cincinnati at the end of the third quarter. What might have been a big 49ers lead now looked like a possible Super Bowl loss.

With the team floundering, the 49er offense finally had a mistake-free drive. Montana engineered an 85-yard drive in four plays, all passes. It started with a 31-yard pass and run to Rice, followed by a 40 yarder to Craig. After an incompletion, Joe found Rice in the end zone from the Bengal 14-yard line for the equalizer.

Three plays into the fourth quarter and the score was knotted at 13-13. A few minutes later, the 49ers forced a Bengal punt and Montana marched the 49ers down to the Bengal 31-yard line. But Cofer again missed the field goal and the score stay tied. The Bengals took advantage of that mistake with another long drive. This time, they went on a 10 play, 46-yard drive, eating up much of the remaining fourth quarter clock, before the 49ers defense held. Jim Breech's field goal didn't miss. The Bengals had a 16-13 lead.

I had given up 50-yard line seats to sit with other family members and friends in the mezzanine of the end zone the 49ers would be driving toward. They were good seats, but they were perfect seats to view what was going to happen next.

There was just over three minutes left in the game and after a penalty on the kickoff, the 49ers drive started on the Niners' eight-yard line. The noise in the stadium was deafening, some rooting for a Bengal upset, while others were pulling for another "Montana moment." Reportedly, Bengal coach Wyche watched Montana run onto the field, then looked at the clock and commented, "We're not going to be able to stop him." All he could hope for was another 49er mistake.

With the Bengals guarding the sidelines to keep the clock running, Joe twice threw down the middle of the field for short gains, before a short sideline pass to Rice stopped the clock. Walsh then surprised the Bengals with two Craig runs, to the Niners' 31-yard line, followed by a 17-yard pass to Rice to put them in Bengals' territory. Another completion, this time to Roger Craig, moved the Forty Niners into field goal range, but only temporarily. An incompletion, followed by a penalty, and suddenly the 49ers were facing a second down and 20 yards to go, from the Bengals 45-yard line. The clock had ticked down to 1:15 left.

Montana again responded, connecting with Rice again, on a 27 yarder that put San Francisco on the 18-yard line. An eight yarder to Craig moved it to the Bengals' 10 with 39 seconds left, and the Forty

Niners called time out. All the action was right below us. The crowd was going nuts. Coach Wyche hoped for a stop and a field goal attempt and possible overtime. But, Bill Walsh was having none of that.

The 49er offense, like many that have since evolved, was full of misdirection. Wyche called for a double team on Rice and Cincinnati was expecting Craig or Rice, Montana's primary targets on the current drive. Instead, Walsh called a post play to John Taylor, who ran a perfect route and caught Montana's perfect pass that barely eluded a diving Bengal safety. We saw the play unfold right below us, and bedlam ensued. The NFL finally had a classic Super Bowl ending, as Joe Montana, almost put out to pasture earlier in the season, just guaranteed his entry into the Hall of Fame.

I eschewed going to the postgame Super Bowl party and chose to take my family to Joe's Stone Crab for a quiet victory party. My mother had seen one NFL football game in her life, and it turned out to be the most exciting Super Bowl ever. The next morning, we bid our Florida family goodbye and headed to the airport. On the drive to the airport, I told Chris "I am ready to resign from DeBartolo now."

Five days after winning the Super Bowl, Bill Walsh retired as coach of the 49ers. It was just another end in the era in which I worked. Bill had been rumored to be ready to leave for the last few years and, he apparently felt he now had nothing more to prove. I sent him a letter congratulating him on the recent Super Bowl win and wishing him the best in the future.

Having made up my mind, the timing for my own resignation was the only issue left for me. I still had a few big projects I was working on for the DeBartolo family and I wanted to finish them. I was aware few people voluntarily left the DeBartolo's and nearly all of those that did were referred to as "bums who were never any good, anyway." I wanted to avoid being thought of that way.

I decided to resign on a Saturday in early February and would give the Company five-months' notice to finish what I started. Early that Saturday morning, I met with Bill Moses at an area donut shop to tell him what I was planning to do.

Bill was very close with both EJD and EJD, Jr., and could advise me on how to successfully leave the company. It wasn't the first time I had spoken confidentially about my future to Bill, and the other times he talked me out of doing what I was planning and would tell me why. That morning, he listened to my reasons and then told me he was sad I would be leaving, but my reasons were valid and he wouldn't try to talk me out of it this time.

"One piece of advice," he told me, "when you leave, don't look back." Later that morning, I left a personal letter of resignation in a sealed envelope for Mr. DeBartolo, as I was leaving for the weekend. I also left copies for EJD, Jr. and Marie Denise.

I had no idea what to expect, but I was surprised at what did happen – nothing! None of the three said a word to me when I went into the office on Monday, and I just decided to keep doing my job as if nothing had changed.

One project I had begun for Mr. DeBartolo was attempting to buy out the concession contract at Thistledown. For as long as I was in the company, Sportservice, Inc. had the food and beverage contract at Thistledown and everyone complained about the food quality and service at the track, including patrons and employees.

Earlier in January, Mr. DeBartolo gave me the go ahead to contact them and see if it could be done. The contract was to run for six more years, expiring at the end of 1995. Our experience in running the concessions at our other tracks, as well as at the Civic Arena, had shown us that the profits were enormous and we could improve quality and service and make a lot more than the percentage Sportservice was currently paying us.

Sportservice had a colorful past. The original company was founded by Louis Jacobs and two brothers in Buffalo, New York as a theater concession company. They later expanded to providing concessions in some minor league ballparks. The name was changed to Sportservice in 1926, and they moved into major league baseball stadiums and then racetracks.

Lou Jacobs, the founder, built up an impressive operation and found he could lock up long contracts by lending money to racetrack owners in exchange for the contracts. Reportedly, that was how they got into Thistledown, and over the years they kept those contracts. An affiliated company, Emprise had been accused of organized crime ties which, to my knowledge, were never proven. After Lou Jacobs died, reportedly at his desk, the company changed names again to Delaware North and the company continues to flourish today.

Prior attempts to get rid of Sportservice at Thistledown were rebuffed by the company, so Mr. DeBartolo didn't expect us to be successful. But, the first meeting I had with the local Cleveland Sportservice representative was surprisingly hopeful, and it wasn't long before I was dealing with the company principals in Buffalo.

After negotiations, Sportservice agreed to allow us to buy out the last six years of its contract for $2 million. Even EJD was impressed. We already had a manager in Mike Dowling from our Cleveland Holiday Inn Operations that we sold, and the rest of our infrastructure was already in place. Our proformas indicated the return on our investment would be 18 months and perhaps as early as 12 months.

Mr. DeBartolo gave his approval, through our legal department. On February 26, 1989, a few weeks before the opening of the 1989 racing season, Bob Roberts of the Cleveland Plain Dealer reported the deal.

"Thistledown has bought out its concessionaire, Sportservice, which had a contract through 1995. Beginning this year, the track will handle all food services, as well as track parking and programs. 'It fits with our operation,' said Tom Rossetti, vice-president/controller for the Edward J. DeBartolo Corp., Thistledown's parent company. 'We control the food services at our other tracks, Louisiana Downs and Remington Park.' No buyout figures were made public, but the deal had to cost Thistledown several million dollars."

A few days later, we closed on the deal. Although Mr. DeBartolo approved the deal, he had done it through one of our corporate lawyers. We didn't meet to discuss it, and he didn't respond to me directly. He still hadn't responded to my resignation letter. Bill Moses told me Mr. DeBartolo had told him about my resignation and he was "deeply disappointed and hurt" with my decision. Moses advised me to let it run its course. I had also spoken to Eddie, Jr. and Denise, and they had also indicated I needed to give Mr. DeBartolo time to deal with it.

March came and went, and the silence from Mr. DeBartolo continued. I got little or no direction from him and continued to get my and his, business affairs in order. I took trips to San Francisco for the final time to tell Keith Simon I would be leaving and flew to Shreveport and Oklahoma to advise the management there.

Since Mr. DeBartolo hadn't yet accepted my resignation, I chose not to tell anyone who my successor might be. Coincidentally, my secretary, Carol, who had been so instrumental in helping me over the last few years, surprisingly asked if I would approve her transfer to another department, and I acknowledged I would. She looked at me and said "So, the rumors are true?"

I told her they were, and that was why I wouldn't try to talk her out of the transfer. That made me realize the word was out, so I called a staff meeting with my people and told them what they probably already knew. Then I went to Pittsburgh and told Paul Martha, Rick McLaughlin, Ed Walter and Tony Esposito. It was now mid-April.

And then I heard from Mr. D. Edy called one morning near the end of April and said Mr. DeBartolo wanted to see me that morning. We met in his office, and he told me he was extremely disappointed in my leaving and asked if I would change my mind. I told him that was unlikely and nobody had addressed what I stated a year ago about not being challenged.

I pointed out the Diversified Operations were shrinking and I had done my job building my department and identifying a successor. I also told him I wasn't happy with some of the changes going on with the company and that my feelings weren't going to change anything. I told him I felt I had gone as far as I could go in the company.

He didn't comment other than to ask if it was "a financial thing." I responded that financial was only a very small part of the problem. The bigger issues were not going to change. He didn't agree or disagree. That was the last time I would ever meet with Mr. DeBartolo in his office.

May and June sped by and I began cleaning out my office. Tony Liberati got involved, and he told me Jerry Wiemann would be promoted to my job, but not the title, which he would have to earn through performance.

I had one final project that I finished, a settlement with a discharged employee at Thistledown. I met with Tony and told him when it was completed. I hadn't talked to EJD in five weeks. He suggested I send Mr. DeBartolo another personal memo.

"He's going to talk to you," Tony said. I left Tony's office and stopped in to say goodbye to Eddie, Jr., who I knew would be heading out of town the next day and wouldn't return to the office until after I was gone. We had a nice meeting, reminisced about the good times and shook hands and hugged.

When I got back to my office, I wrote another note to EJD. I explained I had completed everything I hoped to, and asked for a final goodbye meeting. Excerpts included, "Boss, I've been trying to get in to see you for the last five weeks...I want to leave here as a friend, to you, Eddie and Denise...I want you to know that, if you ever need me in the future, I'll be there for you...Mr. D, please don't shut me out. This has been difficult enough for me, as it is. Let's get together soon. June 30 is rapidly approaching."

On June 18, Bob Roberts wrote in the Plain Dealer: "Tom Rossetti has resigned his post as vice-president/controller for the Edward J. DeBartolo Corp. 'After 16 years, it's time to move on,' said Rossetti, who leaves his Youngstown post at the end of the month to head for Naples, Fla.., where he will start his own sports consulting firm. Rossetti may be best remembered by Thistledown racing fans as the man who announced last fall that the races would go on post time. He made the decision after George Jones resigned as general manager and before Mike Mackey assumed the post."

The June 12, 1989 copy of Barron's National Business and Financial Weekly arrived on my desk as I was beginning to clear out my office. The cover story read "The King of Malls and His Shadowy Realm." It was about Mr. DeBartolo and there was a caricature of EJD and EJD, Jr. that I found offensive.

Although a reader of the headline might assume a tie to organized crime, the mob, or the Mafia, the article wasn't too bad and certainly didn't create the aura that The DeBartolo Corporation was involved in organized crime, but it did characterize Mr. DeBartolo as a "Shadowy Figure."

There are a few references in this book to "organized crime", although none of them indicates any connection with DeBartolo's companies and crime members. Organized crime existed in Youngstown, and it was impossible to avoid dealing with some of its members. Youngstown was a union town and organized crime members were in control of the many arms of unions in those days. If you had to work with the unions, you had to work with members of organized crime. It was a catch-22.

I had heard the rumors as soon as I set foot in Youngstown in 1973. "DeBartolo was mobbed up," they said. "DeBartolo was in the Mafia, "they said. Some said he ran racetracks and that was proof, even though the tracks were licensed by the states and had state representatives there every day.

To Mr. DeBartolo's credit, he fumed whenever he heard the rumors and he fired back at the people who insinuated as much.

"Just because I'm successful and my name ends in a vowel doesn't mean that I'm involved in the mob." I heard him say that several times over the years, including to Bowie Kuhn in the White Sox fiasco, but it never stopped the rumors.

One day while I was in his office, he pointed to a picture on his wall. There were four young men in the picture, including DeBartolo. "We grew up together," he said of the picture. "Two of them got involved in the rackets. Does that mean I have to take down the picture? We were friends!"

In fact, at the end of the Barron's article was the following disclaimer: "DeBartolo has suffered over the years from rumors linking him to organized crime. Not a shred of evidence of such ties has ever surfaced despite a number of investigations. But the innuendo was reportedly enough to cause the American League baseball owners, a group never known for either progressiveness nor acumen, to scotch DeBartolo's 1980 purchase of the Chicago White Sox."

In addition, Mr. DeBartolo's Biography on Your Dictionary on the Internet states the following: "In 1980 he attempted to purchase the Chicago White Sox baseball team, but was voted down by the American League owners, under pressure from commissioner Bowie Kuhn. The ostensible reasons included his absentee ownership and his race track involvement, but many believed the unspoken objection was his reputed link to organized crime. A series of innuendoes followed DeBartolo beginning in the 1950s when there was a rash of bombings at his properties in Youngstown, where organized crime was strong, but FBI and Treasury Department investigations turned up no evidence."

Racing Boards in Ohio, Illinois, Louisiana and Oklahoma investigated the man and his company and approved his ownership of racetracks in their states. He was vetted and approved by The National

Football League, The National Hockey League, the United States Football League and The Major Indoor Soccer League.

Even my own father put out feelers about the DeBartolo's when I told him the company offered me a job. How did he do that? He contacted members of organized crime that ran the unions in New York, and my dad told me it was okay for me to go to work for them. In other words, they told him DeBartolo was not "involved." Finally, in the nearly 16 years I worked for the DeBartolo Family, closely in many of those years, I never saw nor heard of any references to illegal dealings with organized crime.

June 30 arrived. My last day and my office was cleaned out. Mr. DeBartolo's secretary told me EJD would meet me at 10 a.m. Since my company car would be surrendered that day, Chris came in and we packed my stuff into her car, and she went home until I called her to pick me up. At 10 I drove over to Mr. D's office for the last time. His door was closed so I went into Edy's office and waited. A few minutes later, he came out. He handed me a check for $270,000. He had bought back my interests in my four partnerships for the full value, even though I wasn't fully vested.

He also would pay me another $148,000 plus interest over the next nine years on one of the four partnerships that had a 10-year payoff. Although I felt I earned it, I knew I wasn't entitled to all of it since I hadn't spent the time there to get fully vested. Mr. DeBartolo had treated me very generously one final time.

Like a father, he said to me, "This is a lot of money. Invest it wisely." He had tears in his eyes. I had tears in my eyes. Even tough Edy had tears in her eyes as Mr. DeBartolo embraced me. "Will you help me if I need you?" he asked in a shaky voice.

"Just call me and I'll be there," I choked out my answer.

And then he was gone - back into his office and closed the door. Edy jumped up and gave me a hug, and then I walked out her door, down the hall, down the steps, out the front door, and got into my company car for the last time. That was when I fell apart. I sat there for several minutes trying to compose myself. It was one of the saddest moments of my life. A huge part of that life, a great part, was ending.

I had joined DeBartolo as a young man and was leaving as a middle-aged man. For 16 years, I loved my job and my employers. I was challenged, chastised, praised, threatened, rewarded, nearly fired, and promoted so many times over the 16 years it seemed unreal. And yet, even during the few bad times, I was still able to give my best. I looked forward to every day over those years because I knew each of them would bring something new. I gave them everything I had and was leaving with my head held high. I would not be remembered as "a bum." Bill Jaynes' prognostication about my learning curve with DeBartolo had been spot on.

A few minutes later, I was back in my office. I called Chris and she showed up 10 minutes later. I jumped into the family car and she drove me home. I heeded Bill Moses' advice: I didn't look back.

CHAPTER NINETEEN

LIFE AFTER DEBARTOLO

That would not be the end of my contact with the DeBartolo family. For starters, I received a check for more than $16,000, plus interest, annually for the next nine years. In addition, Marie Denise and I exchanged Christmas cards for several years. But, when I woke up on July 1, it was strange to know I no longer had to go to work at 7620 Market St.

We left for Florida on July 4, after a tearful farewell party the day before with neighbors and friends. Arriving in Florida a couple days later, we settled in and my boys, my brothers and I started playing golf whenever we wanted to. It was also nice living near my parents for the first time in almost 20 years.

I made no effort to get work until the boys went back to school in late August. Then I sent out a few letters and got a long-term consulting arrangement with the Orlando Juice Baseball Club, in the short-lived Senior Professional Baseball League. But, the day before I was to start that assignment, I received a call from attorney Carmen Policy, on behalf of Eddie DeBartolo, Jr.

The San Diego Padres were on the market and Eddie wanted me to evaluate their operation to see if a purchase was viable. Policy said, "Eddie looked at the DeBartolo organization and had nobody qualified to do the job."

Carmen and I negotiated the fee and he asked if I could fly out to San Francisco to meet with Eddie the following Monday, November 27. A prepaid first-class ticket was arranged for me at the airport. Monday was the day I was scheduled to start with the Juice, but the GM was amenable to moving it back a week, especially after hearing what it was for.

Monday, I arrived in San Francisco and was chauffeured to Candlestick, where the 49ers were playing the Giants. I watched the game with Eddie and then we discussed the Padres proposal after the game. Joan Kroc had inherited the team from her husband and was shopping the team. The next day, I arrived in San Diego, met with the attorney representing Mrs. Kroc, got a tour of the facility, and got the financial information I needed to analyze the opportunity. In the end, Kroc's price was too high and the numbers didn't work at the price she insisted on, so the deal went no further after I sent my report to Eddie.

The 49ers season ended after another a great year, rolling through the playoffs and into the Super Bowl. My kids started bugging me about going to the game, which was in New Orleans, and I finally relented. I called Keith Simon and he sent me six tickets, five for us and one for a high school friend of Mike's.

We had a tough time getting a room in New Orleans until Keith called and asked where I was staying. When I told him Biloxi, he said to cancel the rooms. The 49ers chartered a Mississippi riverboat for the weekend and he had three rooms reserved for us. Saturday, we went up to the Niners temporary offices so I could say hello to Eddie, Jr. He had Montana with him and Chip and Tommy had their pictures taken with Eddie and Joe.

Joe predicted he would have a 'signature" game the next day. He did, and the 49ers rolled over Denver, 55-10, with Montana named Most Valuable Player. The game was never close after the opening kickoff. It was 27-3 at the half, and the only question was what time the party would start. It was the last Super Bowl party we would attend, and my boys got several autographs on the cards given to game attendees.

In 1992, the Pittsburgh Penguins and Mario Lemieux finally won the Stanley Cup. My oldest son. Mike, home from college, still watched all the games and was an ardent fan, having suffered through all the bad years with me. When the Penguins dispatched the Boston Bruins to reach the Stanley Cup finals, Mike asked if we could go. Again, I relented and called Rick McLaughlin, who said, "I have two here with your name on them."

The next day, Mike and I put the golf clubs in the trunk and headed to Pittsburgh for the first two home games. Our tickets were behind the opposition net, meaning the Penguins would be shooting at that net for two of the three periods. The tickets were also next to the NHL Director of Officiating.

Mike had always said that NHL officials were incompetent and he gave the Director an earful throughout the game. Early in the first period, I noticed Mr. DeBartolo was sitting in the owner's box, a rare occurrence. When the first period ended, I went up to the box to pay my respects to Mr. D. He asked me to sit with him and we watched the second period together. We had a nice chat, but I was sad to say he didn't look well.

The Penguins lost that game, but won the series in six games, with the Penguins winning the last three. We were back in Florida when Lemieux hoisted the Cup over his head and all the years of losing and frustration were flushed away. The Pens also won the Cup the next year, but it wasn't a DeBartolo championship. Mr. D sold the team before the season started, amid rumors the DeBartolo Corporation was in dire financial straits.

In 1993, Bill Moses died suddenly under abnormal circumstances. I received a call from George Jones with the news. I flew up and met George and we went to Bill's funeral, after which we also visited the DeBartolo offices. Again, when I saw Mr. DeBartolo, he didn't look well.

On December 19, 1994, Edward J. DeBartolo, Sr. died from complications related to pneumonia. This time, the call came from one of my former secretaries, Connie Fair, who gave me the bad news. I felt like I had not only lost a good friend, but a father figure, as well. It put a hole in my heart that will be there forever. I think about him every day.

Slightly more than a month later, on January 29, 1995, the Forty Niners once again found themselves in a Super Bowl in Miami, and I got tickets from the team to see the game. Also, once again they won, 49-26, over the San Diego Chargers. Eddie DeBartolo, Jr. proclaimed the win was dedicated to his father, who had recently passed away. With the win, the Niners became the first team to win five Super Bowls, with a Super Bowl record of 5-0.

In 1997, Eddie DeBartolo was accused in a scandal with Louisiana former governor, Edwin Edwards. Eddie was indicted and forced to cede control of the team to his sister, Marie Denise York, while he worked through the legalities of the Edwards matter. He eventually took a plea bargain and was suspended for a year by NFL Commissioner, Paul Tagliabue. In early 2000, he agreed to swap assets with his sister, who took permanent control of the 49ers. The golden era of 49er domination and greatness under Eddie's ownership was over.

In August 2016, Edward J. DeBartolo, Jr. was elected to the National Football League Hall of Fame. Regardless of the reason he no longer had the team, he had earned the honor. He was one of the greatest owners of a pro sports franchise in history. It is also a great ending to this book.

CHAPTER TWENTY

WHY I DID IT

I started writing this book in 2012, at the urging of my three sons, who wanted to know what I really did for the DeBartolo Family. They were all too young to realize it was a real job and not just all the games and celebrations they were a part of, as children and young men. Later in 2012, I was diagnosed with prostate cancer and the book writing went on the back shelf as I dealt with the cancer.

Over the 28 years I've been gone from the DeBartolos, many people asked me what it was like back then, living such an exciting life with some of the greatest sports and business figures in history. When they heard of some of my experiences, many often said, "You should write a book." So, here it is.

One thing you will notice is I rarely criticized the members of the DeBartolo Family. There is a reason for that - they were wonderful people to work for. Yes, they were tough and perhaps a bit unreasonable at times, but the overriding experience over my nearly 16 years was they were generous and caring people, who were extremely family-oriented.

They cared about me and my family and subscribed to the "Family First" philosophy. And that meant not just for their family, but mine, as well. It still blows my mind to think that Mr. DeBartolo called the hospital in Chicago in 1977, to get daily updates on my Dad's condition after the brain aneurism that nearly killed him. But that was the way he was, and when you really think about it, what better way is there to keep people working for you, when they truly believe you care about them? The DeBartolo's not always stressed family, they also practiced it. I stayed loyal to them and they stayed loyal to me.

Another question I have heard often over the years is, "Why would you leave such a fantastic job?" That is a good question that, to this day, I'm not sure I know how to answer. I know I finally got tired of watching my back, mostly from other people working at the company. There were too many department heads over the years that tried to discredit other department heads to protect their own empires. And yes, I think the phone call from Mr. DeBartolo to me in Myrtle Beach in March 1988 may have started me thinking that perhaps it was time for me to move on.

Another possible reason I left was because I sensed the company had really changed over the years, particularly my last few years. When I first joined the company, all the executives seemed to be loyal to the family and we all worked as a team, for the benefit of the company rather than ourselves. I felt if I took care of the company business, it would take care of me, and it worked. But in the last few years I was there, new people came in and it appeared to me they perhaps made some decisions based on what was good for them first and for the company second.

Or, it is conceivable that maybe I was burned out, but I'm not sure that would be a legitimate reason. Another possible reason is I did my job the right way, and in doing so worked myself out of a job. I loved the challenges and when they stopped coming, I started to get bored.

The real reason is probably a combination of these, coupled with my desire to become a better husband and father. While I traveled all over North America, I always used the excuse I was home for my boys' big events and, while that may have been true, sometimes the little events are big events in their eyes, too.

When I heard Mike talking about visiting colleges in his junior year, that's when I knew I needed, and wanted, to be home more, and the only way to do it was to control my own destiny. And, for the last 28 years, that is what I have done. So, I guess in the end it was "Family First" for me, after all.

Regrets? I've had a few, to quote Frank Sinatra in his famous song. It would be impossible not to second-guess my decision, given the power I gave up and my experiences and love for my employers. One of my more obvious mistakes may have been the timing of my resignation. Very possibly, I could have gotten a third Super Bowl ring, and then when I leave this earth, each of my sons could inherit a ring. But, my resignation was delivered before that possibility came to pass, and it was not to be.

Then again, if I had stayed another year, maybe there would have been yet another Super Bowl ring. And if I waited yet a little longer, there would have been a Stanley Cup ring. But where does it stop and what would those extra years have entailed?

Postponing the inevitable would have only been procrastination. I may have left a bit prematurely, but I left on good terms with the DeBartolo Family, and that means more to me than any rings or championships.

I also regret I was never enamored over working with so many of those great athletes and people, like Montana, Lott, Clark, Solomon, Lemieux and Walsh, to name a few. The list could be much longer. To me, they were just employees like me, working toward a common goal.

I never was star-struck about being around them, even though they were superstars.

But, in the end, the great relationships I have and have had with my wife, my children, my brothers and sister, my parents and my beautiful grandchildren have made it all worthwhile. And that is something on which you can't put a price tag.

THE END

Made in the USA
Monee, IL
10 July 2021

73351116R00175